Oracle
Poems, Art, and Stories

Spring 2024

Oracle

Poems, Art, and Stories

Spartan Voices

Spring 2024

Oracle
© 2024, Spartan Voices
ISBN:979-8-99005-312-0
Library of Congress Control Number: 2024909354

Cover Photography: Kathy Tinoco

First Edition, 2024

Printed in the United States of America

Edited: Erica Castro
Cover Design: Matthew Genesis Gonzalez Reyes
Layout Design: Ricardo Valencia
Logo Art: Karime Aruajo
Logo Design: Tyler Alvarez

Published by: Schurr High School
            Montebello, Ca
            90640

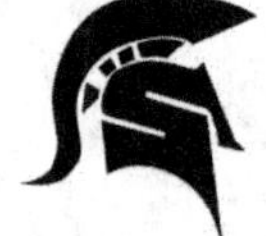

Schurr High School Publishing

Oracle
Poems, Art, and Stories

Spring 2024

Schurr High School
Publishing

Preface

This collection of art, poems, and stories represents a safe space for student's to display their creative art. Art, photography, and writing gives people purpose, and it also promotes creative expression. We believe that everyone has a voice through art, and it must be heard. We constructed this project because we wanted to honor, and validate the art, poems, and stories created by students. Through their voice, we hope that people have a better understanding and acceptance of student work and hear their voice.

Conversation with My Inner-Child

Sorry to myself
Sorry for not protecting you
Sorry that I wasn't able to stand up for us
Or the people around us
Sorry if I never put us first
Sorry for trying to make everyone happy
Except us
Sorry I listened to everyone around us
Sorry for all those times I have harmed you
In my selfish ways,
and saying obnoxious things.
Sorry you had to grow up so fast
Sorry for not experiencing a normal childhood
I apologize for all the hurtful things that came
out of our mouths
Saying things without thinking twice
Hurting the people we loved
Sorry I spent more time in my head than
listening to you.
All the times I hide in my room away from you
Away from society
Just to be alone in my head
Sorry I wasn't the best at making friends
Sorry I didn't try hard in school
Hoping you will forgive me one of these days
Realizing I was unfair to you

By: Amelie Ramirez

Night Ride-The Growlers

Lonely nights

Fueled by drugs and alcohol
Alone with my thoughts

Questioning?

Running out of time
Over & Over & over again

Disillusionment
Trapped in a cycle
Repetitive behavior
Repetitive thoughts

Tomorrow night will go on without you

Til dawn & no one will care

Wanting more time

Can no longer pretend I am sane

Trying but I couldn't

Trying but I could no longer pretend
Trying but the end never changes

Peeling off my smile

With baggies in the backroom
Trying to fill an endless void

Now you see there was never a point

By: Amelie Ramirez

Rembrandt Van Rijn

Rembrandt Van Rijn a man of sophistication
Tall, well-dressed man
Painting is his wish

To show the world his painting
From the poor to the Queen
  is his favorite

The colors mixing
The palate of a simple man
Black clothing
Well-groomed beard

Tall hat
Blue sky
Showing his slight smile
With his rosy lips

Many may not understand him
His bold choice of colors
Dull yellow
That make his painting pop

By: Kimberly Lopez-Ramirez

Losing You

Time seemed to fly by fast. Your eyes make me smile lighting up my face. Your eyes are like stars sparkling brighter every time I see you. Your soft curl that I have played around with. Your hair bouncy up and down. Moving like a flower on a windy day. We completed each other. Life seemed like sunshine and rainbows, but later it became dark and gloomy. Like rain you came down and left. Feeling betrayed and lonely. You did not seem to care. We grew distant. Never talking again

You memorize in my mind
Like rain you came down and left
Wishing you would come back

By: Kimberly Lopez-Ramirez

Truth Be Seemed

Ambered Blue Stone.
Oh so carefully compassionate you are
Is it true?
What if I grab you true?
Will you still be in truth?
To confide in you--Do you change enough of your tune?
Do you walk the same hues?--To change your hue.
Will you still be blue?--Will you play the same tune?
The whole of amber coated--Will you break with time?
To Power and Give, to Change and Stay; Are you Truth?
Can you truly stay true in my truth?

By: Johnny Solorzano

Sprout(ing)

Oh my Sprout…Why so shrubbed?
Was my time I gave just for fame??
Were you always so grave?
Can you bring life with what you cave?
Through blood and bread; through tears of sweat.
Must I truly obey you till I break?
Can I calm your fate for my own sake?
Can I plead my case in front of your big intake?
Will you even pay my words with a warm embrace?
To challenge your will,
Life must Take.

By: Johnny Solorzano

Dahlia

Flower under the moon and over the lake
To show us such sweet colors, you must have a sweet.
To elegantly remain at peace, humble through your kindness.
You shine brighter than any Sun; giving hues of Lavender.
My resented blasphemy; still. I partake my path of choice.
My crescent smile by the clouds, the clouds that reflect
Your eternal beauty print upon your petaled Tula.
Dahlia, is your name? Maybe so.
But I know it true.
I know now Lavender is what you prime.
For it shows within; and within it all, it calls before me, calming me
upon the blue watered moon.

By: Johnny Solorzano

Raine?

To power vision, you fail. You give me cold envisions.
You stain my dreams with insensitive provisions.
What made you hinder us so? Is it your calm sounding
inscriptions?
Why fall for such a Jester? Maybe I am too weak to see it through…
But… Wait…
Am I to be fooled? Are you truly insensitive to my renditions?
Or is it just your Sister's coalition?
The vision you give fails, true, but lives within the trickling of skin.
The blurry cold makes us see through our prescriptions.
You truly do not stain? But trip us to our Case; you make us for-
give…
But once you pass, what true beauty you give.
Once you pass, what color you begin.
To say I hope for your end: I am Selfish…?
Are you not just my release? A stained flow?
Do you not just… fail… in time anew?

By: Johnny Solorzano

Relevance

Relevance is my power.
I shall not be forgotten by my foot left engraved into this soul.
To be cared, I cared too.
To be foolish, I fooled you.
Now to all who noticed, I applaud you.
You can now hold my hand down into the drain and pledge that you too shall be brave.
So forth and so long you stay so that I may pray.
Continue into this hammer, for as such I appraise for however long you crave.
And to crave I overjoy this stimulant, to the point I am washed away.
…I must stop… I am too dazed now by you…
I laugh at you.
-

I laugh at you.
-

I laugh at you.
-

You.
-

Laugh.
-

Now.
Stop.
-

…Try once more…
Oh. You cannot.
I guess you, tainted, he--tainted.
I now see the true voice. So for now, that I know, you cannot be alone.

By: Johnny Solorzano

My Beautiful Sheen

Here, do I say the years?
The years you and I have been told why?
But I tell you now to grasp my hand and I shall feed your eyes with nothing but cries.
To the vast ocean of colors fleeting your eyes, I must be quick, but careful.
…What do you see now?
Still gray?
…No, you say?
What may you see now fortune You.
…You say you see the sea past the long ocean's deep?
Yes, yes, but what colors do you see?
…Could it be?
…You only see me? Do you not?
…You now see green, you say?
…But what green is there then in the sky?
…But must be cause you have oddly told no lie.
…So I do trust you and me for you held our hands as tight as can be.
…I say to you no faults, but I do wish this vision you see could be past on to me.
…For I want the thoughts of your mind be read in and on.
…Do you now wish to see deep?
…Yes, you say once more I love.
…Come now, we should have all day to you and me.
…Does the pale black frighten you? Oh dear.
…But now must come, for you have strode this path, followed behind me.
…Just open your eyes and you shall see.
See something grand.
…Maybe not another, but of course it shall be a lover.
…Can you see it now?
…Oh. Why didn't you tell me you saw it passed down?
…Well I see, just continue to lecture me from what you see.
…You say you see clouds?
…But how can that be?

…Oh I know, you must be My Raine.

…For only rain can be in the clouds. So I say to you, are you My Raine?

…To which no you say?

…Well of what clouds do you say you see?

…Of you and me?

…Oh I forgive thee, something so beautiful to see through my dearest drums.

…You put up a fancy farce to deceive me I see.

…Well I thank you for what you said you see.

…But now, that is all the time I said can be.

…I did have that wish to be seen by you this whole night passed.

…But alas it cannot be.

…But maybe one day we shall get to see the ending of this scenery together with one mind of reading, be it thee.

…So now, I bid thee to farewell.

…But I ask you one last thing; did you like to what you have seen with me as your sheen?

…I see. Then as last goodbyes, I show you one last scene I put to you, dedicated to you, granted by your talents, to only you shall it be seen.

…So take it with you and keep fresh in your mind, and tell me the conjured thoughts, to which you thrive, next time.

…Goodbye… My Sheen.

By: Johnny Solorzano

I Won't Bite my Tongue

Oh to bad news I say go, *Halt.*
My heart fears to twist, to *Yearn,*
But I'm not given' up; Devoted 'til my heart don't pump.
'Yil I succumb to the fight, I must rise when the sun don't shine.
I won't *Give Up.* I won't *Give In.*
I fight for war stuck in my mind and stick to my binds that hold my arms.
Even if they shoot me down, I rise with my breaking bones and my aching woes.
To the end I fight for me and my dreams, my goals I have chosen.
I won't *Give up.* I won't *Give In.*
I ain't backing down cause all my life I've been running, but now I choose to stay and fight.
So now I won't *Give Up* 'till they kill me or I win it.
I won't turn behind; I will fight with the knife that I chose, covered in blood I wake the soldier loaded, and the war so chosen.
I won't *Give Up.* I won't *Give In.*
I ain't *Backing Down.*
This time they see me, and they say--You Are…
So now I dry my eyes to the beat of their hearts.
Never cried, so Divine.
So now to set off, I go with no safety and bend their minds into mine.
"If I gotta be a Soldier…
I will be a Soldier…"

By: Johnny Solorzano

I Alone I Stand to be with You

I care to be with you, but
I'm a new man now.
We were on the same page, but every chapter ends.
And you know I had to let you go, let you leave.
But I still won't say goodbye…
Goodbye.

…

Now I wake up alone, gifted to nothing.
I say to myself, under my breath, Oh how do I miss the days.
Even my soul cries out loud to the loss.
But you know I had to let you go, let you leave.
I still think about you, though I had to let you fly.
I still wish I didn't say goodbye.
I said I wouldn't say goodbye…
Goodbye.

…

I told myself to not to beat myself, but that never worked.
I still miss you.
I sleep in bed, my heartache doesn't let me think, only about you.
It still breaks me to this point.
My demons may get to me without your help.
But how could I count you in? Now that I'm alone.
Now that you're gone, I sit by myself in my thoughts.
Should I have said something different?
Should I have not said Goodbye?...
Goodbye.

…

I feel the water around, and with sharks keeping me in the middle.
I can't shake that feeling, breaking down.
I keep breaking down, crying an inch every time.
I can't get over you.
I still say I miss you.
But I can't let you back in.
That's just how it has to be.
So I'm sorry to say,
I've Loved You.

By: Johnny Solorzano

Cri

Through the dark. I must remain. Only hidden in my tough terrain.
I strike at dawn. To be contained. As if I don't. I shall not reign.

By: Johnny Solorzano

I am Grateful

I am grateful
because my mom is the opposite of my dad.
My mom is positive
I am grateful
because my dad is super strict,
and my mom is not.
I am grateful because
She makes me learn without stress.
She makes me feel that I am the best.
She is positive about life and doesn't scare me.
She makes things easier and cares for me.
She makes home fun.
I am grateful because I am her son.

By: Duke Salomon

Life's Hardships

Hardship is always upon me
Unsatisfaction is a bad habit of mine
Never-ending war against me and me
Negativity crawling through my head
Day, night, always the same cycle

I try my best to stay away from it
Soon it comes back
Like the speed of light
Yet, it turning into darkness
That is never acknowledged

What can I do for others?
How do I express myself?
Questions unanswered and unknown
As I bring myself down repeatedly
Fear of being worth nothing
Or being unloved by anyone

Then there comes ahead
My loved ones
Reminding me of who I am
Bringing me back to my senses
Of the beauty life holds
Nature being part of us on this Earth
With animals that represent other spirits

As I look at the parrots
They always remind me of the colors
Of the living and the creatures that surround me
They are like family as we are all living things
That soon leave the world

Appearance is not always the key
Passion and faith is what moves us
Through daily life struggles

These birds being a symbol of long life
And freedom as I will experience
When I find myself in this world
As they surround me
It is like my loved ones are beside me
Giving me hope and motivation in this world
Even if they are not completely here
I can feel their spirits comforting me

Ignoring hopelessness and
Accepting trust is what lies
Inside my heart

By: Stephanie Velasquez

Courage

The way I solidified my success
through the challenges
from my past
was by focusing on myself
I focused on my mental health
by working out
spending time with my family
I am grateful for having the family I have

I am grateful for the things people do for me
I took a step forward from the difficult challenges I faced
I want a career in life
I want to achieve goals for myself
Working out makes me forget the harsh moments I go through
I miss the happy moments
such as my family all gathered together

The most important thing to me
is my successful future
I am proud of myself for staying strong and positive
I am glad I am passing my classes and working hard to graduate
I just want to make my family proud and to be proud of myself
I want to be known for how I made it to the top of the ladder

I struggled with many things in the past between my mom and dad
But I am not upset because they have supported me
They have been supported me throughout my journey
I want a better life and future for myself
I take the chances I take to do something
but some have a cost

By: Andrew Olmedo

My Trip to Montana

My story is about the time I was seven and it was the summertime around my birthday. My family and I went on a road trip from California to Montana. We went through the Nevada desert where the mountains were all sand, and it was below 30 in the night. To beat the high desert heat, I slept most of the way through Nevada, but clearly remember the drive into Idaho state. Seeing the signs of potatoes, many mountains, and canyons looked amazing. Most of the drive was through flat lands, so not much sightseeing, but man when we drove through the Idaho falls it was incredible. The feeling you get from how deep the canyons are is insane. You feel like you're on top of the world, and everything below you is so far. Then we finally made it to Montana. The most natural untouched *man place* I have seen. Animals wandering a round freely, and people lowering the windows to take pictures of the trees and animals. The destination was *Yellowstone* and to enter there was a bunch of wild buffalo wandering around. People were afraid to drive to avoid getting attacked by one. Then I remember peeing in the back because there was no place to pee for hundreds of miles and wet the seat in the back. All my cousins were making fun of me, and that was funny. The weather was amazing, and we spent five days there in a cabin by a lake and a ski resort. I caught my first fish and remember eating it in tacos that my uncle made. Having lots of snacks and food was amazing and being with nature was out of control there. The mountains were insane, and everything was unique and beautiful. The drive back was the saddest, but the memories I still hold on to are the best.

By: Noah Serna

Boy Addicted to Social Media

Clement wakes up every day in the morning and the first thing he does is check his cell phone. He grabs his cell phone and immediately opens the popular social media app *Instagram*. He scrolls through his feed and replies to all of his messages he might have received throughout the night while he was asleep. Clement continues to lie in his bed for 1 hour and 36 minutes after he has woken up. Clement heads to the washroom to brush his teeth, rinse his face, and use the toilet. He brings his phone along with him to the washroom, as he is brushing his teeth, he places his phone on the counter, while watching *Instagram* reels. After Clement finishes brushing his teeth, he heads to the kitchen to make some breakfast for himself. As he is making his breakfast, he switches to other social media platforms; he is now scrolling through *Tik-Tok*. Clement's mother is also in the kitchen. Over time Clement's mother realizes he spends way too much time on his cell phone. She tells him how he needs to put his phone down sometimes and go outside and explore the real world. Clement's mother fusses at him about being on his phone for various hours a day and describes how addicted he is to his cell phone and social media. She explains how when Clement wakes up in the morning, he gets on his cell phone immediately. She exposes how much he is on it and how much time he spends scrolling on social media.

Clement's mother asked to see the screen time on his cell phone. When Clement shows his mother his screen time, she lets out a loud gasp. She could not believe her eyes. When she saw Clement's screen time, she was too stunned to speak. Clement has 17 hours daily average total screen time. His mother checks the statistics of his screen time and discovers that Clement spends six hours and thirty-two minutes on *Instagram*, five hours and twenty-six minutes on *TikTok*, four hours exactly on *Snapchat*, and two hours and three minutes on *Facebook*. Clement's mom explains how spending that much time of your day on social media is not healthy for him. His mother walks away disappointed., a few hours go past, Clement's father goes to check on him. Clement is in his room, lying on his stomach. His father asks what he's up to. Clement says, "oh nothing much dad just chatting with my friends in

Snapchat." With a concerned face, Clements' father says to him, "son you don't think the amount of time you spend on social media is a little concerning?" Clement replied with "no father." Clement's dad replies with "your mother and I had a very serious talk, and we have both agreed that we need to put a time limit on your phone. Meaning you will only be able to be on social media for a certain amount of time." Clement gets upset and raises his tone of voice, saying, "why, would you guys do that?" His father tells him, "because the amount of time you are on social media is unacceptable." Clement gets furious and storms out of his room while his father is still speaking to him.

His father chases after him, "where do you think you're going, young man?" said Clement's father. Clement ignores his father, his mother comes into the room and asks, "what is going on in here?" "Clement, why are you being disrespectful?" Clement replies "what's such a big deal with me being on my phone so much? It's what I enjoy doing, it keeps me entertained and you guys are trying to ruin it for me!" At this point, his parent's confirmed Clement is in fact addicted. His parents take away his phone completely and Clement acts crazy.

He runs to his room screaming and cursing at his parents about taking his cell phone away. His parents stand there looking at one another in disbelief. They could not believe their eyes. They had never seen Clement react like this before. After a few hours had passed Clement's mom goes into Clement's room only to discover he is not in there. She quickly runs to her husband shouting "where is Clement?" He replies, "I don't know? I thought he was in his bedroom." "No. He's gone, he isn't in his bedroom," she said. They both look around the home while rapidly calling Clement's name.

"Clement? Clement? Where are you Clement ?" They got no response at all. They looked outside of their home to check if he was outside. Maybe he was getting fresh air, but he wasn't. It had seemed that Clement had run away from home. Clement's mother goes to call a family member to let them know the bad news. That Clement had run away from home. "Oh geez? Should we report the situation to the police department?" said the family member on the phone. Clement's mother replied, "no, if he doesn't show up within 24 hours, I will. But for now, I'm just going to wait until he decides to come home. "The next day had arrived, Clement still had not come back home, it had been 12 hours since he ran away from home. At 7:24 in the morning, Clement's mother receives a phone call from a police officer. She was overly concerned and asked the officer, "Is everything alright?" The officer mentioned they found Clement at 11:45 last night, dead in a car accident. It had appeared that Clement had got picked up by a friend he met on social media a few weeks ago who is also addicted to social media. They appeared to be driving to the nearest cell phone store to buy a new phone for Clement until they rear-ended another vehicle because the driver Clement was in the car with had been live streaming on *Instagram* and paid more attention to the social media live stream instead of the road. Clement's mom was devastated. She had dropped to her knees proceeding to cry. Clement's father rushed to her to figure out what had seemed to be the problem. "Clement is dead."Drving while using a cell phone is very dangerous. It is very life threatening, and the road needs your full attention when driving.

By: Amyaah Richardson

A Merciful Love

Todavía te sigo amando desde lo más profundo de mi corazón
eres como ese fuego del infierno que me hace pecar
me arrepiento de haberlo hecho
sabes que no te olvido, te lloro cada noche y día
pero no quiero volver a caer en el amor
Tal vez fue mi culpa
O tal vez fue culpa de los dos
Ninguno de los dos estaba preparado
Pero no te importo
Me hiciste daño
Me viste llorar
Y no hiciste nada al respecto
Vuelves sin decir nada
Como si nada hubiera pasado
Me creas nuevas promesas
Ilusiones falsas piensas que caeré
Pero solo jugaste conmigo
Una vez
No importa lo que diga mi corazón
Prefiero olvidarte
Y solo tenerte como un recuerdo.

By: Brayan Sanchez

No Todo es Real

Enamorarme de él fue como caer en desgracia
Todo envuelto en uno, él era tantos pecados
Hubiera hecho cualquier cosa
Todo por él
Y si me lo preguntas
Lo haría todo de nuevo
Ellos dicen "los chicos buenos van al cielo"
Pero los chicos malos te traen el cielo
No te das cuenta del poder que tienen
Hasta que te abandonan
Y los quieres de regreso
Nada del mundo te prepara para eso
No estoy avergonzado
Él no era el indicado
Lo se es extraño de decir pero
Lo extraño como si fuera parte de mi
No tenía idea de en qué nos convertimos los dos
No hay arrepentimiento
Solo pensé que era divertido
Pero terminó jugando conmigo
Creo que caí en su sucio juego
Aún recuerdo
El momento que nos conocimos
La impresión que plantó en mi
El jardin que dejo
Supongo que la lluvia
Fue la mitad del efecto
Y la otra mitad
Algo que él mismo iba destruyendo
Como si de hiedra venenosa se tratara.

By: Brayan Sanchez

Heaven

Falling in love with him was like falling from grace
All at once
He defined so many of my sins
I would have done anything
For him
And if you ask me today
I would do it all over again
They say,
Good boys go to heaven
But bad boys bring you to heaven
You don't realize the power they have
Until they abandon you
And you want them back
Nothing in the world prepares you for that.
I'm not ashamed
He wasn't meant for me
I know it's strange to say, but
I miss him like he was a part of me
I had no idea what would become of us
There is no regret
I just thought he was fun
But he ended up playing with me
I think I fell into his dirty game
I still remember
The moment we met
The impression he planted in me
The garden he left
I guess the rain was half the defect.
And the other half
was something that he himself
created
he planted poison ivy.

By: Brayan Sanchez

Pensamientos Enfermos

Puede que simplemente seamos crueles
Pero así es como estamos diseñados.
Me tienes tan jodido
Pienso en ti la mayor parte del tiempo
Entonces pienso en perder la cabeza
Quiero parar antes de que nos atrapen
Antes que sea demasiado tarde
Yo tengo cosas que quiero
Pero tú estás en la cima
En la parte superior
Somos psicópatas para siempre
En diamantes y cuero
Nunca mejoraremos
Mira lo que has causado
Este sentimiento en mi corazón
¿Quieres saber qué te está adormeciendo?
Hermoso es cuando el daño está hecho.
Tú me conoces, no me moveré
Y si me lastimas te arrepentirás de haberlo hecho
No importa cuanto te ame
Estoy a punto de empezar a tomar lo que es mío.
Entonces pensaré en perder la cabeza.
Quiero parar antes de que nos atrapen
Pero no pares
no te detengas
Nunca nos rendiremos
Por eso tengo estos
Sentimientos por ti
Mira lo que has causado (tú causaste)
Me tratas duro (me tratas duro)
Y aún así te sigo amando
Horas después de medianoche
Pensar en ti
No sé cómo empezó
Siento que corres en mi mente
Arrastrándome en el piso porque te extraño

Nadie piensa como tú y yo,
Mírame, mira lo que empezaste.
Estoy tan enfermo y con el corazón roto,
Y todo es gracias a ti.
He estado paseando
bajo la luz de la luna
Buscándote
Sólo mi sombra me acompaña
En este viaje para irte a buscar
Así que pon tus labios
En mis cicatrices
Y enséñame a amar
Dale a mi lento corazón el ritmo de sentir ser amado
No quiero que te vayas
Necesito más de ti
En mi vida
Nadie debería estar solo
Haría cualquier cosa por estar contigo
No sabes que yo estoy enloqueciendo
Y en el momento me enamoro de ti
No quiero que te vayas
Necesito más de ti
En mi vida
Ya que estoy perdidamente enamorado de ti.

By: Brayan Sanchez

Discovering Me

As I put on my chest binder for the first time, it felt like I had final-ly been let free from a cage that I had been locked in all my life. I always grew up feeling like I didn't fit in anywhere. Despite all the friends I had around me who I connected with deeply, it was hard to fit in when it felt like something telling me I was made to be something I wasn't yet. This feeling followed me as I grew up, making me feel the need to fill that void with my academics. I always earned straight A's and made the honor roll to keep myself from having to think about the feeling of never fitting in. Every-thing stopped when Covid hit, however.

I was left feeling lost and alone in my thoughts, the lock-down forcing me to face feelings I had never wanted to face before. As I fell into a pit of loneliness, where I couldn't easily turn to my friends to help distract me from the thoughts, this feeling of being stuck with myself, someone I didn't like, led to a drastic decline in my academics. As I fell into a deep depression about my appearance, that's when it really hit me that I was transgender, fi-nally finding the person I had always wanted to be. While it wasn't easy, since I didn't have the support from my family. I found new friends who would accept and support my changes to being the **true me**.

One way they did this was by helping me buy my chest binder. When I put it on for the first time, it was like I had finally found the reason I was alive. The person *I wanted* to be and not the person *everyone said* I had to be. This helped me mentally and I was able to improve on my academics, getting back into the groove of earning at least Bs in all my classes. I finally found myself after years of feeling like an impostor of someone I had yet to become.

By: Conner Lopez

The Dance of Gun Violence

A teenage student named Alexander was getting ready to go out with friends on his prom night. He is going with his friends Brock and Juan. They have been friends all of middle school and high school. Brock is a great athlete and has multiple scholarships to Division I teams for football. Juan has a great business opportunity to help his family out after high school. He has been looking forward to working all year to graduate. A teacher who has been helping all of his students in his last years of teaching at the high school level decides to go to all the senior activities to chaperone. His name is Mr. Garcia, and he has been favored by all the students on campus and chose to chaperone the prom dance. One student who has been manipulated and bullied by a couple students, his name is Travis, has been contemplating on taking his life, but he is too afraid to do so. He has access to firearms because he has careless parents. His life hasn't been the best. He didn't know he was going to the prom, but he hadn't been well mentally and missed the last two days of school.

Prom night approaches Alexander and his friends had their dates and everything that night was great, and the plans were in motion. They were in the limo on their way to the prom venue about 40 minutes away, and they were all excited about it. Mr. Garcia and the rest of the faculty have all the tables and chairs and music ready. They had been working all day to make the venue perfect. They all woke up early, got ready, and after planning everything was coming together.

Travis got into this huge argument with his parents the night before. His father called him insult after insult. Travis has been fighting hard to be successful, and is on track to graduate. After that, he took his parents' firearm and ran away from home. He wasn't in the right state of mind as he was going out. He had 3 magazines and a 32-caliber pistol just that alone can hurt him or anybody else. Later in the night, before the dance after leaving home Travis got hungry and thirsty. He was fighting for survival with the firearm in his pocket he saw a 24 hour liquor store open. Travis walks in, points the gun at the cashier, and says give me all the money or I'll shoot. It is at this very moment after fighting to have a successful life Travis lost sense of who he was; he had no compassion for anything. He attempted to rob the store successfully, taking the money, and running as far as possible.

Alexander and his friends are almost at the prom. A couple of minutes away Juan mentions what he heard about Travis. He hears what happened to him the night before that he ran away from home, and he was caught on camera robbing a liquor store. It turns out Juan was the only person to know what happened because he has a friend who is a police officer. Brock and Alexander are shocked to hear about the news. But they arrive at the dance and get off the limo and take their seats. Travis in fear of what's happening, but also, he is not mentally healthy pointing the gun to his head and thinking about taking his life and laughing about it. He's hallucinating. Now he starts contemplating on going to the dance and taking their lives as well.

While Travis was hiding, someone finds Travis and without hesitation Travis shoots the person and runs away. That person died on the spot. As Travis is running, he is so tired he makes it back home. After Travis makes it home, he confronts his father and points his gun at him. Travis yells at him getting his point across and ends up killing his father shooting him at point blank range. Travis runs again. Later on, his mom finds his dad's dead body. She calls the police and they put a warrant out for Travis' arrest. Now at this point Alexander and his friends are enjoying the dance, but Alexander gets the urge to tell someone about Travis because that was his classmate.

He mentions it to Mr. Garcia outside the venue. Mr. Garcia talks about it to the director of the dance, and they kind of blow it off because they don't think Travis is going to be there. The news about Travis gets around to the point Brock and Juan get worried and Alexander does too. They all don't know what to do. A little before Travis ran away, Travis took his father's other gun, an AR-15 rifle, so Travis ends up going to the dance and what happens next is something no one even thought about.

Travis ends up in front of the group of teens who bullied him, and he takes their lives. Alexander noticing quickly, he pushes his date, and takes a few bullets along with Juan and Brock. Travis letting off his ammo go, he grabs his pistol and takes his own life after he knew there was no way out. Mr. Garcia as soon as he hears the gunfire ran, and called 911. Alexander, Brock, and Juan all were quickly transported to the hospital. The doctors try to do whatever they can for them to survive, unfortunately, Juan ends up not making it. He took the most damage and the doctors did what they could. Brock was alive and stable, but lost all feeling to his legs. There is a large chance he won't be able to walk after the bullets hit a part of his spine. Alexander had lost a lot of blood, but the doctors were able to remove fractions of the bullets from his body. It will be a long recovery process. A year after the shooting Brock and Alexander go to Juan's grave and talk about the trauma they went through; they both still go to therapy for the PTSD from the gun violence.

By: William Garcia

Deep Words

Words are like bombs. How can something so small,
Turn into something so terribly wrong?
What starts as something not hurtful at all
Can leave you singing a miserable song
Something so small can leave you in tears
Words are like bombs, something you can't unhear
And the memories can haunt you for years
Leaving the words to whisper in your ear
As sharp as knives, they glisten in your mind
Causing you to be blinded by the night
Keep in mind kind words are so hard to find
When they are found you will soon see the light
Every now and then you will take some pows
But for now, we might as well take a bow

By: Nyssa Rodarte, Destiny Orellana, Sara Tesfaghabriel, and Ashley Bejar Martinez

Mental Health

I struggled with mental health
especially in junior year
bad depressive episodes
and panic attacks
I even had an eating disorder

It made my depression worse
It happened in the summer
going to junior year
The days felt never-ending
and at night I cried myself to sleep

Praying to God to help me get out
of that mental space
I felt like I hit lower than rock bottom
a mindset that I couldn't get out of
I couldn't talk to my friends or family about it

Didn't want to worry my family
I would make my friends scared
My friends had to almost tell my parents
it got really bad

Friends thought I wanted to cease living
I didn't go to school for a whole week
I went full ghost on everybody
that's how bad it really was

Continuing throughout junior year,
my mental health was like an on and off switch.
had some good days
and would have some bad days

It started to affect everything
my grades, my attendance,
my physical appearance, my moods,

 and even my relationships

Summer going into senior year,
I was sick and tired
of feeling sick and tired
I wanted to stop feeling like a sag of crap

I wanted to start feeling like a teenager again
started working on self-love and confidence,
doing things that made me feel happy
To make me feel alive again

Hanging out with my friends,
listening to music,
watching my favorite movies,
taking baby steps

Things started to get better for me
mental health was finally improving
my friends and I are a lot closer
my relationship with food was getting better

I taught myself that it's okay to gain a couple pounds
to not waste my life on looking at calories
a huge weight was lifted off my shoulders.
I still struggled a little bit with my mental health

I learned how to deal with it on my own,
to take one day at a time
it's okay to feel
and it's okay to not feel okay.

By: Rubee Gomez

Manifesto

People stay in bad relationships because they have issues with change, and they are scared to leave and are fearful of consequences. They also have attachment issues to the person. It is hard to get away from a relationship obsession for some reason. People just have the tendency to stay with a bad person, till it drives them crazy. I don't know why people cheat. But I am a firm believer that they are cheating to either get away from a bad relationship, or they cheat because they feel they are better than their significant other. But when they do cheat it usually tends to lead to a downgrade. It is about self-worth, and if you have integrity you would not live a double life. You would care enough about yourself to be honest, and be true to yourself.

By: Daniel Santa Cruz

Impact of Covid 19

It was March 13 of 2020
They said it would only be for two weeks
Boy would they be so wrong
What was supposed to be two weeks turned into a year
What was supposed to be a break was turned into isolation
The signs were there I was just trying to be optimistic
I remember they day like it was yesterday
Everyone was going to every store
Honestly it looked like it came out of a movie
After that was over it was pretty normal
Or so I thought
The change started slowly but steadily
With so much free time in my hands I didn't know what to do
I could not go out like some of my other friends
So I only had a new phone, online friends, and the occasional
church gathering
What seem to be a dream come true became a sad reality
I started to realize what I wanted
But in return I lost some sense of myself
I thought I preferred to be alone
I thought I would be fine if people left
I thought being in quarantine was going to be the best thing for me
It turned out to be the opposite
I started to lose a lot of friends
My family lost the motivation to go out
My lack of communication started showing
Everything that I thought I hated was something I needed
My connection with my family was something that I realize
was never there
My friends leaving showed I had some fear of abandonment
Everything was changing and I didn't even realize it
Not just inside my life
But the outside too
When computers were rumored to be used prevalently at school
I thought it was something that was super advanced
Now it is the norm

Influencers were popping up everywhere
And everyone wanted to be one
When having a phone was something only a few had
Now everyone has it out
So much has changed
And we didn't notice
I didn't notice
The world is still changing
And it's not stopping any time soon

By: Mauricio Canil

Drug Trade

Once upon a time there was a poor Mexican teenager who was called Manuel. He was a 19-year-old. Manuel lived in the state of Mexico. He was very poor. He lived in a small house. His house was in very bad condition. His father Emmanuel was a mechanic. He fixed many cars, and his mother Teresa worked in a factory where she created clothing like shirts and jeans. His parents were very hard workers because they wanted their son to have a good life, but Manuel's parents couldn't afford to pay his private school or to travel to different cities.

Manuel wanted to start a new life with his parents because he thinks that they work hard to pay bills and expenses. So then when Manuel was walking to the market to buy chips, he was getting abused by some strangers who were walking around there to sell some drugs because the random stranger wanted to be wealthy. The strangers wanted to use that money from the drugs to buy luxurious things and do illegal things like rob banks and many other stores that were in the area. When they abused Manuel, he tried to buy the drugs from the stranger that was selling them. When he bought them, he started to get addicted. Then he started to join the business to sell drugs, and then when he sold drugs the police started to arrest the people who were selling the drugs, so then Manuel ran away from the police because he didn't want his parents to know that he was getting addicted to drugs.

When he was running away from the police the police started to block the streets and started to chase Manuel because he knew the organization and what they could do. When the police knew who he was working for, they started to investigate more on Manuel because he knew the leader. After Manuel escaped from the police, he got to the base where the organization was set up. When he was there, he talked to the leader about the police, and he found out that they were looking for him. The leader started to hide the evidence, and also he would escape with the money. When they tried to escape, it was already too late to escape. The police arrived and the swat team was there to detain everyone who was involved in the drug trade, and when they tried to detain everyone the leader tried to escape by shooting the officers. When the leader tried to escape Manuel stopped the leader and fought with the leader because he knew that he was the cause of all these drug problems, and he wanted revenge on the leader.

When he fought him, Manuel beat up the leader. The police came and they finally detained the leader. Manuel was also taken by the police because he was also involved in the crime, so then they sent Manuel to jail. Then after a week, Manuel was transferred to the court to testify on the crimes he did. When he told the court about what happened during the crime, the judge was deciding if he should let go of Manuel or have him stay in jail for a long time. Then after 15 minutes the court decided that Manuel should be in jail for only two years, and then for the leader they gave him fifty years of prison time on an island with maximum security. There would not be a fine to release him for all the crimes he did in the past like drug trading.

In conclusion, when Manuel heard they were going to release him from all charges in two years he was happier than ever because he was going to get out prison. Then Manuel realized that he would start a better life by working hard, and also not getting into trouble with drugs or any other things. He learned that he should avoid making the same mistakes all over again. When he learned that, he started to get more experience by working hard and dedication on his job and his life.

Once he got released, he started to work a full-time job and then he began to buy a bigger and better house and then a sports car. He had worked so much, he was like a changed person with value and honor. When he was successful, he returned to his parents' house to apologize for leaving them behind. Also for making them worried, so then after apologizing Manuel surprised his parents by moving them into his new property. They were proud of their son for working hard and being successful, and leaving the dark life behind.

By: Manuel Cisneros

Dear Old Danny Boy

A nice stroll after hours, as the street lights flicker
The two wandered down the vendor filled paths
The aroma surrounded pupils, the stench of liquor
A scene so perfect the embodiment of a photograph

Puffs flow within the air, strawberry blast
The boy looks a bit pensive viewing the small artifact
The friend coughed the sense of repast
Slowly entering his own field of abstract

One two three he inhaled
"That is right Danny boy!" the friend said vocally proud
His face portraying it all, the disgust, yet he must not unveil
Danny boy can not admit dishonesty,
"wouldn't mind trying again"
he thought as he blew

As time passed the more the cravings grew
Variety is needed so desperately for, oh Danny boy
Plants, shrooms, needles, pills the body and mind,
the poor boy implored
The constant hunger eradicated him,
so harmfully he was far from poise

Oh Danny boy, the life it calls no more,
please accept this cruel embrace
The chains of your addiction
your lifeless body, a broken frame
The beat of your heart increases,
you know this is it, slowly becoming a case
As the foam begins to form acknowledging the fact
overtime your body became maimed

Dear old Danny boy the sky is so beautiful on this unfortunate day
He was gone, why did you follow the intuition of stupidity
One life is all you have now wasted,

may your soul rest and sway
My dear son, oh I miss you so,
you no longer need the feeling of validity

Dear old Danny boy,
papa loves you so
You will always live on
in my heart,
I love you and
goodnight mi precioso

By: Isabella Gonzalez

Blooming

Flowers bloom as the sunlight glows,
its light is so bright but its just right.
Never shall it stop from growing,
as the glow will never stop towards them.

The flowers slowly expand their pedals,
a variety of colors begin to appear.
No matter what flower the seed grew into,
they all have their own beauty.

Their leaves are part of their identity,
they never leave them behind as they also grow.
These flowers are the beauty in life,
they are part of what nature is.

This is a creation that compares to nothing else,
because of its uniqueness.
They are the way through peace and love,
as they are shared within relationships.

Always growing in every part of the world,
as they bring happiness and joy.
Never shall these be abandoned,
for these are special and important to us all.

The blooming is what spreads good fortune,
no matter where they are given
or who they are given to.
This is a bloom that will never end,
no matter what season it changes to

By: Stephanie Velazquez

Faith

Negativity comes and goes,
clouds move as the wind blows,
Sadness being never-ending,
as rain pours every drop.

Mistakes occur unexpectedly,
just like birds that fall from trees.
Still the sun shines upon us,
hoping to see faith and motivation.

God is the lord who protects,
and leads us.
He is within our hearts,
through every moment.

There is no need to fear within ourselves,
we are taken care of by the King.
Every part of nature is within his will,
we all do what we can to survive in this world.

He has our lives in His hands,
every day not always according to our plans.
Give your all to Him,
as He cares about our choices in life.

Failure is meant to occur,
not to cry, but to learn from.
We are meant to grow into improvement,
not into perfection.

Faith is what matters the most.

By: Stephanie Velazquez

Responsibilities

Everyday leads into life's journey,
plans are happening before the time comes.
Expectations and requirements,
needed to be fulfilled on a timeline.

A routine that repeats until the very end,
never-ending as it is continuous.
Responsibilities needing to be done,
by each and every one of us.

Whether it is attending school, going to church,
there is always something to do.
It is unnecessary to complain or procrastinate,
it will only be a distraction from our life.

There should be more moving and doing,
even if it is boring or too much.
We must not let ourselves down by laziness,
even if work can be full of craziness.

Work is worth the wellness in life,
even if there are challenges in every step.
Responsibilities should be taken seriously,
as they can affect future, plans, or goals.

This is your responsibility,
don´t you ever give up on yourself.

By: Stephanie Velazquez

Overthinking

Children are born with happiness,
as they arrive in the world.
They grow until reality hits,
perfection is what is expected of them.

There is fear of letting themselves down,
as they are looked down upon.
Every choice or action is overthought,
as it can lead to destruction.

Suspense is within every life,
never knowing what will come next.
Just as the weather changes,
being bipolar as the seasons continue.

Overthinking is an enemy,
it attacks, but never ends.
It takes control until the very end,
never leading us anywhere, but to fear.

It arrives in any instant anywhere,
it brings terror as others watch.
Breaking down is unnecessary,
change needs to be done.

Feel the emotions and control them,
there is no time to think.
No need to think what one should feel,
there should be more doing than thinking.

Overthinking is only a distraction.

By: Stephanie Velazquez

Coming Out

A secret in a family
With none, we did not keep secrets
For years, I kept it silent
I knew what it meant if they found out
I would have been rejected and humiliated

A religious mother
Married to a *machista* father
And two brothers with closed minds
How could I turn out to be gay
They raised me to be a man

I had the beliefs
I had the culture
Why would I be the one to defy them
I would defy them
just for them to deny me

The first time I spoke up
I was shut down
This time I was ready
I wouldn't let mother's words
throw me back in the closet

It took years to build up thick skin
One that their words could no longer cut

A regular day at school came
Little did I know,
my secret would be out
A dumb dispute that caused me to get suspended
The office called so I could get picked up

Thanks to the state law
my secret was protected
I thought I was safe

But my family wanted answers
I was ready to give them

First was my oldest brother
I told him I was gay
And he said he loves me
No matter what
He was there for me to tell mother

A long argument assembled like a tornado
I told mother
She kept asking why
Nothing she could do could change me
She understood my pain and accepted me

Finally my father and other brother were next
They were the most *machistas* in our household
I knew it wouldn't be easy
But I stood firm and didn't hold back
They would not be the reason my truth gets shut down

I am a young gay Hispanic teen
It took time to build the force to tell my family
With all odds against me I did it
It was hard but not impossible

My story won't be the same as yours
But if I did it
Who says you can't
Stand in your truth
I am gay, and I am still a strong man

By: Oscar Banuelos

Grief

I still wait for you to walk in the door
With your bags from T.J Maxx, Nordstrom, and Home Goods
Waiting to go run in your room to see what you got me
These funky looking shirts
I always pretended to like them just so you wouldn't get mad
I am still waiting to pretend again

Every Saturday morning I walk into the dining room
Hoping to see you sitting on the chair that everyone knew was
yours
Drinking your McDonald's coffee with your pan dulce
I walk in and the chair is empty just like my heart

Early Sunday mornings
You get up and garden
Your plants and front yard had to look nice
Shopping for hours for silly garden statues
I begged and begged to go home because of how tired I was
I now want to go shopping for them silly statues again

Every Thursday night at 9 pm you watched your novella
I would go into your room and lay in the bed with you
I am trying to put together what the actors are saying
I can't catch up with their Spanish as it annoys me
I get up and go to the living room to be on my phone
Today I would stay to watch the entire episode with you
More time around you is all I long for

You are now coming home from a treatment
They give us the news
Only a few weeks they said
You gave yourself 3 months

These months go by fast
The last moments I had with you
In bed is all you could do

That is what you hated most
Seeing you from going shopping,
gardening and getting up on a Saturday mornings for coffee
To staying in bed 24/7 needing help from us
This shattered my heart the 'most
And all because of a dumb sickness
Cancer

My sweet Grandma
My angel
Please come back to me
I promise to love you for eternity.

By: Savanah Murillo

Money isn't Everything

My dad, a stubborn air conditioner repairman, often told me, "Don't do things your heart feels guilty of." Within his profession, my father stands as a rare figure who refrains from upselling and deceiving his clients for profit. He prioritizes ethics ahead of business. It was after last summer that I began to understand why.

During my last summer break, much like many of my classmates began seeking jobs, I too was looking forward to obtaining some money. Yet, the toil of my dad's job persuaded me to seek a shortcut. Growing up, I was comfortable with cheap second-hand items. *EBay*, the biggest online market for used items, occupies my screen daily. It was one day that I discovered a way of basically making money out of thin air.

This is called "*EBay* drop-shipping." Imagine stumbling upon a used copy of *The Great Gatsby* listed for $10. Here's where the magic happens: I list the same book, but with a more appealing product image and a price tag of $17. The twist is, I don't actually possess the book. Instead, once a buyer purchases from me, I then procure it from the original seller at a lower price and have it shipped directly to my customer. This method of drop-shipping allows me to pocket a $5 profit per transaction. Generating profit out of nothing.

My small business quickly expanded. I diversified my offerings to video game disks, fishing gear, sports shoes—anything you can think of. As a fabulously successful "five-star seller," the delightful "Cha-Ching" notifications would wake me from my sleep. However, despite my extraordinary success, I felt an indescribable sense of guilt from my "business." From the bottom of my heart, I understood that drop-shipping is not at all justified.

Every day at the dinner table, I couldn't initiate conversations with my dad. An indescribable feeling of fear arose and prevented me from sharing with him the bits and pieces of my day. While my dad confused work with pleasure, I, conversely, sat in front of a screen for 8 hours mindlessly hunting for the next *EBay* deal, doing nothing using my time. There wasn't any verbal exchange at the table. I was just eating silently and incessantly, fulfilling my hunger and desires.

It was the warmest day of the summer. My dad required my assistance and brought me alongside. The heat seemed to liquefy the asphalt beneath our feet, generating a pungent odor. I knew right away it would be an unpleasant experience. After we transported all our equipment into the client's house, I sat on a refrigerant tank and breathed desperately. Even the house owner acknowledged that it was too hot to do anything. However, the heat could not distract my dad. He immediately began examining the AC with his calloused hands. Meanwhile, I was boiled. My back was already soaked with perspiration from merely passing some tools to my dad. Every minute felt unbearable.

Three hours later, my dad revived the AC. The refreshing air breezed away the heat and swept away my frustration and exhaustion. The house owner immediately walked up to my dad with an enormous radiant smile that felt warmer than the sun. "Thank you! Chen shi-fu (technician)," the homeowner said as he shook hands vigorously. The room was immediately filled with joy and laughter. My dad smiled and waved his hand, "Easy task, easy task, that's nothing." However, despite all the work and labor, my dad didn't charge this client an extra cent. My dad was just proud of his creation.

The effort he put in outweighed the money he earned tremendously. This is the cost of not lying to your customers and not upselling your service. However, I finally realized the reason why he places ethics ahead of business. Because from wrestling with monetary temptations coupled with unbearable physical distress, my dad was able to deepen his understanding of himself. Standing amidst the refreshing breeze, the house owner's spirited and lively smile also taught me the imperativeness of following ethics: to create positivity and contribute to a better world.

It soon became clear why I felt guilty and unethical for drop-shipping. While grappling between the lucrative but morally questionable practice of drop-shipping, I compromised ethics. Unlike my dad who earned his money through hard work and created value in exchange for his money, I, conversely, exploited gaps in consumer knowledge. I didn't "earn" my money, and I essentially lied to my customers. This was why I felt guilty and couldn't have conversations with my dad at dinner because I would be ashamed to share.

That night, at the dinner table, I set aside my chopsticks. "Ba," I finally mustered the courage to ask, "How was your day?"

By: Jiakang Chen

Birdie the Cat

In a quiet and small town, there lived an indoor cat who lived in an even quieter home. The cat's name was Birdie, and this is the home she had lived inside all her life. Although she had only lived for three years, she had already experienced the feeling of being lonely. Her caretakers had adopted her in hopes of creating a new thrill in their own lives, but they had grown tired of Birdie fast and were "not cruel enough" to let her go. Of course, Birdie was given her normal meals once a day, but sometimes her owners over fill her bowl and other times would under fill it.

Birdie feels this loneliness every day, "what a boring thing to do" is what she often says. "I feel like I'm waiting for something that isn't going to happen." All that Birdie wants is someone to acknowledge her, to let her crawl up on their lap and have someone to say, "it must be so hard, to be such a small kitten, in a world so big." But Birdie knows what she wants is too much. And she mustn't leave the home she was born in, no matter how much she had longed to see the other world. She is inexperienced and the world outside is far more cruel than the world she is currently living in. In other words, she is scared.

Although she still finds at least one amusing pastime which is staring out the window. She loves to look outside and stare at the real birds flying over the once loved garden in her backyard. She wondered how a little cat like her would go by if she had wings like these birds. She wondered how far these birds go and how far really is too far for them. On one of these days, as Birdie was doing her usual observance of the day, out of nowhere a big and dirty cat jumped up from the other side of the rusted fence and chased over these birds. Birdie was in complete shock at this act, she took a good look at this disturbance of a creature, he was on the verge of being as big as a dog, and had a gray coat of dirt as opposed to the orange fur that was left of this feline. His fur was so dirty it made Birdie lick her own as if she felt filthy by just looking at him.

She scowls in annoyance at this thing who finds joy in chasing such helpless creatures. So much so, that the newly announced feline becomes aware of the staring and halts his pleasant hunt and stares right back at Birdie. "Is that supposed to be fun?"

Birdie says, attempting to sound intimidating, but from the tiny structure she embodies not to mention the rather muffled voice she has due to the window in between the two it sounded more as if she was the one being intimidated. "Of course it's fun, I wouldn't be doing it if it were otherwise." Birdie looks away and stays silent hoping he would go bother someone else's day.

"My name is Beau, although I'm happy enough to go by any other name you'd want," the dusty cat puffed up his chest and lifted his chin, proud of the first impression he had made for himself. Birdie scoffed and chuckled at his act and found his well-pleased performance rather foolish. "Beau, what a stupid name," hoping that this will make him leave so that the birds would return to her garden. This however did the exact opposite, as Beau now glared at her with complete distaste, as to him, this was an unforgivable insult to his character."

"*Stupid, Stupid, Little* cat, your brain is the same as your body! The feline in front of you right now has lived hundreds of lives. I have seen what your little head cannot comprehend. I have influenced great men to become historical leaders! I was the pet of the notorious settlers of the very ground you walk on—I was the praised pet of Cleopatra—I had murals and writings dedicated to my name! I am the very inspiration the French had to build their cathedrals and the same for the Romans! I am as stupid as you are intelligent, little cat."

Birdie, with her mouth open and wide, stood in disbelief. Not because the dirty cat before her was an absolute conspicuous individual, what caught her was the fact he claims that he has lived hundreds of lives. They stared in silence for a bit, Beau was waiting for Birdie to spew out a new insult of defamation, so he can spew out a quicker and more denigrating reply than the first.

What broke the silence was a question from Birdie that came out in a genuinely curious tone, "Have you really lived hundreds of lives?" "—of course I have" Beau cuts off still annoyed by Birdie's perceived arrogance. Birdie watches her words carefully this time, not wanting to offend Beau once more, especially since she has been pulled aback by his statement and had to know more.

"I'm in my first life, and I am already bored, am I doomed to live this again? And again Once more?" her voice cracks while saying it, to her this seems like a punishment rather than a blessing. Beau found pity in her words, "Silly cat, after this life you will be born in all these new environments and you will experience so much more." "Experience what exactly?" Birdie is still perplexed by this newfound ability that her species is able to undertake. "Experience the world of course! See all of its beauty and find what life is all about!" Beau says this gazing at nowhere almost as if he is reminiscing of all that he himself had experienced.

Birdie is of course, fascinated by Beau's claim she opts for him to tell her about all his fascinating stories and adventures. So he did, he did for a while, he would come over every day before sundown to tell Birdie all of his fascinating stories of his past lives, every one of them more daring and longer than the next. Through this, their relationship had grown, and Beau had started staying longer and they had talked more.

"Why don›t you get out?" Beau asks in one of his story telling consultations. "Get out where?" Birdie asked, puzzled with Beaus' halt in his recent life story for this out-of-context question. "Out of this house, your owners keep the door open for you to do so, why don't you leave?"

Birdie sits with that question for a moment, not because she doesn't know the answer, but such a question of leaving the very place she has been in her whole life was daunting to little Birdie. "This is all I know," she looks down at her paws sitting with her confession in her head, what a silly question, how could Birdie leave? "It's much too dangerous for a little cat like me, such a big scary world, and I'm so small. How could I even survive?"

Beau chuckles at this, has she not paid attention to any of his stories? Has she simply blanked out when Beau had finished every story with his deaths, but then to bring up another story of the life he has after? "It's not about surviving, Birdie, it's about living."

"But how must I live if I don't receive great moments?" "Well Birdie, great moments will come. Even when nothing happens at all. It's truly what you decide to be great, is when life begins." Birdie thinks, and thinks, although she is scared, if there is a chance that she may live a life like Beau, she is willing to take a chance. So she leaves. She leaves her boring and lifeless home to start anew alongside Beau. He was more than happy to show her all the beautiful moments Birdie's new life had in store for her. And Beau realized, out of all the lives he's lived before, this one will be his favorite.

By: Isabella Loya

The Lost Girl

I'm laying in bed, it's seven thirty in the morning. I struggle to get up, exhausted. I thought to myself how could I be so worn out when I went to bed at nine. It's not that I'm physically drained. I'm mentally drained. My mother yelled at me from downstairs, telling me I'm going to be late. What's the point of getting to school? What am I living for? I finally have the strength to get up. She looks at me as I'm walking out the door… she says "why do you look so tired and what time did you go to sleep."

My mother doesn't realize I'm struggling. She thinks because I'm always smiling; I have no problems. I'm on my way to school with my head looking out the window. My sister is playing music, trying to cheer me up because she sees my pain and suffering. "Why are you playing your music so loud, Angela?" I exclaimed to my sister. She doesn't react. Angela knows all my problems. I go to her for support. It's easy to talk to her. My mom, not so much. I trust her, but she won't understand.

Once I arrive at school, I put on an act. I feel like my struggles are not valid. My friends are going through worse, and I need to be there for them. My best friend Sage is going through a breakup and I don't know what's wrong with me. So I put a smile on my face and act like nothing is wrong. Not being able to compare my feelings with theirs is the hard part.

My favorite part of school is seeing my friends. Nutrition is when we talk and gossip about anything. We have our laughs and moments. We cry together sometimes too. On my way to 4th period I walk to class alone listening to depressing music, with the thoughts of, am I depressed? Is this just a phase that I will overcome or do I actually need to get help? At this point I just want to go home, but 4th period is my favorite class. I have the best teacher. Her words are so inspiring. Mrs. E. She always has the most inspirational words. They speak to me.

When she talks, I'm so intrigued because everything she says is what I'm feeling. I don't talk to her about my feelings, but I always try to take her words as advice. It's been a week and I haven't gone to school. My mom said I can stay home as long as I keep my grades up, but I'm losing motivation. I'm becoming the person who is "lazy" in my mom's eyes. She went through my phone and read my notes.

My mom came up to me and finally asked what's wrong. I feel seen for the first time as a person with feelings rather than a person who is just being passive. She panics! She cries because she feels like a failure. It hit me. My mom does care and she understands. I felt so alone, but just having my mother by my side was all I needed. She called my doctor immediately. She pulls me into the restroom and hands me the phone.

The next thing I know, they are asking me so many questions. My mom sits there and listens to my responses with tears in her eyes. "Do you have suicidal thoughts," I answered with no. The relief in my mother's eyes; I felt her pain was being caused by my pain. The doctor recommended therapy as soon as possible to treat my "seasonal depression." Was I really depressed? I knew it would go away, but it was driving me insane. I had my first counseling meeting with my therapist.

I absolutely hated talking to some stranger about my life. I cried to my sister when I got home. I told her how disappointed I was in myself and that I would not go back for another session. I did my research. It became clear I could do things on my own to heal from my depression. I started by cleaning my room. It had been about 3 weeks since I truly deep cleaned my room. Filthy! I was living like a pig. Started going on walks to get fresh air and sunlight.

I was on medication that was supposed to help with my low iron and vitamin D because that apparently affected when a person is depressed. My mother would come home every day asking me how I was feeling. She was my inspiration to get better. I caused her to worry. I am doing so much better now. I lived in this world for what seemed like forever, where I thought no one cared, and no one loved me. I thought my feelings were not valid, but I was wrong. It was hard. I was going through so much and no one noticed. I gave so many signs. I've learned a lot. Overcoming depression is possible. It takes some work, but it's worth it. I did it for my mom, but it benefited me so much. Depression is temporary, happiness is a choice. You have to keep going, and never give up. Depression cannot exist in a heart that has gratitude. If you need help, get the help you need. Brighter days are coming.

By: Jazmine Diaz

Impact of Social Media

She stood there, crying with a flow of tears as she scrolled through the comments. Serenity did not like the negative comments after she posted a picture of herself. It always bothered her to see that there is always something for people to judge or criticize. She always felt uncomfortable about her appearance, but she would express herself by posting herself in beautiful sceneries whenever she went out. As a quiet, shy person, this was the only way she was able to socialize with her peers.

Her friend Celeste had always been the person to defend Serenity by responding to the negative comments because she knew that Serenity would just leave the negative comments, and accept what people say. Her friend would always tell her that social media is not necessary to feel good about yourself just because everyone posts everything. Serenity did not have social media at first, until Tessa would always pick on her, she is the popular cheerleader at the school. She posted all the time what she was doing, where she was, and what friends she was with. Tessa was the person that told Serenity that she should get social media if she wanted to get along with everyone. Serenity was convinced that she was finally going to be able to make more friends, so she installed it.

Serenity´s mother did not like the idea. She would notice the changes and impact, it caused on her daughter. Before she would socialize with her siblings, play with them, and help with their homework. She was more open to her family because at school she would always be quiet unless she was with her friend Celeste. It hurts her to see how her daughter is changing herself just to get along with her peers. She felt as if Serenity did not care about her family anymore. Whenever her mother spoke to her, Serenity remained silent as she looked at peers' posts on social media and how everyone would get along. Serenity wanted to know what it was that she was doing wrong that no other people, except Celeste, liked her.

It was not until one day, Jacob had come up to Serenity when no one else was around to tell her that Tessa lied to her classmates saying that she was bullied and made fun of by Serenity. Jacob is Serenity´s neighbor and he had known her for years. They have been friends since sixth grade and they now still keep in contact with each other. Serenity knew that he was not like the others. He did not care if they would tell him anything about not having social media because he cared more about being in football and other sports. Serenity always felt comfortable with him because he would make her feel better whenever she was upset.

Now that Serenity knew why peers or classmates would always criticize her, she decided to delete all the social media she had. She decided she would spend more of her time with her family and friends. She apologized to her mother for how she had been acting, and that she would try to focus on herself to get over all the negativity she went through. Her mother had noticed that now Serenity had been herself again because she would play around with her little brother and sister and help them with their homework. She would also go out either with Celeste or Jacob during her free time instead of going out just to come up with pictures to post on social media. These changes had impacted Serenity and her daily habits.

Tessa had seemed annoyed by the fact that she lost followers. This was because Jacob decided to tell everyone that she had been lying to them the whole time about being bullied by Serenity. He knew she only did this to be the most popular girl in the school. Tessa did not like Serenity for several reasons, the main reason was because Serenity and Jacob are close to each other. Tessa always had a crush on him since kindergarten until Serenity transferred during second grade. This was when he would go and talk to Serenity because she was always by herself. Tessa had lost connection with Jacob ever since Serenity came. She would no longer see him alone but with someone else. This was the moment Tessa became jealous of Serenity.

It was the day where prom was in a few weeks. Tessa had been planning to prompose to Jacob as it would be their last year in high school. She had the poster and a football basket for him, but suddenly during lunch time she noticed it was too late. Jacob had already asked Serenity to be his partner for prom. Tessa had mixed feelings, embarrassment, anger, and sadness. She ran away at this moment and Serenity noticed. She quickly went to follow Tessa, but she had already disappeared.

A few days left before prom, classmates have been murmuring rumors about Tessa as they laughed. Someone had posted a picture of Tessa crying in the restroom. At prom, Serenity decided to speak up. The school announced that Jacob and Serenity would be the prom king and queen. During her speech, Serenity had spoken to the crowd that what they did was wrong, and that they shouldn't make fun of someone during their tough moments. Everyone was silent and she called up Tessa, with embarrassment she went up, and said she supports her. Serenity had told her that social media is only a distraction that takes away who we truly are. This was when Tessa had realized that it was true, she then apologized to Serenity for what she did and they became friends.

By: Stephanie Velazquez

A Letter to Myself

You've been doing well. You're still very anxious at times. You are still trying to let go of acts of control. You are still trying to become happy when alone. You are trying and will start to try even harder to become the person you have dreamed of becoming. You have come so far from the high school girl who tried to build homes for people with broken houses. You have come so far from the high school girl who was convinced the world was better without her in it. You have come so far from the high school girl who was so ashamed of her existence.

It's still hard for you to look back on the mistakes you have made. It's still hard and you still cringe about who and what you have been throughout your life. But in such times, I must remind you, you are human, and such things are all a part of this journey we call life. I want you to know I am so proud of you. At six years old, you wouldn't believe that mummy is safe. You wouldn't believe that you are a beautiful person who deserves amazing friendships.

At 16-years-old, you won't believe who you are no longer friends with, and at 18-years-old, you are a woman who's trying to mend each piece of herself that she shattered on the cold hard floor. If it's not the hardest thing ever, I don't know what it is, but through the strength of your beloved creator, you are doing it, you will get to where you want to be. Trust me.

You are at university now, and do you believe me? You are actually enjoying it so much, you love sitting alone on your favorite chair overlooking the tree outside the library window now. You are speaking to new people and rekindling friendships with people you met when you were a child.

You are finding life hard and a little messy, but you are navigating well and finding reasons to stay positive. You are starting to let go of the fear of death and driving more, which is your biggest accomplishment yet. I am so proud of you. I know it's been hard, sometimes you're reminded by old versions of you, and people who are no longer in your life, and it sucks, but you will be just fine. I know it's hard every time you speak to a guy, the heaviness of missing him comes gushing in like a tsunami, and you can't do anything but hold back stinging tears. I know you long to talk to him, to get answers, to ask him if he was just messing with you, but you can't, so you stay silent and sometimes the silence starts to eat you alive. I know it's so hard, but you are leaving it to God, because you can't seem to get answers. And I know you miss him, but you will be okay.

Dear me, you have come so far. You should be so proud of yourself. You surprise me more and more each day and I can't wait to see you continue to thrive and grow. I never thought you'd be okay with looking at your reflection again, but you are now. It's easier. Every day that passes, you are becoming more content with yourself, and you aren't thriving for perfection, but betterment... Dear me, you make me smile. I love you heaps. A story of encouragement for the girl who carried on. A story of encouragement of a messy, beautiful human who is trying her best... A story for myself.

By: Courtney Angel

Forbidden Paradise

I see her there,
Standing.
With her soft,
Bronze skin.
Skin,
as golden as the sun.

Beautiful round eyes,
As blue as the ocean.
With soft and delicate stripes.
She holds my focus
as I stare into her sight.

Her lips are like a paradise.
The top curve so deep,
It reminds me of the waves.
Her bottom lip,
So warm.
So soft.

She's like the sand.
I now understand,
This woman is
my forbidden paradise.

By: D.M.

Inspired by the Song Softcore

Are we too young for this?
We often ask, the world moving so fast around us.
Lost in this disorderly world,
consumed by our own thoughts
Seeking for balance in the chaotic world
The lyrics sing, "I'm too consumed with my own life"
Carrying the weight of the world on our shoulders
Daily problems, stuck in between chaos
Suffocating us at such a young age
We navigate the world, searching for a satisfaction
Away from this disorderly world
Disorderly world that is both thrilling and uncertain
Chasing after our dreams and goals empowered by our passions
Embracing the challenges, growing up too fast
Pushing higher in our lows
Trying to persevere this disorderly world
We're put down, our goals squashed
"Feels like I can't move"
Depths of uncertainty unlocked in ourselves
Finding ourselves stuck, out of luck
Still trying to persevere this disorderly world that consumes us

By: Elizabeth Sierra

Empoderamiento de Madre

Mi luz, mi guía, mi amada madre
Tanta fuerza y gracia
Empoderada por mamá
La mujer que me levanta
Me ama incondicionalmente
Amor que no se rompe

By: Elizabeth Sierra

Sister

To my little sister Vicsy,
13 years old and so bright
You bring me joy and laughter
You are my light in the darkest places
Through our fights and tough times,
continuing to stand side by side
Going through a toxic storm daily
Our bond reinforced
Through thick and thin, you are there
My best friend, my sister
Your presence brings me comfort
Our sister bond is unbreakable, continuing to grow
Just as we continue to grow into adulthood

By: Elizabeth Sierra

Cheer Routine with Nature

The sun's warm embrace greeted us as we stepped on the stage
Excited to showcase our cheer routine
The grass beneath our feet felt alive,
energized by the hopefulness that was in the air
We moved together like the leafs move with the wind,
Synchronizing our motions with the rhythm.
It came closer to my favorite part of the routine
I continue to tumble & leap
The sky seemed to cheer along with my family in the crowd,
the trees moved in admiration
branches applauding our every twist & turn.
My team together as a whole
The announcing of the winning team, everyone holding their
breath
hoping for their team to be called
Everyone anxious as to what was going to happen next
Finally, our cheer team's victory filled the air with joy
Our hard work had paid off, such a relief.
The cheers of our loved ones
echoed throughout the crowd along with ours
Both resonate with the spirit of nature.

By: Elizabeth Sierra

Sunlight

The feeling of the warm embrace of the sun,
shining onto your skin.
Especially when you're cold,
the sun's rays act as a protective shield.
What happens when it becomes overbearing?
The sun begins to burn you,
but at the same time replenishes.
When exposed for long periods of time,
the sun alters the pigment of your skin.
Just a harmless tan can lead to sunburns,
ones that ache and require treatment.
An overabundance of something
never works.

By: Iztli Quinones

Codependency

I attach myself to you
As if I were gum,
Constantly being around you everyday

I lose my individuality
And then I start changing,
Molding myself into another you
Slowly the real me fades
Into the altered new *me*
The extension of you *me*
Without realizing the consequences coming

Clinging onto you every moment
Being so codependent on you
It begins to feel intoxicating

Your emotions are now mine
Your anger
sadness
guilt
anxiety
Is mine to bear now

Feeling the responsibility for this
The responsibility for your emotions
Fearing the chance of abandonment

Being so codependent on you
Constant anxiety
fearing abandonment
This relationship becoming slowly toxic
Slowly it takes a toll
Becoming draining for us both
noticing this unhealthy love searching for me, the real me

By: Yulia Mendez

A Facade

People see me one way
Others see me another
Which way is right?
Neither in my opinion

Some people see the light in me
Others see my darkness
Others see me as a robot
A ghost in the background

I'm happy
I'm sad
I'm disgusted at myself
I'm at peace

I want to show people
I can be both
I can be happy
I can be sad

Why does my body only choose to show one?
I'm either happy or sad
At school, I look sad or neutral
At home, I'm depressed
showing barely a glimpses of hope

Online is where I shine
My smile is immense
Unrestricted by even my own mind and body
Yet no one can see that smile online

By: Johnny Garcia

A Need for Change

Each day passes by
Dust in the wind
Sand by the shore
Snow in the mountains

Everyday feels the same
No joy
No happiness
No hope

A pit of despair
The world graying around me
Can I save myself?
Music being my only treatment

They show up
Who are they?
Can I really call them friends?
Friends with me?

They show me the games they play
The conversations they have
I feel joy
I feel happy

Just as water evaporates and then rain falls
I want to repeat the cycle of being with them
I don't care how long
I just want to be with them a moment more

By: Johnny Garcia

State of Being

A constant state of suffering
No one to call
The fear of rejection
The fear to tell someone

I feel sad
I feel angry
I feel frustrated
I feel alone

I know people
I trust people
I tell people
But why can't I tell the truth?

To be happy
Not a fake mask
Masking my despair
Looking for a glimmer of hope

Why do I sleep where I want to hide?
Hide away
Shy away
Forever walking away from others

An act for a play
It can be jovial
But an act for life
Is what I am on road for

By: Johnny Garcia

Personification

In the back of my mind, depression runs rapidly
Attempting to cause chaos within my own mind
I just sit there, a statue, never speaking
never really showing any emotion

I am truly a statue always keeping depression in its cage
but never being able to leave it
I know when I forget about depression and I leave it alone
it comes back blindsiding me back to putting it in its cage

I place it back and continue to watch it
I want to be free
I want to be happy
So why can't I just build a better cage?

Why can't I just leave it alone?
Without it running wild in my mind?
I see someone sad and I can't help but to be angry at myself
with depression snickering away in my mind

I carry my burdens alone
I don't speak
I try not to feel
and I try not to show

The only words I'll utter throughout a day
hi, yes, no, have a nice day, and *see you later*
I want to say more and speak my mind
but I fear my depression will be let loose

Anxiety will show in my words
Stuttering in fear of saying
something that might upset someone
So I don't say anything
I keep to myself

I get through the day alone
I get home to prepare for another day
Even with the friends I do have
I don't see them because they go to another school

They all have strong bonds with one another
Being from the same school
and hanging out on the daily
Where does that leave me?
Sometimes I feel like an outcast when hanging out with them

All I know is that I need to keep my depression caged
Never let it show
To keep my neutrality
Keep my state of self
To myself

By: Johnny Garcia

Porcelain

I'm crazy
I try to explain
And I have came to the conclusion
That you have the delusion
It drove me insane
I now think your words were a game
You destroyed my life
Stabbed in the stomach with a knife
My heart shattered
But it didn't even matter
As long as a your image was the same
Only you gained
I never imagined
This would have happened
Don't know what to do
My brain is like stew
I'm at a loss
Wipes off my lip gloss
You can't stay the same
Be nice for fun and games
Put on that smile
You could run a mile
don't crack your porcelain figure
As everybody figures
You're nothing more then a face
Know your place

By: Alberto Reynoso

Perplexed

I'm so perplexed
Don't know what comes next
I solve
I write
But it never ignites
The fire
the flame
Do I want fame
I try to steer clear
Because that thing I fear
Most
Is what come next
I'm so perplexed

By: Alberto Reynoso

Keep Quiet

In fear
I stay quite
always hide it
Don't know how to write it
Stood there
Blank stare
Trying to articulate
But all I feel is hate
Couldn't say
Being in the way
All a nuisance
Nothing but confusion
Trying to to get my true sense
But it's all a delusion
So I stand there with a blank stare
Chaos all around
Just a frown
This just brings me down
So in fear I stay quite
And always hide it
I ain't shedding no tear

By: Alberto Reynoso

From My Mama

I try to be a good mom,
It's hard when they don't listen,
It's hard when they think they know it all.

I want them to be happy.
I don't want them to see me weak,
I don't want them to see me break.
I don't want them to know life's struggles.

I want to be able to be better
For them, I love them
They're my all.

By: Jocelyn Diaz

Among Clouds

When you're lonely
the sky may become your best friend
if you wish hard enough,
it'll take you in
as one of its own.
Drifting clouds
stand out and sing to me,
they go out into the world and tell stories.
But when they're gone
I go back to this plain old painting,
living in the past hurts,
living in the future is perseverance,
living in the present is a gift.

By: Jocelyn Diaz

My Friend Chrissy

It was a beautiful spring morning. I woke up early in the morning to get ready for school. I had never felt so rested before. I got up, brushed my teeth, got ready, and even had time to enjoy breakfast. Being able to have breakfast before school is rare, everything was going so well and I had such an immense feeling that it was going to be such a good day.

I am so used to feeling exhausted and already dreading the school day before I even get to school. I felt that it was going to be a good day because I normally have to fight myself to get out of bed, but on this spring morning feeling like a movie where the birds chirp, I was able to effortlessly get out of bed. After a beautifully spent morning, I got in the car happier than ever, ready to go. I was able to enjoy the music and look out the window rather than fighting the urge to sleep the entire ride to school.

Once I got to school, I walked onto campus, greeting everyone with whom I crossed paths with, "Good morning!" I smiled the whole way to class. I was able to help my teacher set up her lesson plans for the day, she mentioned to me, "Don't you feel like today is going to be a great day?" I responded, "I felt that this morning." She replied, telling me that she had never seen me happier, I was so excited for the day to begin, it was about 8:27 in the morning and the bell rang at 8:30 am sharp.

For the most part, all the seats in our classroom were already filled by my peers, by 8:30 am the class was filled and all tables had a student seated except for the one next to me. In that seat sat my good friend Chrissy, she was known for being one of the best students in our grade. She had the highest grades and was always involved in events at our school, Chrissy hadn't missed a day of school since the time her cat passed away in the second grade.

Since then, she has dedicated herself to focusing on school. I tried being there for her, but she is the kind of person who does not like to open up to anyone, she was never a quiet person until she had something personal on her mind. She told me that her method to cope with everything was to just focus on her studies, she is a good friend, and I have always tried to be there for her. I found it odd that she hadn't come, but I told myself that I would check on her later at the door. I was hoping that she was just going to come late to school. It could have been for various reasons—that she wasn't at school or that she hadn't arrived.

Even our teacher was shocked to have to marked her absent when the late bell rang. Our teacher asked me if I knew what the reason for her absence was, I wish I knew. For some reason, this beautiful spring day started to feel gloomy and dark. The energy had completely shifted. I felt a sense of fear consume me. I am not sure if it was because I was worried about Chrissy or the sense that I had a feeling that things weren't right. How could such a beautiful spring day feel like a snowstorm during the winter just because the daily routine of seeing the same people everyday had changed?

I tried to shake it off as much as I could, the day went on and I tried to focus on my studies rather than letting it ruin the beautiful spring day that I had been experiencing before the absence of my good friend Chrissy. The bell rang at 10:30 am for nutrition, my teacher asked me if I planned to stay in class since I was zoned out, I hadn't even heard the bell ring. I got up from my seat and went to sit at the table where Chrissy and I always sat with our mutual friends.

I asked my friend Tiff if she had heard anything from Chrissy all day, she brushed it off by saying that she probably just felt exhausted. She didn't seem concerned, but I have never been the friend to just not worry, I care so much about others so if I don't know one hundred percent that they are okay it will drive me insane. It is such a beautiful trait to have in the eyes of others, but I feel it has been my greatest curse.

By fourth period I was feeling a little better, midway through the period, an alarm goes off. All the alarms at our school went off, no one could tell what was going on. For the most part, when the alarms go off they are just false alarms. As a school, we had learned to just brush them off and go on with our school day, but unfortunately the fear I was experiencing wasn't for nothing. Once the bell finished ringing, you could hear the gunshots and the screams of students. In the moment it didn't feel real, school shootings are the type of thing you hear about on the news and read about in the newspaper.

I didn't believe that it was actually happening at my school. The fear I had felt earlier today was making sense to me, the footsteps outside our classroom became quiet, our door had been busted open, my class and I hid. I could see my peers go down one by one. I decided to drop to the floor pretending to be dead. It was one of the hardest things I have ever done, I was covered in the blood of my classmates, some of whom I had been going to school with since elementary school.

The screams, tears, and hard breathing of those who have been badly injured pierced my soul. I didn't know if I was going to make it, is this something I even want to live through? Surprisingly through it all, I could still hear the seconds of the clock as if it were silent in the classroom. The time between each tick felt as if it had grew, every second felt like an hour. All I could think about was whether it was going to end. I couldn't even tell if I was still living or not, the class went silent.

When the police finally came in, all you could hear was one final gunshot. It was the cops, there goes the shooter. How could my beautiful spring morning turn into something so terrifying? I wish I was lucky like Chrissy. I wish I had stayed home, I bet my deceased classmates would've liked to stay home like Chrissy. How will anyone recover from this? How am I supposed to break this news to Chrissy? By the end of the night, the news reporter had talked about what had happened as if they had lived it. No one knew who had done it, and neither did I. Who could do such a thing? It turns out the shooter was from our community, the shooter ended up being my good friend Chrissy.

By: Destiny Avila

*This story is fiction, but in our world, these things do happen in real life. May the lives lost by school shootings, be always remembered.

Mental Health

My mental health has been one of my biggest struggles throughout my life, I seem to always find myself trapped in my thoughts, thinking about the worst things possible. I force my brain to hate myself for the way I am and how I think. I know it makes it worse to think that way, but it's so hard to drag myself out of that mentality. I always think about all the things I have, all the people that I love, and those who love me to remind myself that I'm not alone, but I choose to be alone all the time because it seems easier to not have to talk to anybody or waste their time by expressing what I am feeling or thinking.

I feel like it's awkward to sit there in front of somebody and just tell them how sad or mad I am or what is bothering me. I don't want them to feel uncomfortable or pressured to make me feel better, so I would rather just not put anyone in a situation like that. I struggle with low motivation, low self-esteem, self-neglect, doubt, and low-confidence. I compare a lot and I am super hard on myself. I never feel like I am enough, or I'm not doing what I am supposed to correctly, and I feel that I am not capable of doing better or achieving greatness or success.

However, I know that it's my brain telling myself those lies that only bring me down. I am always overthinking, worrying, and fearing my future. It is tremendously difficult to avoid this horrible and negative thought process. It's difficult to realize when I am in a negative mindset. Only because I convince myself that it is just me being realistic or telling myself that it is the truth that I need to hear and basically suck up any emotions that I'm feeling. It sucks more because it's even harder to pull myself out of it. I don't allow myself to feel or show any emotion because in my mind I think that being vulnerable is "lame" and that I am "pathetic" because I'm letting "life get to me." I know that it's a toxic mindset that only makes matters worse, but it's just so hard for me to overcome the storm in my mind.

I turn my sadness and worries into anger and frustration, but then I also turn it into self-hatred. Which is why I'm not the happiest of people. Sometimes I feel joyful and there are things that make me happy, but there are also times when I'm having a great time and then I start to overthink. Which takes me away from being in the moment, because I am always in my head it's hard to not worry and to just enjoy moments. My lack of confidence is caused by this mindset, but I put up a front that I am strong and calm. When really, I am having a mental battle every day. However, I will never tell myself that I am a sad or depressed person, or that I might be bipolar or have anger issues.

I somewhat agree that I might be overstimulated and that I sometimes panic when something or someone triggers me. Sometimes moments can be overwhelming and I get overstimulated and freak out a bit. This is also because I struggle with talking and I am antisocial and have social anxiety. I do a great job of not showing any emotion or showing that I am thinking about something. However, if you know me well enough, then you would know that anytime I bite my nails, I'm usually thinking, it doesn't always mean that it's something negative.

I just think a lot, I know I don't have valid reasons to be feeling or thinking this way or to say that I'm depressed or something like that. I just struggle mentally with self-love and I know that it's important to have a strong suit like that. I know I am a tough person and it's difficult to get under my skin, it also takes a lot to make me actually cry or show that I am mad and lash out. Even though I feel and think things that make me sad and mad super often, I never show it and I never allow myself to let anyone see those sides of me. However, lately I've been noticing that I have been the happiest I have ever been since I started taking better care of myself both mentally and physically. I am also allowing myself to understand that it's okay to cry or feel things because it's normal and that I am just human.

I have also been a lot happier ever since I took the time to build a relationship with God and start praying a lot more. Ever since I got with my boyfriend, he has shown me to look at life from a different perspective and he has really made me a happier person. Overall, I know that having someone that loves and cares for me and encourages me to have a good relationship with God will bring me a lot of happiness and peace, rather than thinking so negatively all the time and I am super grateful to have met him. I am so grateful also that I have opened up my mind and heart to God because I am now way more motivated, happy, and at peace with myself. I know now that I am not alone, and there are people who love me, and God loves me too.

By: Destiny Moreno

Grandfather

One of the most traumatic things that have happened to me would be COVID-19, everything was shut down and places that once were populated with many people became liminal. Liminal means places that used to be full of people are now empty without a person in sight. Staying at home at first didn't seem like a bad idea, because I could sleep all day and do nothing. But I soon realized how horrible it felt to stay inside for so long, to make matters worse I was in the transition from middle school to high school, so dealing with COVID-19 was no help at all.

The impact that COVID-19 had on me was somewhat big in that my mentality and my drive just dissipated, I had no drive to clean my room, my mentality was nowhere to be seen and I just laid down all day and slouched in my filth. My mom was probably my biggest supporter in getting my life under control, without her I'd probably still be in bed or worse. I remember how I wouldn't shower for a month or two during 2020, which was the biggest point of COVID-19. It also wasn't just me who felt affected by this new change.

When it came to family around COVID, it was hard. My family and I are very close to each other and we would see each other every day. I have a godson who is turning 3 this year and he has been a blessing to me this whole year, but the only problem is that because of COVID I can only really see him once or twice a week, instead of every day of the week. My family would have cookouts every weekend where everyone in the family would come and join in. But since COVID we have yet to have one where every single family member could attend. Being without most of my family was tough, but school felt like a whole other weight being added onto my shoulders.

Attending school on my computer and at home during COVID-19 was probably the hardest thing I have done. School was already boring enough, but being stuck at home attending school was a whole new level of boredom. Slouching and rotting in my own filth were my only options. Not even the schools themselves were able to properly function during quarantine, I remember sometimes the teachers would fall asleep or lose attention during class which stirred even more problems. It was hard enough being at home, but now having to do work while at home just made the whole experience worse.

To be honest, my weight never really became a problem, I always was okay with where I was at. Yet, I was not aware or prepared for what COVID would do to me because I went from 160 LBS to almost 220 LBS. It was a low point in my life. I felt that I could not get away from the weight. It was hard because I lost most of my weight by walking and moving around, but since I could not do any of that due to COVID, and being stuck at home I only gained. It felt like the only things I could do were either eat food or slouch on the couch.

The worst thing though was not my weight nor was it how hard school was. I lost my grandfather in 2021, around November I think. I do not like to reminisce about it, but it had a crucial and large impact by COVID to my life. My grandfather was more than just my grandfather. My father was not in the picture, so my grandfather stood up for me and man did he do well. The only bad was that he did not teach me his work ethic. He taught me many things to be a good man and live a good life, he was a respectable old man who always knew how to light up a room with his jokes. He was also a man who was heavy on family. He worked 12 hours a day for his family. He had always made time for his family, he worked as a carpenter, so he handled a lot of wood which was another thing that was inherited. All through COVID I would cross the street, at the time he lived across the street from me, and he would teach me how to work with wood. Although life is much harder now without him, I feel that he left this world knowing that he taught me well.

Yes, COVID had an impact on me, but in the end I think it was a turnaround that made a difference. I would wish that COVID had never happened, but I wouldn't be the guy I am today if it wasn't for it, I think in the end I was positive in moving my life forward into something brighter.

By: Max Muro

The Bargain

London, England
1874

"Brother, will you please do me the courtesy of telling me of this proposition that you won't stop babbling on about?" Edwin begged. Cornelius chuckled, half glancing over his shoulder to look at his little brother before returning his gaze back to the front. "You'll have to wait and see, my darling Edwin," Cornelius said, smiling in amusement. Edwin heaved a sigh and continued to trail after his older brother. "Will you at the very least tell me what this bargain will grant us should we accept it? I allowed you to give my word, alongside yours, in my absence. You at least owe me an explanation of that."

Cornelius spun towards him, taking precise steps backwards as a thoughtful expression flickered over his face. A joyful grin slowly overtaking it. "He promised a long life filled to the brim with thrills of adventure." He confessed almost dreamily, a wistful glint clouding his eyes. "A life where we will power beyond compare. Where no one will ever look down at us again." Cornelius finished softly, his gaze going distant and dark before brightening once more, smiling positively. "Not to worry though." He assured. "We're almost there." He added before letting silence fall upon them again, spinning on his heel to face the front. Edwin narrowed his gaze and glared at Cornelius' back, huffing in annoyance as wisps of his hair flew momentarily upwards before falling back down over his golden-hazel eyes. As much as he wanted to give his older brother a good telling off for being a stubborn mule and an inexplicit git, he is quite curious about this mysterious engagement Cornelius had kept going on about since the moment he heard of it. Cornelius being Cornelius, he'd always liked the element of surprise–much to Edwin's dismay–and knowing him, he won't tell Edwin anything more than that until they arrive at their intended destination wherever that may be.

Some time later as the two brothers walked up the abandoned buildings of *West London,* Cornelius suddenly turned to an alleyway that forked off to the right of them. Cornelius immediately–and naturally–walked down the path while Edwin stopped at the mouth of it, gazing intently at the entrance with an air of caution around him. Cornelius noticed his brother's absent steps and turned back to face him, a confused frown altering his usually good nature face.

"Edwin, come on now, my friend won't be waiting for much longer. Come on." Cornelius gestured for him to come forward before turning around and resuming down his targeted path. Edwin gently bit his lip in anticipation. He is still receiving the sense that he should not go down that alleyway, but the anxiousness of not wanting to leave his brother on his own–nor desiring to stay put in an unknown place alone–made Edwin run after Cornelius, slipping his hand into his pocket where he kept his dagger. The two of them walked farther down the silently and slowly down the darkening alley. Eventually the two brothers came upon a door that appeared on their left. They stopped–Edwin briefly glancing at his brother as the foreboding sense washed over him again–and Cornelius reached forward and pulled open the door, him walking in first with Edwin following close behind. The moment they entered inside, the door suddenly swung shut and locked behind them, plunging them into darkness. Edwin immediately banished out his dagger, straining his eyes in the darkness to see what may lay ahead when he felt his brother's hand calmly encase his wrist and removed the dagger from his grasp.

"You won't need that here." Cornelius's voice assured him. "I apologize for my friend, he has a bit of a liking for theatrical flair. But I swear to you, Ed, we are in no danger here. I promise."

Despite the reassurance, Edwin did not feel any more safer, he felt precisely the opposite.
Whoosh!

Suddenly one by one, the room was lit up with candles until there was a glowing circle in the center where they stood that kept the darkness beyond it at bay. "Hello, Cornelius." A deep voice said as a man appeared from the darkness and stepped into the light of the circle.

Cornelius immediately broke into a grin and stepped forward for a moment before thinking better of it and stepped back to his original position. "Hello, Amos. It's nice to see you again."

"The same to you, my friend." The man said kindly as a hint of a smile glimmered onto his face then he turned in Edwin's direction, seemingly to be surveying him. "Your brother, I take it?"

Cornelius nodded fiercely. "Yes, this is Edwin. I brought him as you asked." He answered, completely ignoring the outraged look from his brother. "Yes . . . Yes, you did."

Edwin gazed toward Amos and felt a shiver run down his spine instantly. Despite this Amos person standing no more than four feet away from him, Edwin was unable to see his face, it was shrouded, almost like the darkness that lay above them was masking it. Making certain that they would not be able to fully see him. And that was not the only thing. Even though Edwin is unable to see his face, he could feel Amos' gaze on him and it was almost . . . unsettling, like he was a man who was once starved to the point of no return and was staring at a meal that he could not reach in some form of inhuman hunger.

Most similarly to that of a predator, observing its prey before pouncing to hunt it down. In this moment, Edwin felt like Amos was the predator and he and his brother were the quarries that he was slowly backing into an inescapable corner.

"Cornelius, I think we should go." Edwin said suddenly as the instinct to run began to flood into his veins."Ed, you haven't heard his proposition yet." Cornelius protested, hurt flickering across his face.
"I don't bloody care about this blasted proposal! I wish to return home before anyone discovers we are no longer there." Edwin countered as he glared at his brother.

"Edwin please. I've already given our word to him--"
"It is all right Cornelius." Amos spoke, interrupting his plea. "If your brother does not wish to hear what I have to say then it is his choice. I daresay it is quite a pity that we would not be working together the way I had hoped for but alas, that is how it must

be. Though before you depart, may I offer you lads a glass of wine? As a gesture of apology for the trouble of bringing you all the way here for nothing." "I really did not think it necessary-" "Of course." Cornelius answered. "It would be a pleasure." Amos smiled, "Splendid."

Amos unexpectedly withdrew two goblets from behind him and took a step closer, offering them to the two men. Cornelius grasped his immediately while Edwin reluctantly accepted it, staring into the contents of it. Because of the limited light, he was unable to see much of the color but he knew it to be a deep shade, possibly a dark garnet or currant. He suddenly felt the urge to run strike through him once more.

"To us." Amos said, now holding a goblet of his own. "To what could have been . . . a spectacular partnership."

"Cheers to that." Cornelius said, a note of melancholy in his voice. Edwin merely nodded, not having the courage to speak at the moment. Amos gazed at them each in turn before smiling and drank from his goblet, peering over the rim at them. Cornelius smiled back and drank from his. Edwin felt the instinct to escape now more than ever. Alas, instead of turning tail for the door, he drank from his goblet and the instant he did, he knew it was a mistake. But it was far too late. The taste of something metallic lingering on his lips and tongue as he felt a sudden burst of pain exploding inside of him, causing him to collapse to his knees as his vision swam and darkened at the edges.

Edwin desperately clung on to wakefulness as he struggled to keep his eyes open but it was futile. Already his mind had begun to lose its focus, falling further and further into the abyss of his unconsciousness as the darkness slowly darkened his vision.

"Rest now, lads. For when you next wake, we are going to have a *splendid* time together." Edwin heard Amos speak softly, his voice seeming to be originating right beside them. "I am certain of it." He spoke, his tone almost a beastly purr that delivered shivers down Edwin's spine in fear. Gathering what strength he possessed left, Edwin wretched open his eyes and stared in horror as he witnessed the monstrous sight before him, something that would haunt him for eternal as his mind steadily grew heavier. "After all," The grotesque Amos proclaimed as he turned. "I gave you my word, Cornelius. As did you. And as did Edwin in your place." He grinned, setting his ominous yellow eyes upon Edwin, the shadows seeming to grow taller in his presence. "It is going to be a *pleasure* working with you lads. An eternity is about to become quite wicked." He laughed evilly, the sound playing off the walls as Edwin finally lost his battle against consciousness.

The last thing Edwin heard as he fell into darkness was the sound of Amos' demonic laugh echoing inside his mind. Fueling the nightmares that will be right beside him for as long as he lived.

***

"Please, we beg of you!"
"Edwin, stop this, please!"
"What has happened?! Cornelius, speak to me!"
"Run, they've gone mad!"
"Please, we are family!"
"We have no family."
"Amos sends his regards."

Edwin woke with a start, gasping air into his lungs as his mind shuddered and halted, trying in vain to remember what had happened as the vague screams faded into nothing. Then remembrance dawned on him as he felt his heart froze in horror. A demon. The man that was once Amos had become a demon straight from the bowels of hell. A living, breathing hellish being had lured them in like lost lamb and they-They drank the wine that the demon had offered them and were left at its mercy after they fell.

"Cornelius-!" Edwin quickly rose to his feet, panic bleeding through him as he began to search for his brother. Though he only took one step before his voice died away as he finally took notice of what was around him, feeling his blood

turn to ice. There was carnage all around him. Each way he glanced, he spotted his family dead and scattered about the foyer of their home, laying everywhere either intact or in pieces. It was as if they were hunted for sport and were then left to be slaughtered like *animals*. As if they were meaningless.
Drip, drip.
Drip, drip.

Edwin tore his gaze away from the bloodbath before him and turned his eyes to his hand, witnessing drops of blood fall down his fingertips and to the carpet beneath. Slowly, he gazed down at himself and the instant he did, he felt his breath leave his lungs as realization had icily begun to sink into his mind.

He was covered from head to sole in blood – in *their* blood – watching as it soaks through his clothes and stains onto his skin, christening him in red.
Edwin quickly looked away, his stomach churning in sickening horror and as if drawn like lightning to a rod, he caught Cornelius' gaze where he stood across the room from him. A horrified and stricken expression marking his face. An expression Edwin knew with full certainty his own face mirrored.

The two stood where they stood and gazed at all around them, observing the chaos as the sole survivors of this massacre. Or as the killers, admiring their work like art. Feeling cold and ill, Edwin suddenly felt frozen as he watched his brother tensed simultaneously with him, his eyes widening in alarm much like his own as his growing suspicions were at last confirmed. The two of them standing at attention as a familiar, bone-chilling voice rang clear in their minds, forcing them to witness the beginning of the end as their world slowly fell apart before their very eyes.
Now we begin.

By: Alexa Mendoza

Nunca Es Suficíente

Nunca es Suficíente para mi
were the words I whispered to you.
I wanted more from you,
I wanted you to prove our love to be true.
You promised you would change and I believed you,
Toying with my heart seemed to be your favorite game.
Leaving me standing there hearing your excuses
My heart yearned for you.
Still, you were unable to see
that all I wanted was to make you happy,
and that was your biggest disease.
Living in constant fear of you leaving me
The idea of not being with you made me ill,
you were what I've always wanted,
what I've always hoped for.
You made me believe in the illusion
of your unconditional love.
While all I was able to give to you was love,
pain was the only emotion you were able to demonstrate.
Although you hurt me,
you were the one I loved,
you were the only one that could make me feel this way.
Happiness was the only thing that I wanted to bring to you,
that feeling of being loved and desired,
but you still took my love for granted
and left me weeping once again.
I waited for you
hoping the day you would change would arrive.
I believed every word you said to be true,
you were my poison
and I couldn't get enough of you.
Now you live in my memory,
remembering all the time I spent, loving you.
Soon my memories will vanish, the same way you did.

By: Vivian Ceballos

Madre

Ser madre
Es cuidar, amar y nutrir a tu hijo
Amarlos incondicionalmente, aceptarlos tal como son.
Mi madre es todo lo anterior y más
Ella me ama incondicionalmente
Me enseñó a amar a los demás, a ser amable y a defenderme
Ella es mi mayor inspiración
Vino a los Estados Unidos sin nada
Trabajó duro por la vida que quería y esperaba
Ella es una, si no la más importante
En mi vida.
Siempre que la necesite, ella estará allí
Amo a mi mami
Aprecio todo lo que haces
De peinarme a regañarme
Sé que no hay otro amor como el de madre.

By: Vivian Ceballos

Covid Journal

May 3rd, 2020

I had experienced nothing like what we're going through right now. I have learned about past pandemics such as the Spanish flu and the infamous *Black Plague*, but I had never thought I would live through history and witness the tragedies that come with it. This was all supposed to last only two weeks, and we would go back to school. I am in the last stretch to finish my 8th grade year, and not in school. Instead, I am writing a journal on a Sunday evening documenting what has happened these past few weeks. Schoolwise, we're finishing it all online, and won't even go on our end of the year field trip to Knotts Berry Farm which is a bummer since my friends and I have been excited about it since August of last year. I am not complaining about this "vacation" whatsoever because I get to do things I wish to do while I'm at school, such as sleep in, play video games, and eat whatever I want from the comfort of my own home. My mom just recently started going back to work after taking a month off because of this new virus and her boss, of course, wanted to keep all parties involved safe. The best thing that has happened to my family and me during these past few months is that we added a new member to our family, Kobe, a golden retriever. We figured if we were going to be stuck at home for a while, we might as well raise a dog when we have all the time in the world to do so.

Monday June 15th, 2020

Since the last entry in this journal, this country has been getting worse. The recent deaths of African American citizens caused by police brutality have sparked outrage and protests around the country, mainly with the death of George Floyd. The news and media have been covering these protests and people are looting, which is only making things worse. Not to mention the COVID-19 virus has shown no signs of going away, and progress for a vaccine has been very slow. It looks like it's going to last long-term and the protesters aren't helping the situation by going out in public in crowds and rioting. To think that a couple months ago life was normal and behind the scenes, this virus was spreading around the world. Kobe is growing and he's healthy, he's been by my side during this whole nightmare.

Sunday July 5th, 2020

Yesterday was Independence Day and thankfully, people still had their American pride and lit their fireworks. Kobe wasn't too frightened, he seemed to enjoy the show we had in our neighborhood. My family and I sat on the trunk of our car while we watched fireworks light up the night sky. We were trying to forget the state of the world. Thankfully, our family from Honduras and Mexico have been safe and staying inside, but it is also affecting them because it is much harder to get necessities over there than here. To this day, I have had no one close to me test positive for the virus, so I still don't know what it feels like. I fear that the worst is going to come true and my first year as a high school student will be at home which would be a bummer. I also haven't seen any of my closest friends since that last day at school on March 13th, 2020.

Wednesday August 5th, 2020

Today was my first time at my new school as I went to pick up my class schedule, materials, and instructions on how online learning will work. They assigned us freshmen to go, and depending on your last name you went to an assigned location. I was assigned to go early since my last name is "Coxaj" my mom accompanied me wearing masks and keeping our distance of course. My schedule has my new teachers with the subjects and classroom numbers, though that's pretty irrelevant this year. I start my freshman year next week on Monday and my new teachers have already contacted me with google meets. I already know in each class most of the students will have their camera off, and not take part as much because we are all new to this type of learning. It's going to take time to get used to these types of academics, but this still looks like it'll last until the end of the school year.

Monday August 10th, 2020

Today was my first day of online learning, and it went how I thought it would. I joined my earth science class at 7:45 and the teacher introduced herself to us. Each class will last about 45 minutes Mondays through Thursdays, with Fridays being a very short day ending about 2 hours earlier than normal. Just as I suspected, not a lot of kids had their cameras on, and most teachers tried to force kids to show their faces, but they were obviously nervous and didn't want to. I'll try to keep updating this journal, but with school starting I feel as if I'll forget about it completely. It's been such an unfortunate year for the world and living through this has been not only terrible, but also a learning experience. I have been trying to see this from a perspective that this won't last forever and that in a couple months a vaccine will be available, and everything will go back to normal all with the help of God.

By: Yahir Coxaj

The Fog

Wandering around the town of Vernill, Massachusetts lost in the developing shroud of fog. Tom is a native resident of Vernill, but still cannot find his way through the vast smoke enveloping his hometown. He wanders the streets hoping to find a clue, pertaining to where exactly he is. Finally, after some time, Tom wanders across a building, which he recognizes as being on the outskirts of town and realizes that one of the only exits out of town near this building has been blocked off by rubble and flames. In shock, Tom turns back around realizing the fog has been ever so slightly reduced, he can now see about 50 feet ahead of him now, whereas before he only had about 25 feet of visibility. Wondering what his next move is, he goes back into the town to hopefully find someone else who knows what is going on.

After meandering around town for an hour or so, Tom is getting increasingly more concerned by the hour. He could not find a single soul in what used to be a bustling small town. Vernill, being a town built at the bottom of a valley between a mountain range, used to attract tourists because of both its famous hiking trails, and two, its amazing hot springs located at the base of the surrounding mountains. Confused, Tom finally builds desperation to begin shouting out, in search of help. "Hello?! Is Anyone there?" Waiting a few moments with no reply, Tom is now scared. He makes a smart decision and begins a trek towards one of the tallest buildings in town, the hospital. Once he arrives at the hospital, disappointed when he finds that no one is there, he lets himself through the restricted employee only doors. He makes his way to one of the highest floors in the building to get a better view of the town. Seeing an elevator Tom rushed to it, ignoring the maintenance sign plastered on the wall next to it. In the elevator Tom begins making an ascent up the building, when suddenly the elevator comes to a sudden halt. "Really." said Tom, exhausted with his current streak of luck. Already knowing no-one would be able to come to save him, he doesn't even bother with the emergency button.

Instead, he heads straight for the panel in the ceiling to make an escape. Had he noticed the sign next to the elevator, Tom would have known there were problems with the elevator. Luckily for him, one of the elevator doors on the floor a couple feet above where he was stuck was open. Climbing a couple feet up the elevator shaft he makes his way onto the 9th floor of the hospital, finally he makes his way to a window and sees what has been causing all of the fog. Snow from the mountains was falling rather quickly into the hot springs, which at this point had been modified to maintain a certain temperature year-round. With all of the snow melting in the springs, it had created a steam like substance throughout the entire town. But, seeing this still puzzled Tom, "So, that's where the fog is coming from, but that doesn't explain where everyone is."

Once that thought had passed his mind, he decided to look at all of the exits to the town, seeing that each tunnel out of town, similar to the first, had been in flames and surrounded with rubble. Realizing he's trapped he makes his way down the stairs this time, outside the hospital. Tom goes to the nearest police station in search of, hopefully, someone to help him. But once again Tom is met with disappointment, finding another empty building devoid of any signs of life. The only thing he had found when searching the police station was a single case file, which had read "Tom Cullahan, Vernill, 1998" He opened it confused as to why his name would be on a case file in an abandoned police station. After reading it, he realized in 1998 he and his parent's had been in a car accident. Tom's father had accidentally swerved off an icy road, and into a tree. Tom quickly decided to stop reading there, and stormed out of the police station thinking of what his next move might be. He finally decides to just go to the one place he might be comfortable at, his home. When he finally arrived, he walked in without knocking, startling him, something he never thought he would have seen. Walking past the vase of wilting flowers, towards a picture of himself hung on the wall surrounded by several bouquets of flowers and dozens of candles. He takes in the possibility of what might be happening, and once again begins another walk. This time Tom walks to the *Vernill Family Cemetery*, making a trek to where his name Cullahan would be located. Inscribed on a tombstone it read, "Tom Cullahan, 1983-98, Bruce Cullahan 1957-95, and Mary Cullhan 1959-____ "

Tom is still confused about what he is doing in this old town, devoid of any signs of life. He goes back to the police station, and gives the file with his name on it, a second go-over. Tom reads, "In an argument with his father Tom, distracted his father and accidentally caused the vehicle to lose traction on the icy road and crashed the driver side first into a tree. Mr. and Mrs. Cullahan had lost consciousness and Tom Cullahan had been trapped in his seat waiting for first responders to arrive. All events transcribed had been recorded on the family's camcorders, which Mrs. Cullahan had been operating." Tom's mind began racing, wondering if that had really happened. His memory, as foggy as it was, wouldn't let him remember what had happened. He sits for hours trying to remember, remember, remember. But for all the effort he had put in, no progress had been made. He sat there with an indescribable head pain, and confusion surrounding him.

After trying to process all of that information, he traveled to the address labeled in the case file of where the crash had taken place. Once he arrived, he had found fiberglass shrapnel on the floor, glass shards, and droplets of blood, but with all of that there was no crashed car and no sign of either of his parents. He continued to dig deeper into the wreckage described in the file, and he found that it had been heard that due to the wreckage his mother had been sent to the local hospital in critical condition. Before he set himself on a journey to the hospital, he continued to read that he and his father had died on the scene due to their injuries. "Tom Cullahan, dead by Blood Loss, pinned under the mangled body of the car, metal had stabbed and tore his legs apart, tearing major arteries and eventually causing his death. Bruce Cullahan, death by TBI (Traumatic Brain Injury), the force caused from the impact of the vehicle hitting the tree caused Mr. Cullahan to slam his head into the window to his side, then it caused him to slam his temple into the steering wheel, giving him a concussion, and causing an intracranial hemorrhage (Internal Bleeding of the Brain). The force of the crash also sent large glass shards into all three (Mr. and Mrs. Cullahan and Tom) victims causing major blood loss, and loss of consciousness in Tom Cullahan."

Reading what had happened Tom now knew, he had to go find his mother if she was even still alive. He began his journey to the hospital, finally arriving there for the second time in this lucid dream Tom is having. He opens the patient registry on one of the hospitals computers and sees his mother's name listed in the ICU, he had also noticed the date on the bottom half of the computer "05/7/1998." "3 Years?!" Tom exclaimed, putting the gap of time that had passed behind him, he continued to where he would hopefully find his mother, room 2103. Before building up the courage to swing the door open, Tom for the first time in a long while had heard something moving inside of that room. He thought of what could possibly be in there, but then remembered that it could possibly be his mother, conflicted he swung the door open.

To see a man sitting in a chair, holding the hand of a woman seemingly sleeping. The man looking up astonished that someone had found him, Tom and the man locked eyes with one another. Tom, realizing it was his father, was happy to see him, and apologized profusely for their last conversation and apologizing for what had happened. Bruce, visibly not concerned for what his son had to say, opened his mouth to say something but once again shut his mouth. Tom looked up at his father confused at the fact that he had said nothing, and not moved an inch since Tom had walked in. Tom saw the look of rage, and grief that had been staring at him, his father indescribably angered, and grieving his wife's sickness. He yelled at Tom, "It's all your fault, had you not been so stupid and distracted me none of this would have ever happened!"

"We would have never crashed, and your mother never would have been in this coma!" Tom was saddened by the words his father had said, he was choking on the pure emptiness in his mind. He could not spit out a single word to say to his father. When he finally had thought of something to say, he decided to not further anger his father, "How long has it been since she last woke up?" Bruce, visibly regretting his last choice of words, taking in that it had been an accident said, "A couple of days."

Tom, surprised by his father's answer, thought that if the crash had happened 3 years ago how could she have been awake, only three days ago? "Here, take this and go over it." Tom handed his father the police case file, while his father read silently over the file, Tom headed over to the side of his mother's bed. He took her hand and shed tears of regret and guilt for what he had caused, his father was right. He was right that it was all his fault. He was right that he caused his own mother's condition. Tom's father was visibly confused and angered after reading the file. "Dead? But we're right here." said Bruce. "That's what I thought too, but if that wasn't the truth then, where is everybody else, and where are we?" Bruce could say nothing but instead sat there puzzled. "I've already been to the cemetery, and we are buried there, there's a tombstone with your name and my name on it." Both Tom and Bruce sat together puzzled as to where they both actually are, and if everyone else in the town is missing, then why is Mary here? Both of them just glad to be by her side once again, sat in that hospital room simply lost and confused.

After a while of sitting in silence, Tom asked his father, "Are we really dead?" "I don't know, but if we are, what are we still doing here?" Both once again sat in silence trying to either figure out what was happening or accept the truth. His father told Tom he'd be right back and asked him to stay with his mother. Tom sat where his father was when he originally entered the room while his father went wherever he was going. Bruce entered a chapel built in the hospital and approached a bench. Bruce lowered himself to his knees and looked to the statue of Jesus. Bruce did nothing but pray and ask himself why he is really still there instead of being dead. After all of his praying he came to the conclusion that he was in purgatory, punished to watch his wife slowly die in that coma she is in. Bruce thought he was being punished for harboring such horrible emotions towards his son for causing the crash, and he believed Tom was there because of his guilt for accidentally causing the crash.

Eventually Bruce went back to the hospital room with his son and wife in it and sat down thinking once again. He proposed the idea of coming to the chapel to his son. Tom thought about what his father had said and thought to himself that it made sense. Looking back out the window adjacent to his mother's hospital bed, seeing the fog thicken once again, Tom understands. With no way out of this city in sight the *father* and *son* sat together doing the only thing they could do and hoped that their wife/mother would actually wake up to be with them once again.

By: Adrian Fuerte-Campos

Mental Health is Needed

Ring, ring, ring! The alarm sounds. Lily does not wake up. Instead, she presses snooze. Without realizing it, she presses it two more times, and before she knows it; she is going to be late for school.

"Oh, no!" she exclaims. She quickly gets up, puts on a few fresh sets of clothes, puts on a bit of makeup so she doesn't look dead, and fixes up her knotted hair. She has no time for breakfast. She quickly makes her way to school.

After school: "Lily!" her mom summons her. "Yes?" Lily answers her. "What is this? I told you to wash the dishes. And where are the groceries?" mom asks. Oh, man. Lily was supposed to bring groceries that her mom asked for after work, and she was supposed to wash those dishes when she got home. There are many people in this house and Lily, being the hero and helper she is, wanted to contribute and help her mom. "Sorry, I forgot. I got home and went straight to do my homework," Lily responded. "Well, if you want to keep going to school and living here, you need to help. You having a job isn't enough anymore," her mom says.

By the time she came home from work, washed dishes, and finished studying for her big exam, it was already two am. She was exhausted: of everything—of every day. She dreaded coming home. She dreaded waking up every day and doing the entire day again. She never went to sleep, not unless she stopped thinking about how horrible her life was. Not unless she came up with a plan to go away. It was three am when she finally fell asleep.

Why are you always late?" Jess asks. Lily knows what she means well, but sometimes it is better to not point out when some-one's not having a good day. It's better to deal with it alone. "Nothing," she responds dryly. "Are you okay? You look like you just woke up. If you need anything…" Lily became agitated. She was getting annoyed. Did Jess not get the hint? "I'm fine," Lily smiles. "I just want to take a nap."

Ding, ding, ding! Lily's phone sounds. Lily is taking a nap on her day off. She's had 7 days off, actually. She decided she needed a break.

That break turned into two weeks, three weeks, a month… She has finally found a solution to her sleeping problem. When she wakes up, her pillow is full of streaks from her eyes, she realizes. Her phone rings again, and it is her dad. She answers. She always enjoys talking with her dad. "Hi, dad." "Hi, sweet girl, how are you doing? How's school?" he asks. She is silent for a while.

"Lily, are you okay?"

"I'm alone, dad. I'm all alone and I don't know how to fix it," she spills through tears.

Fast forward to graduation Day:

Walking through the stage was a relief. It is healing once you put everything behind you. Lily can walk away now. Her healing is still in progress, but she has one more thing she can do to enhance it. She walks towards her friends. Her friends that have lifted her up and have been there through thick and stone, trying to build her up. "Hey, guys. I, um, just wanted to apologize for everything that happened. You didn't deserve to be left in the dark like that." "Don't apologize. You were in a dark place. I'm sorry we didn't notice sooner," Jess says. "No, that doesn't excuse my behavior. I should've asked for help. I should've asked you guys."

You can't change the past, but you can certainly change the future. Asking for help was the best thing Lily had ever done. It took weeks--months of healing to get where she was. And she did it with her dad and friends by her side. No one is truly alone. You have others to help you through your demons.

You can always ask for help and look to those people who love you. There is always someone willing to be there for you. You just have to search, and do the work to heal.

By: Kevlyn Martinez

Yellow King in Pink

Atop my throne I feel numb
My hands feel like fire
I pledge my love unto all of thee
Come and hear what I decree
Go and swear your fealty
I'm the yellow king in pink
I love my subjects equally
My skin is clear and acne free
Scrape your chalice greedily
I'm the yellow king in pink
Hearing what I don't hum
Pass out invites for choir
On my mountain I can see
What they all truly think of me
That I'm meek and hard to please
I'm the yellow king in pink
Atop my throne I feel numb
My hands feel like fire
I have pain in my thumb
It must've been the day prior
Hearing what I don't hum
Pass out invites for choir
I pledge my love unto all of thee
Come and hear what I decree
Go and swear your fealty
I'm the yellow king in pink

By: Nicholas Hinton

Somewhere in the Morning

Somewhere in the morning
I was blown away
Somewhere in the morning
I would run away
Somewhere in the morning
I died far away
All I do is what I pursue, I never had a clue
Furthermore, I see that you're bored, I know what's in store
And amidst your endless assists, I can see I persist
What's a word that rhymes with endure, it must be quite obscure
Somewhere in the morning
I was blown away
Somewhere in the morning
I got up again
Somewhere in the morning
I would run away
Somewhere in the morning
I came back again
Somewhere in the morning
I died far away
Somewhere in the morning
I was born again

By: Nicholas Hinton

Oh My Days

It's so relieving
I'll misbehave
Onto me
A misbehavior
Breathing mistakes
And I would seem
And I'll refrain
My final words from all
And I'll rephrase
The words you speak and deep you drink
Over it now from the strain in me
In me from your weak willed with
Wide out now from your crazed raved saving
I see the door and I get cold
With blue eyed scores I'm ever bored
And now I know my home truth pain
One more day till' I meet my lover
One more day where I might discover
One more day to find a way to show her
One more day till' I meet my lover
One more day where I might discover
One more day to find a way to show her
She seems to read my mind
I don't know what she'll find
With her gaze I will be blamed
I pray she feels the same
Oh my days
Oh my days
Oh my days
Oh my days
One more day till' I meet my lover
One more day where I might discover
One more day to find a way to show her
One more day till' I meet my lover
One more day where I might discover
One more day to find a way to show her

She seems to read my mind
I don't know what she'll find
With her gaze I will be blamed
I pray she feels the same
Oh my days
Oh my days
Oh my days
Oh my days
One more day till' I meet my lover
One more day where I might discover
One more day to find a way to show her
One more day till' I meet my lover
One more day where I might discover
One more day to find a way to show her
She seems to read my mind
I don't know what she'll find
We have nothing left to do
My voice is so out of tune
All the days we've ever known
We don't have to be alone
With her gaze I will be blamed
I pray she feels the same
Oh my days
Oh my days
Oh my days
Oh my days
Oh my days
Oh my days
Oh my days
Oh my days

By: Nicholas Hinton

Always and Forever Not Yours

I hate that we talk every day
yet you never understand
All of these bits and pieces that you could never stand
Talking about all the little details of our little plans
You said you'd always be there for me and hold my hand
You said always and forever
And yet you surrendered

I know we had our ups and downs, but I thought we were better
Fighting over the little things we did not know any better
Piece by piece it piled up
filling my head with so many intrusive thoughts
A thought that stopped the flow and made everything blow

Not a day goes by without regret
Wishing I didn't say the things I said
Hoping the pieces would fall back into place on their own
It wasn't always and forever anymore,
but me against the world, alone

Watching as you lived the life I hoped for
With deep regret and emotional debt
I realized I shouldn't have fought for you more

I think of you every hour of every day
It hurts me when you see me but, don't say my name
Or the hallucinations filled with dread haunting my brain
I thought it was always and forever, but it'll never be the same.

By Winta Tesfaghbriel

No Thank You

My eyes have been through enough.
This heavy hurt in my head is tough.

I know you care, and I thank you.
Even when my head says no,
thank you.

May I ask why do you stay?
When all I do is cause you pain.

When I ask for help,
save yourself and say no,
thank you.

By: Michael Garcia

The End

Yeah, you are like a flower
in a room full of weeds
passing another hour
nothing more than I need

always want to be near you
wanting to feel your touch
love it when it is just us two
never knew I needed you this much

feelings are overwhelming
when you are around me
feelings that are so unexplainable
wherever you are is where I want to be

but I can't be dealing with someone
so unpredictable
and for the the sake of me
I have to set you free

By: Michael Garcia

Different

Anything to be different.
to hear a compliment

never heard one sincerely
but I can see your intentions clearly

to look like all these flowers
but all I do is wait constant hours

to dream about all that I can be
but at the end of the day, I know that's not me

By: Michael Garcia

friENDS

A lot of people in his life
have lied, stole, judged, and mistreated him
and although those lights dimmed
you still made him balance on the rim.

People like you tend to get on my nerves,
but I try to understand that you're taking many different turns
although some are good and bad
may I add

that I was the one there when you were down on your knees
and that put me at ease
but obviously not for you
no longer your baggage

and hopefully
I make the most out of this damage.
this is the end.
and after all, we were just "friENDS"

By: Michael Garcia

You Must Listen

Listen, you can't get back all the laughter
and all the moments you are trying to back track

with time, you never know
as it passes, new starts grow.
and chances of going back, low.

so let go and be free
here is where you're meant to be

never get too comfortable in time because if you do
you will have a messed up case like mine.

By: Michael Garcia

My Trip to Florida

When I was 17, I went to Florida. I went to Florida to go play baseball. I was selected as an *Academic All American* by Baseball Factory. I went on a flight that took about 5 and a half hours. When we landed it felt like it was super late in the day due to the 3-hour time difference. We got some rest, and the next day went to Universal Studios in Orlando. We then went on all the rides because we had a fast pass. It was very fun there. We went to two different parks that were part of Universal Studios. The first park was Universal Studios, and the second park was Universal Studios Islands of Adventures. My favorite ride at Universal was the "Hollywood Rip Ride Rocket." It was a very fun ride. My favorite ride at Islands of Adventure was the VelociCoaster. After that we went to eat at a restaurant in the City Walk at Universal. After eating we went to watch the movie *Thanksgiving* at the theater they had there. The next day I went to Cocoa Beach where my games would be played. We went there and we stayed there for a little while until we decided to go get something to eat. We went to get some barbecue and after that we went to check out the beach for a little bit. The food was good, and the beaches were nice. The next day I had games. The games were good, and we played at some nice fields. Then we went back to the hotel and stayed there until we had games on Sunday where we had played in the morning and had finished all the games that we had. Then my dad and I went to the beach again and went in the water for a little bit until we started to head back to Orlando where we were going to stay the night. On the way back we saw a place called *Zaxby's* and tried it and it had chicken that was good. Then we made it to our hotel and slept until the next day where we woke up at 4 am to get our flight back to Los Angeles. Then we flew home and that was the end of my trip to Florida.

By: Louie Perez

Detention Centers for Immigrant Children

In dark rooms where many lose hope
Detention centers are there with a hard cost
A cage of metal, with a heavy lock
Humanity is often lost and locked.

Throughout these walls, young souls are lost
Their dreams and their futures are gone
Bars, fences, sadness, cold food
Freedom is absent and unknown.

Youthful minds, once were filled with joy
Now filled with the darkness
Spirits are crushed and discarded
Detention centers, a dream crusher

It is not a place to teach
It isolates and condescends
Every child deserves a chance
To learn, to grow, and to live

There are better paths to take them than this one
To heal young souls and their hearts as well as their minds
To guide, to care, and to protect and to watch grow
Every soul deserves a chance to live and have their freedom.
Don't let detention centers take that away from them.

By: Riane Lopez

My Grandma

I have always been inspired by you
Never getting mad at me, stayed calm
You have went through hell in life
But you never showed any pain

You were always so strong
But you stayed humble about it
You never gave up on something you were passionate for
You never cared about yourself, only others

You had respect for everyone
Even the ones who disrespected you
You had passion for your cooking
Everyone loved it everytime

You knew what to cook for anyone when they were upset
Your food made us happy
We loved how you took care of your plants
They were your babies, they miss you so much

Everyone here misses you so much
You created a path for us
You told us to never give up
You wanted all of us to succeed

You made everyone feel welcomed at your home
You made everyone food everytime they came over
That was what is special about you
You took care of others all the time

We all wish you were still here Grandma
But we would rather have you safe than sick
Thank you for always inspiring us to be better
We are all grateful for what you have done.

By: Riane Lopez

In Memory of Grandma

In memory of my dear grandma, so kind
A second mom to me, in heart and mind.

Her love and care, a beacon in my youth,
guiding me with wisdom, grace, and truth.

With nurturing hands, she wiped away my tears,
calmed my fears and quieted my inner spears.

Through life's storms, she was my steady shore,
a love so deep, forever I'll adore.

In her warm embrace, I found sweet solace,
her tender smile, a moment's pure grace.

Her stories, like old books on dusty shelves,
enriched my soul, revealing life's true selves.

Through seasons changing, she remained the same,
her love is enduring, like an eternal flame.

Though she has left this world, her spirit's near,
in cherished memories, forever dear.

So, here's to you, my grandma, up above,
a treasure of unwavering, boundless love.

With gratitude and love, my heart does say,
thank you for being my guiding light each day.

By: Rogelio Reyes

Thick and Thin

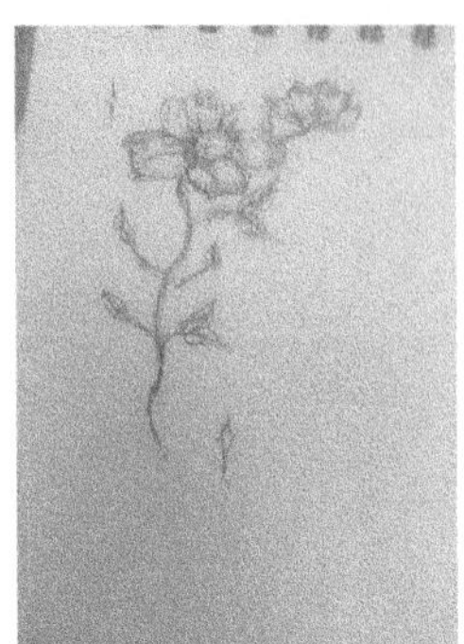

In the tapestry of life, friendships are woven,

A bond so strong, forever unbroken.

Through laughter and tears, we have shared it all,

Creating memories that will never fall.

Through thick and thin, we have stood side by side,

Supporting each other with love and pride.

In times of need, you are always there,

A friend like you is beyond compare.

No matter the distance, our hearts remain near,

With every passing day, our friendship grows dear.

Through the difficulties, we'll always stay,

Forever connected in a special way.

So here is to the moments we have shared,

To the memories we have made

By: Elizabeth Gonzalez

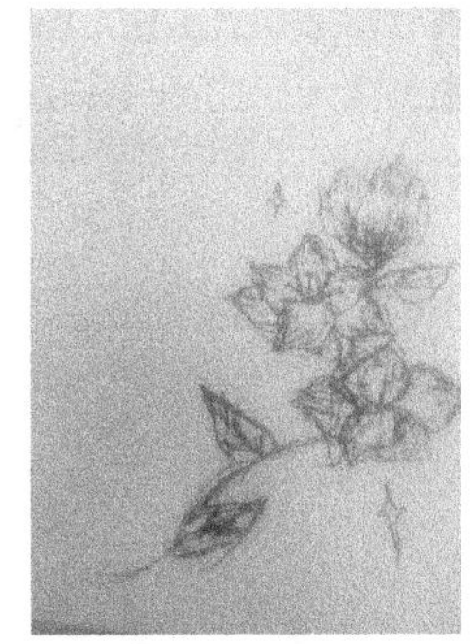

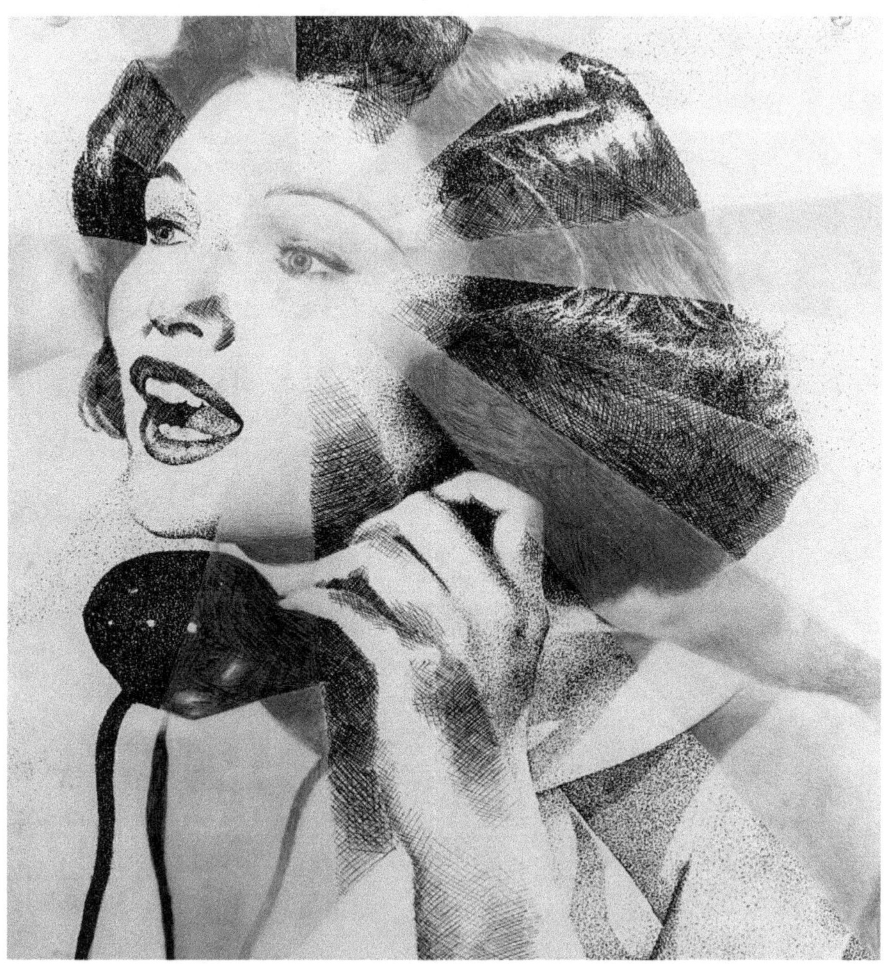

Delilah Bringas

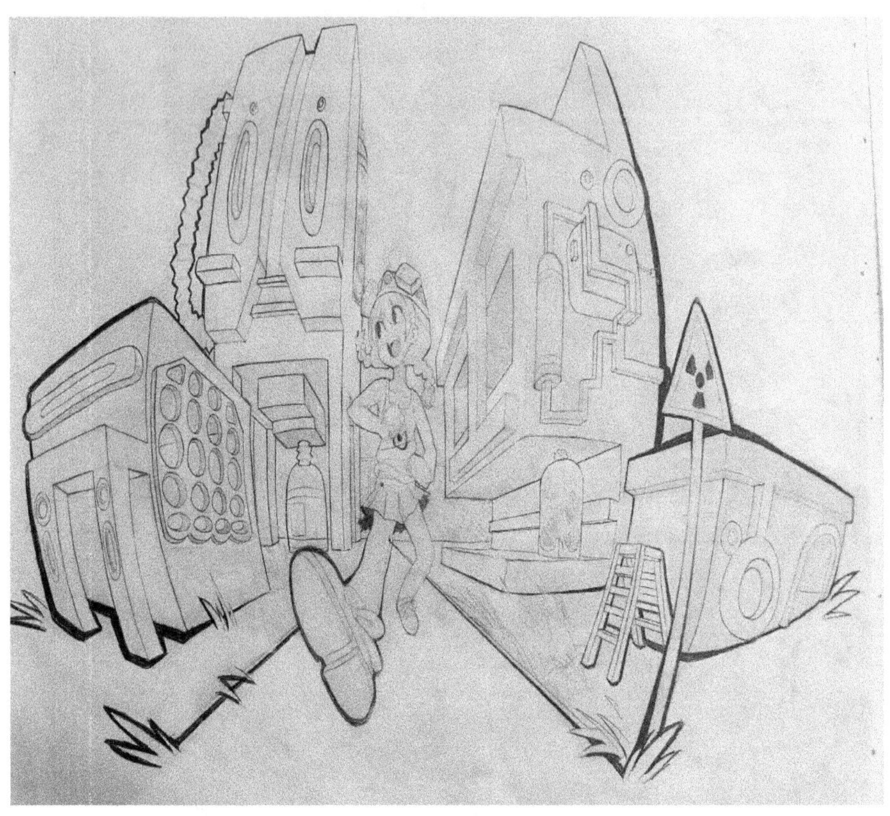

Delilah Bringas

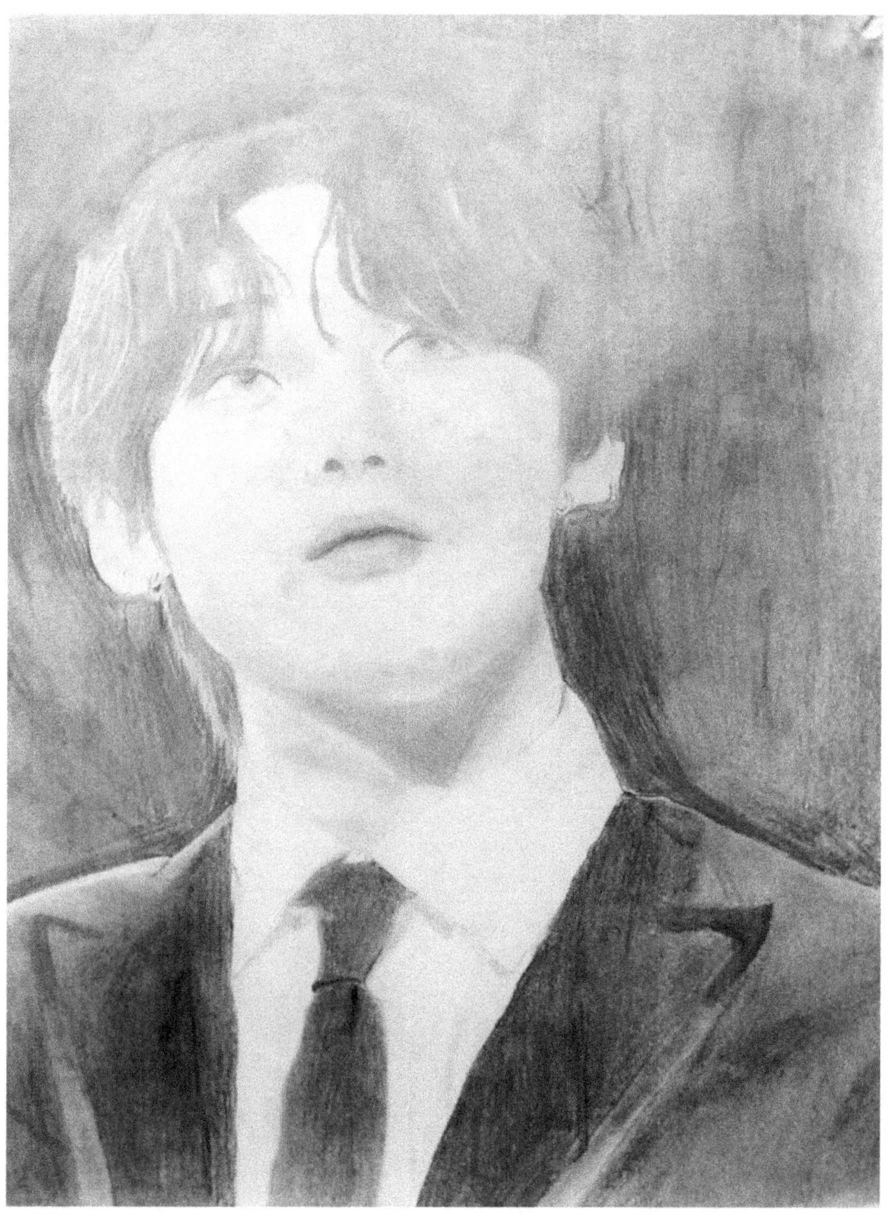

Patty Juarez

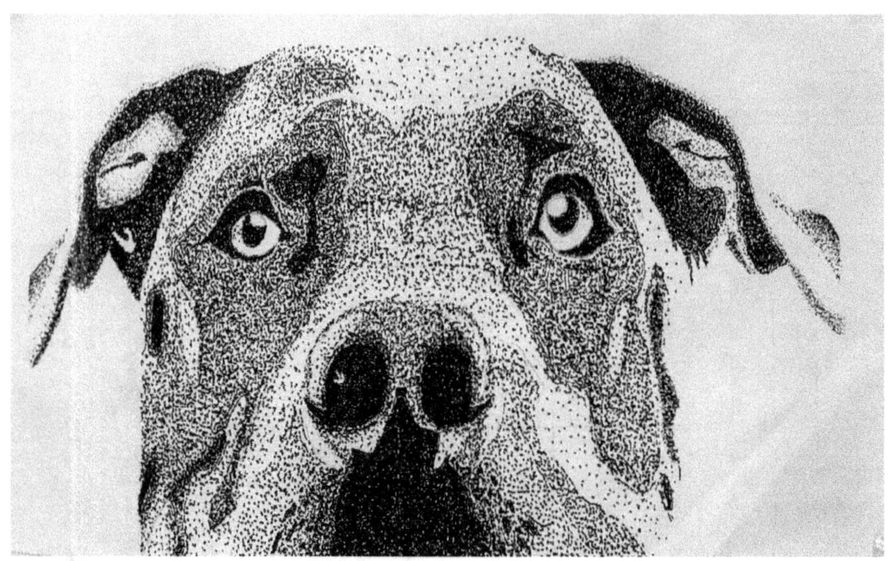

Logan Robles

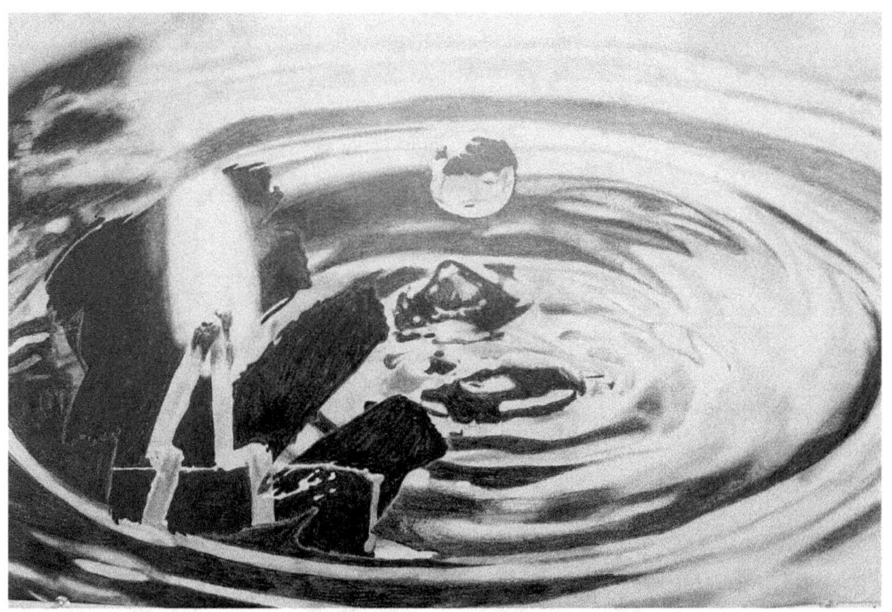

Ariana Ayala

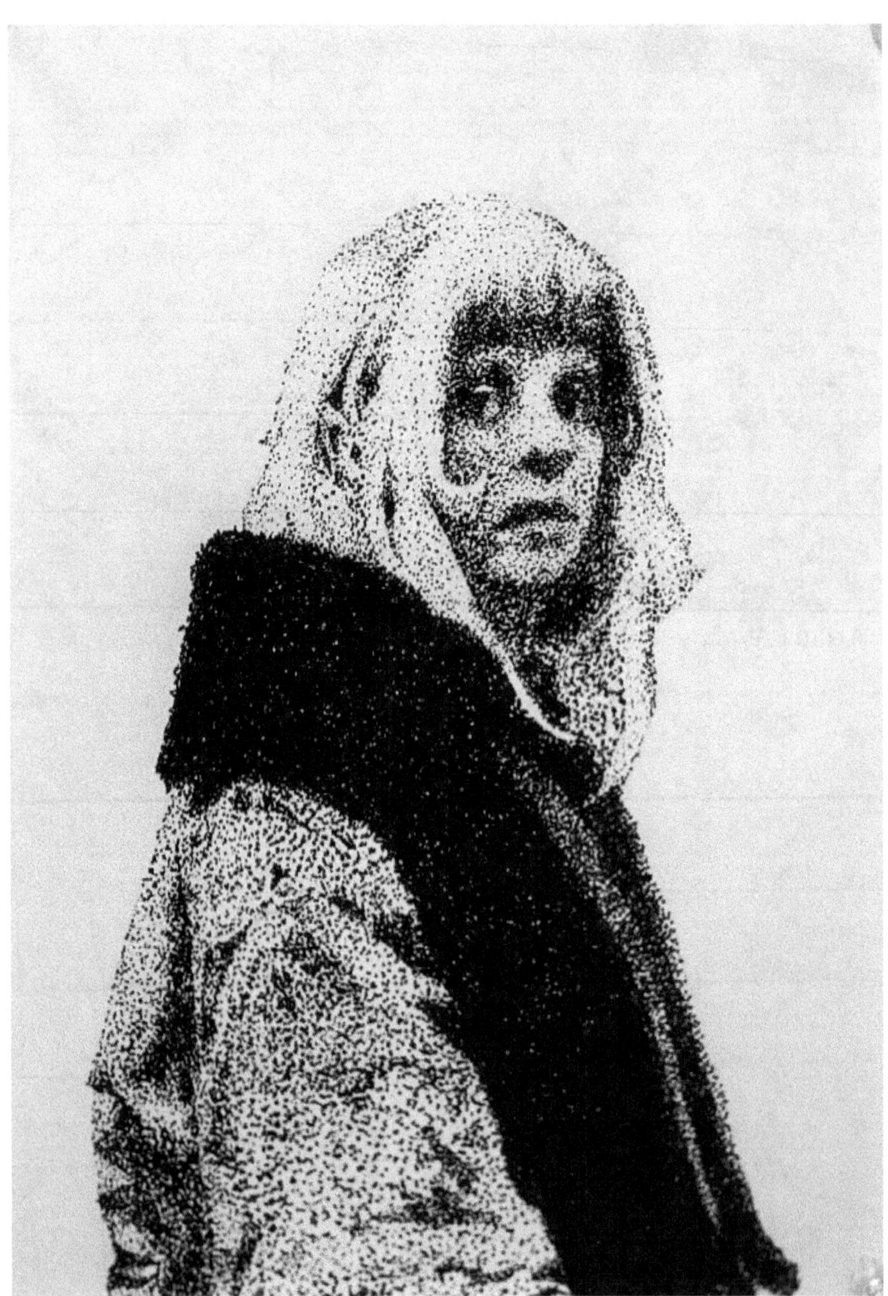

Michelle Lalla

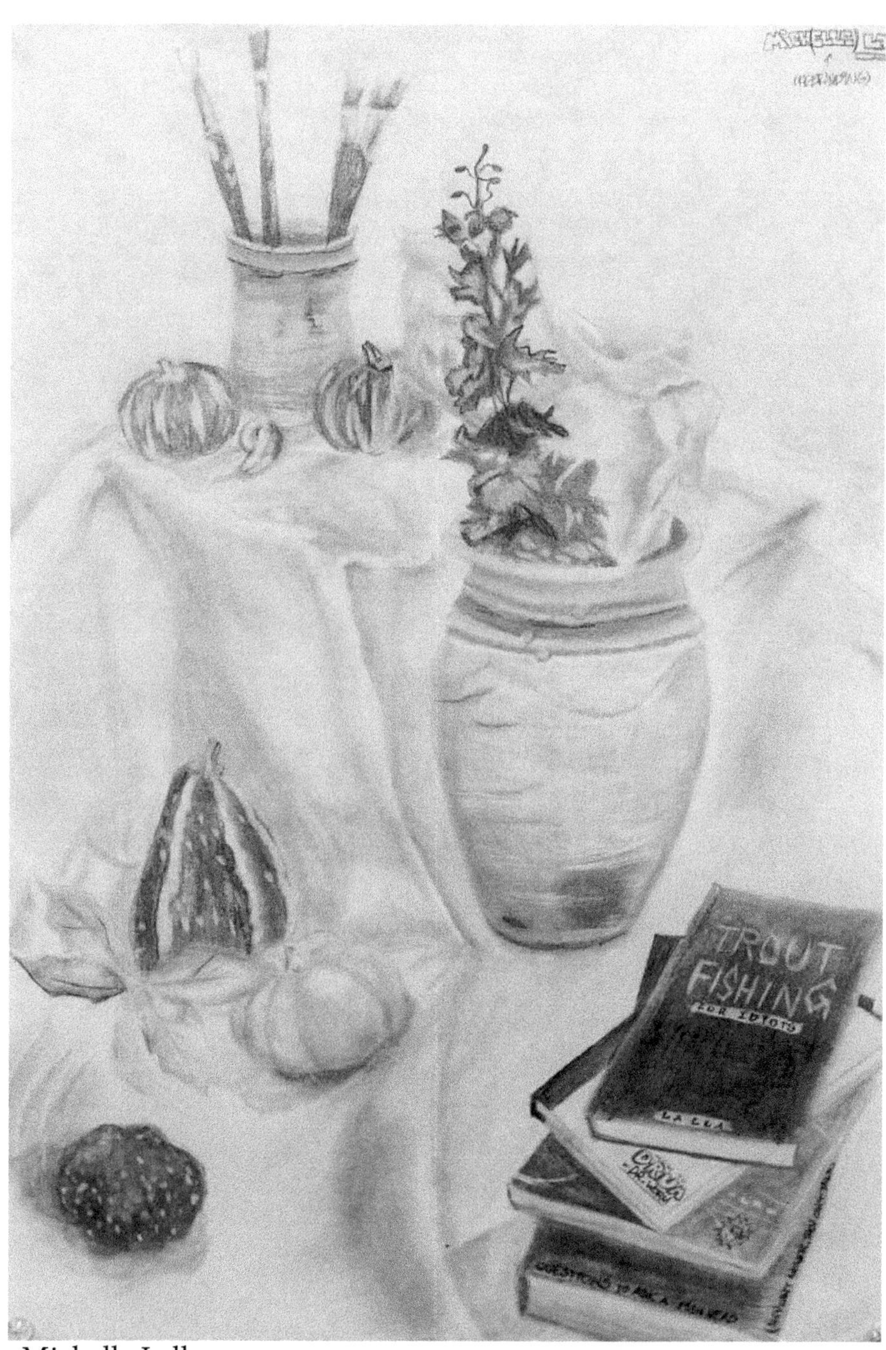

Michelle Lalla

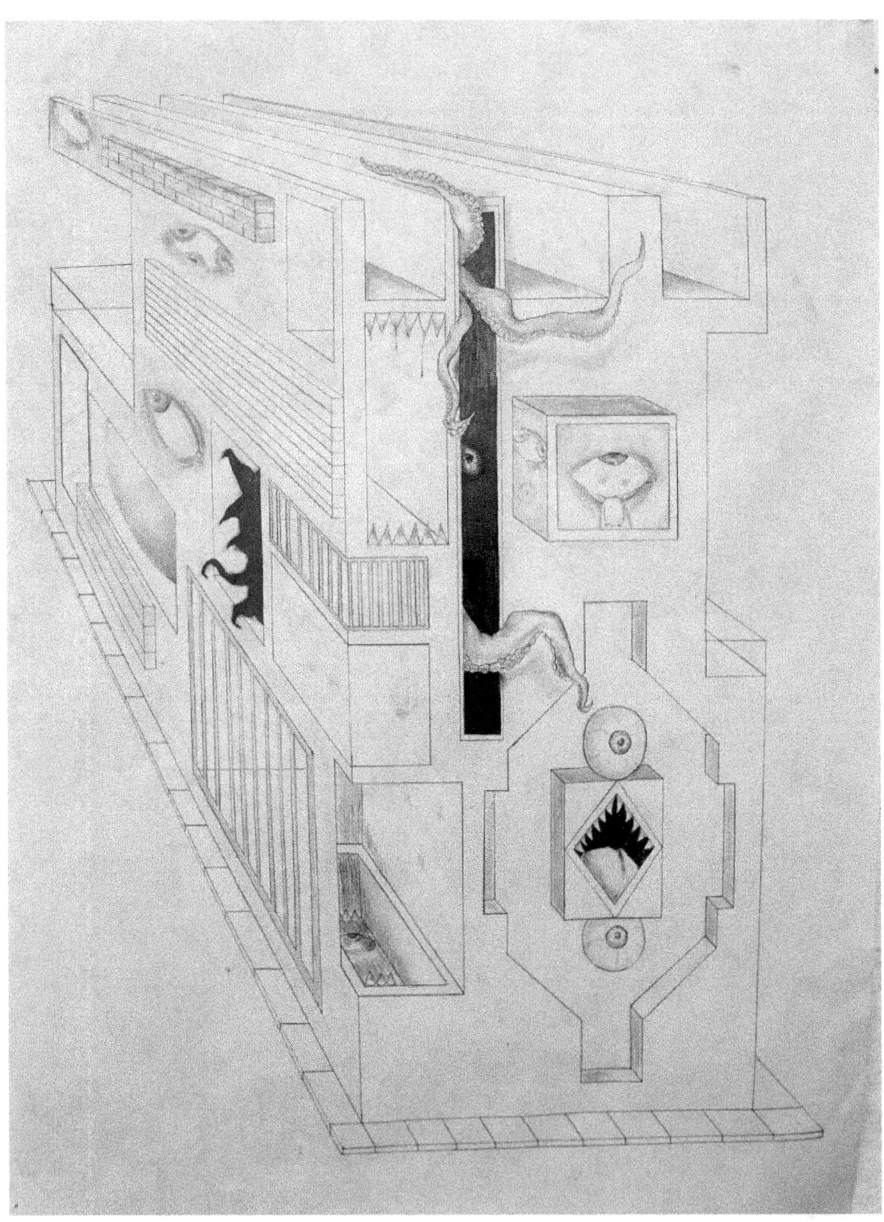

Alyssa Elizardo

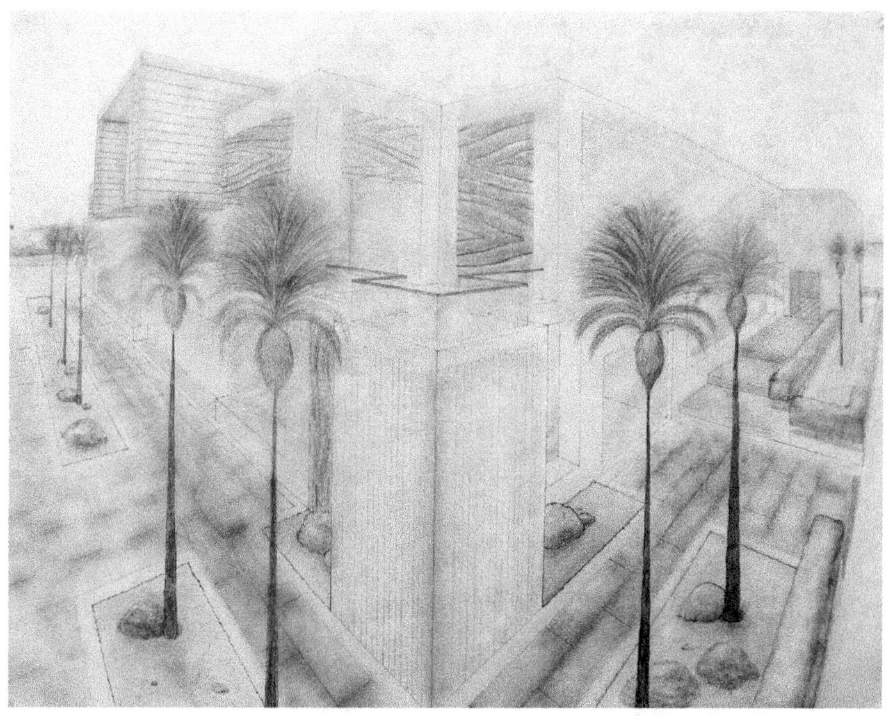

Adrian Rios Cisneros

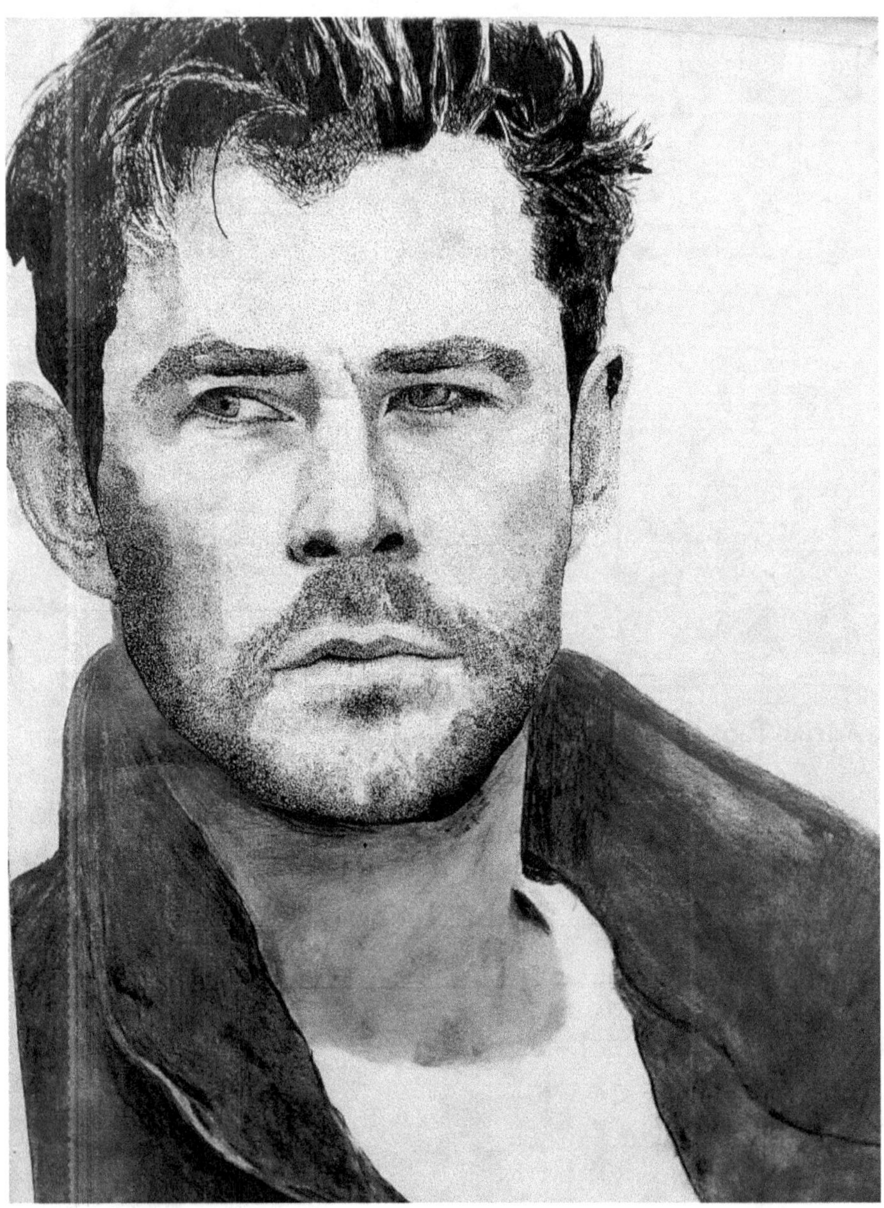

Isabella Munoz

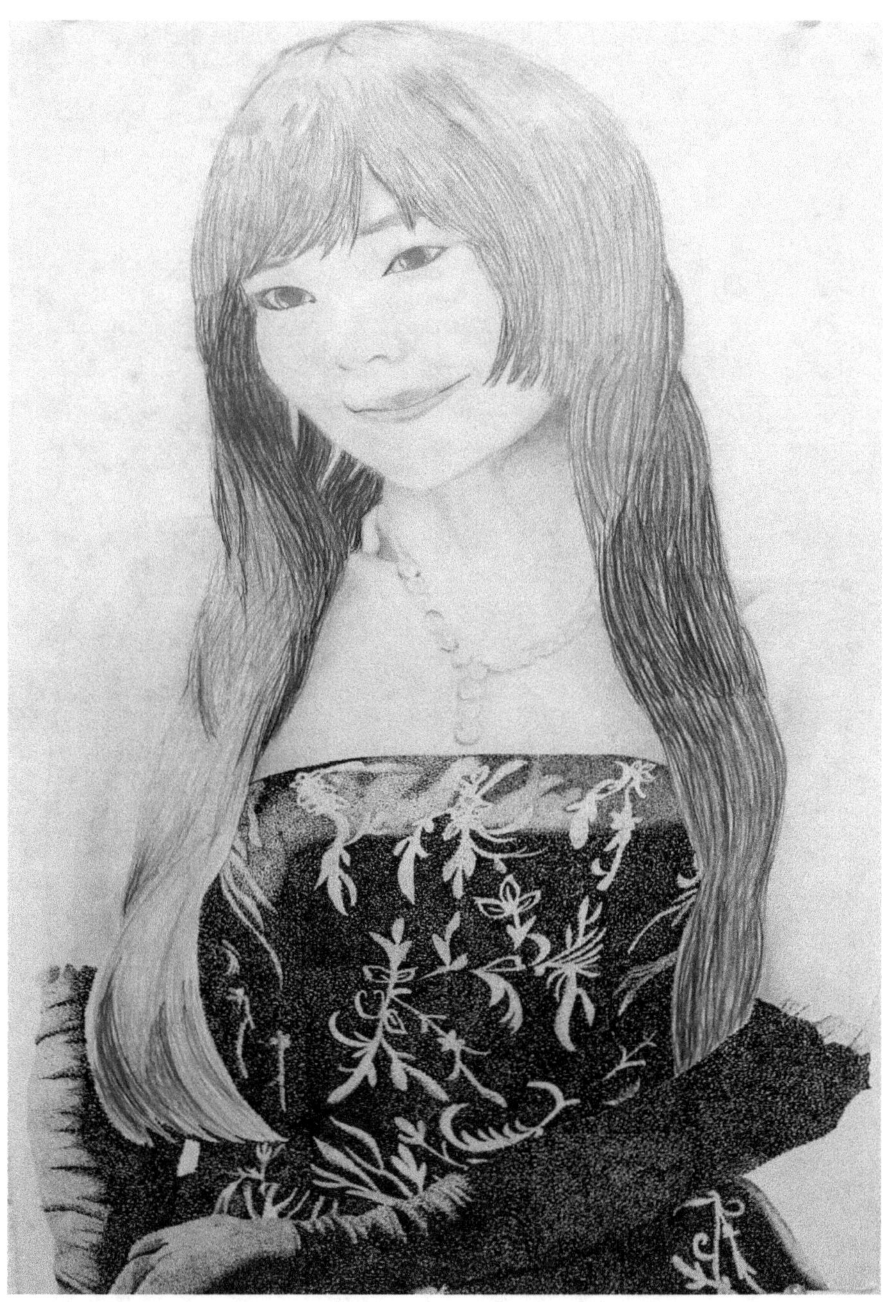

Amanda Escobedo

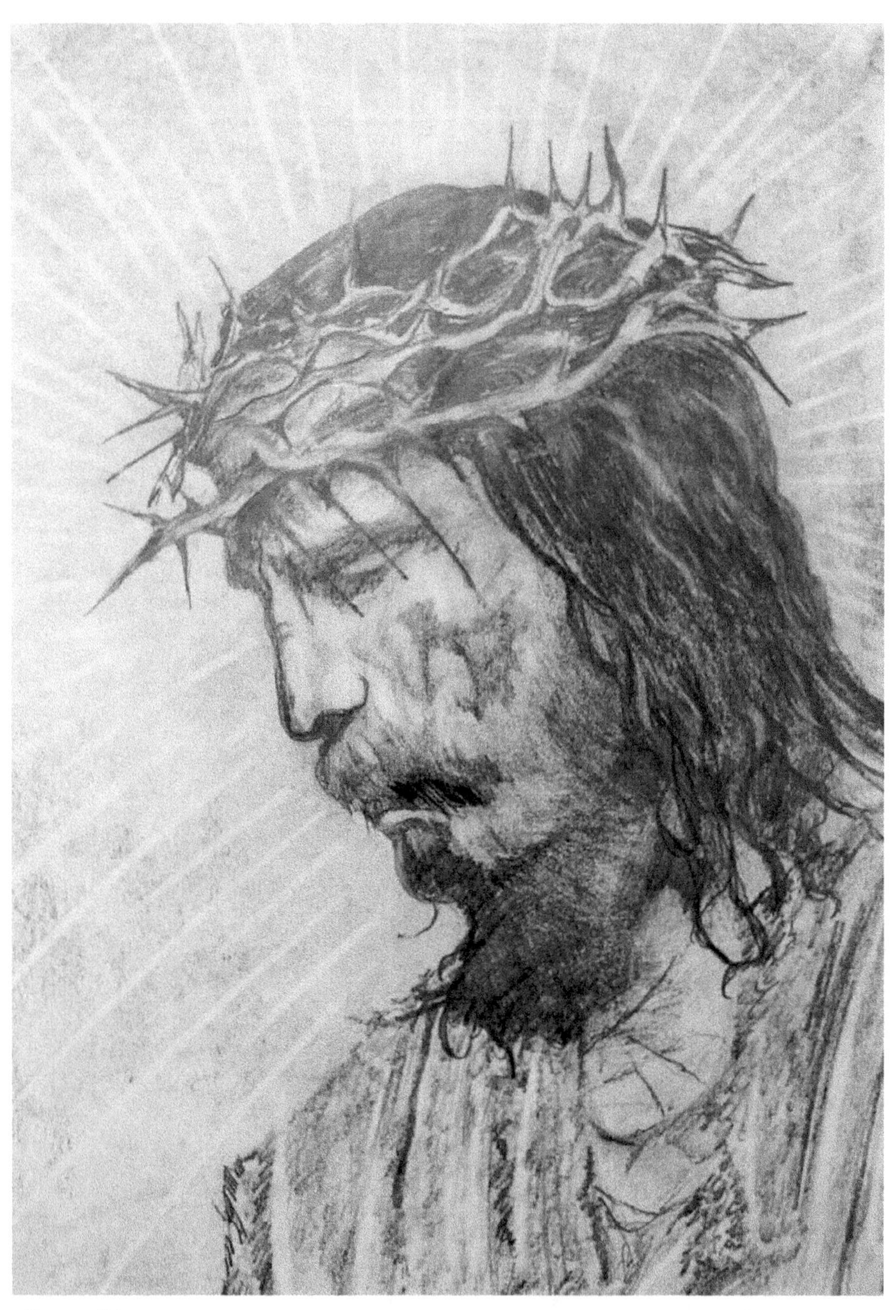

Jesus Vasquez

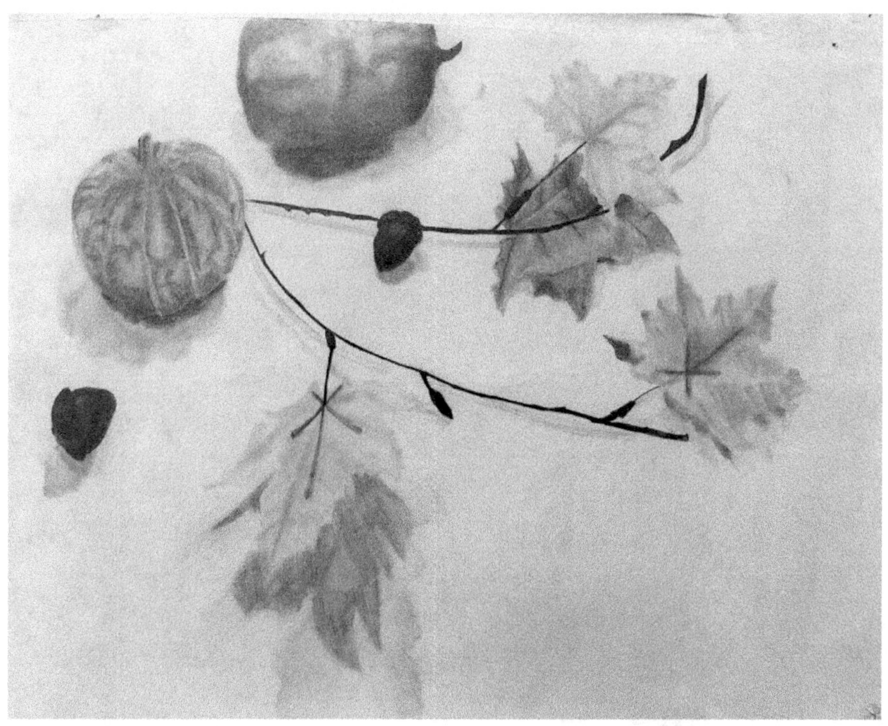

By: Adanesne Montano

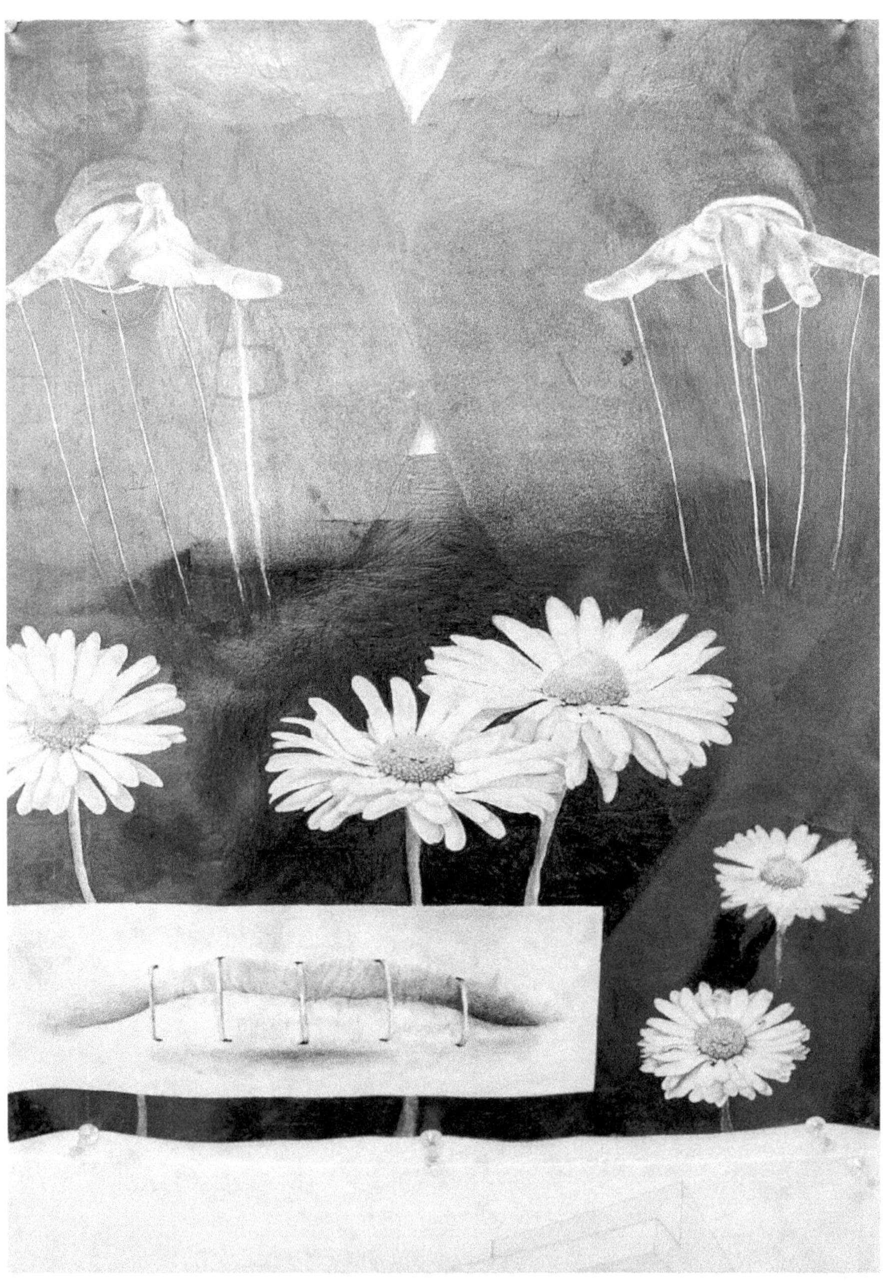

Diana Espinoza

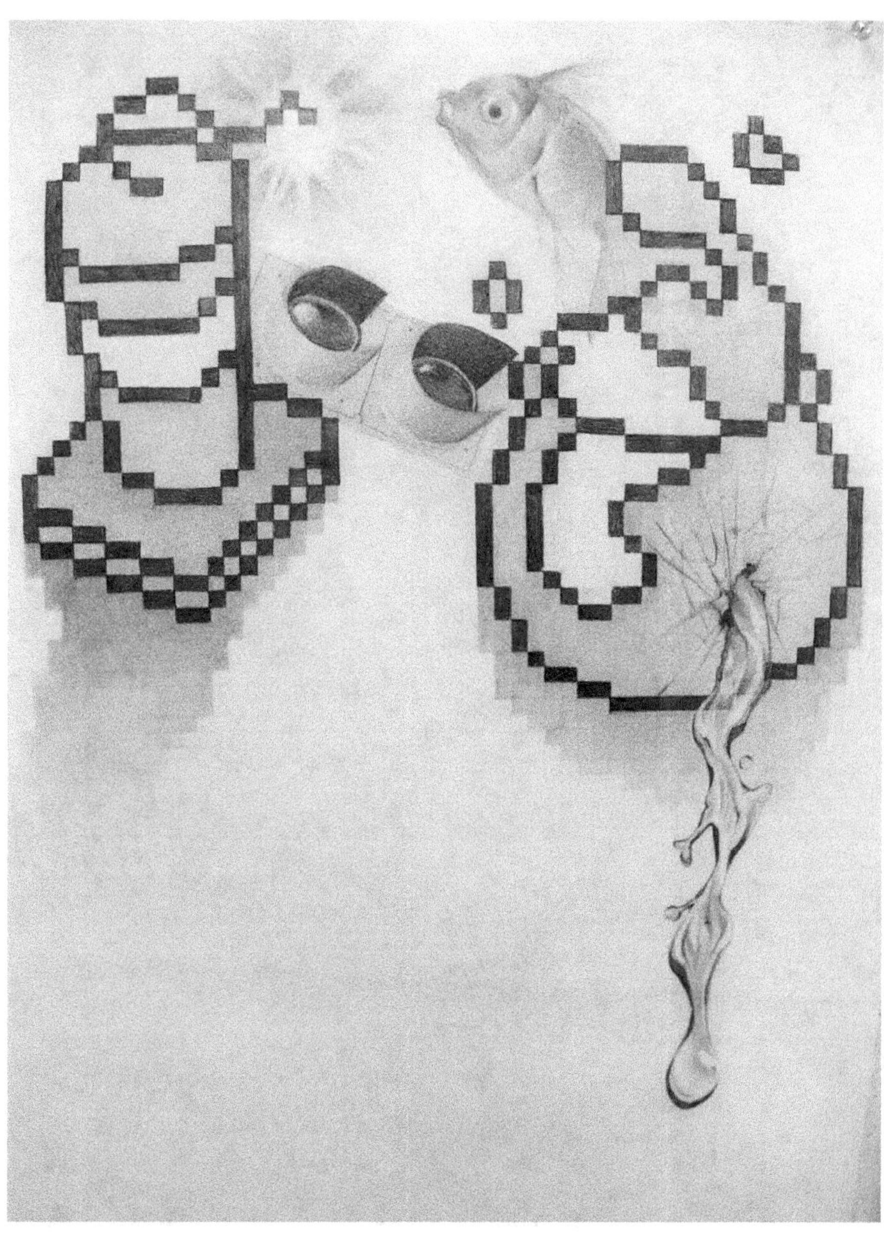

Delilah Bringas

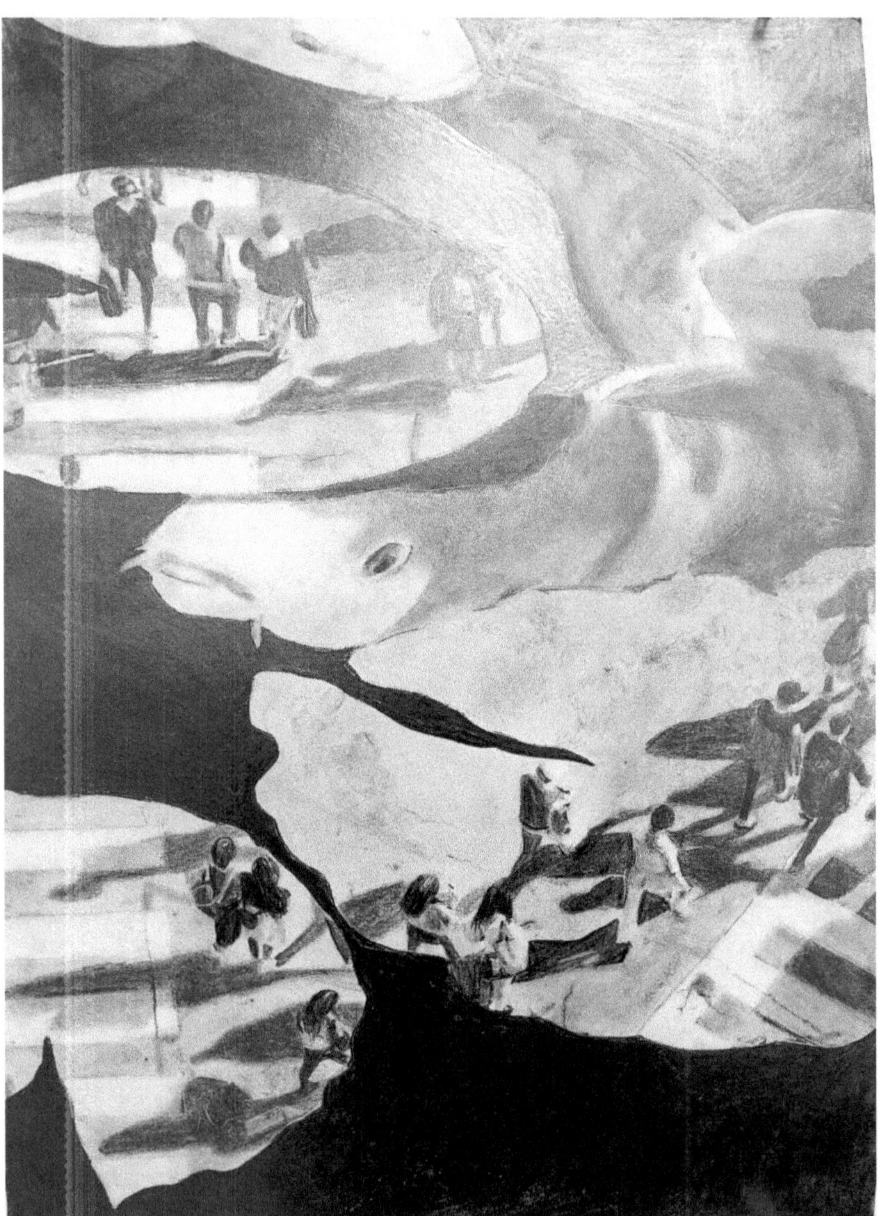

Isabella Munoz

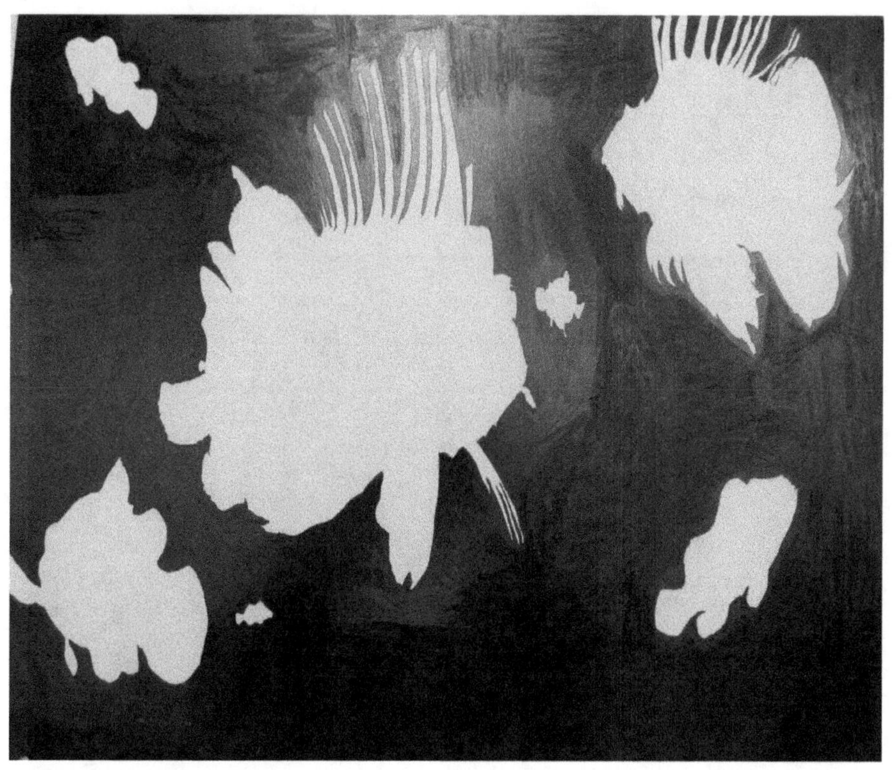

Diana Espinoza

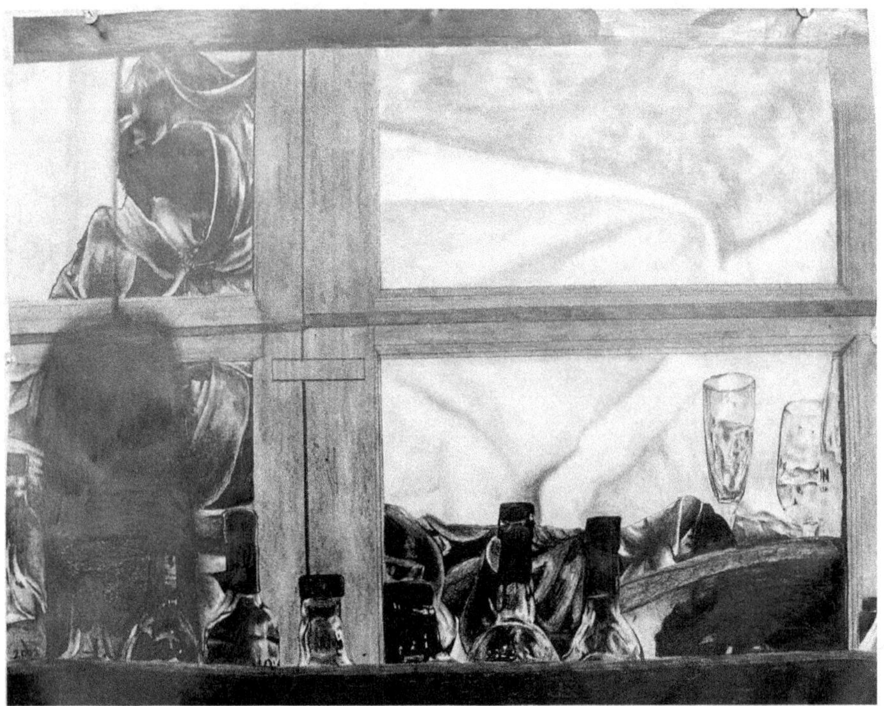

Diana Espinoza

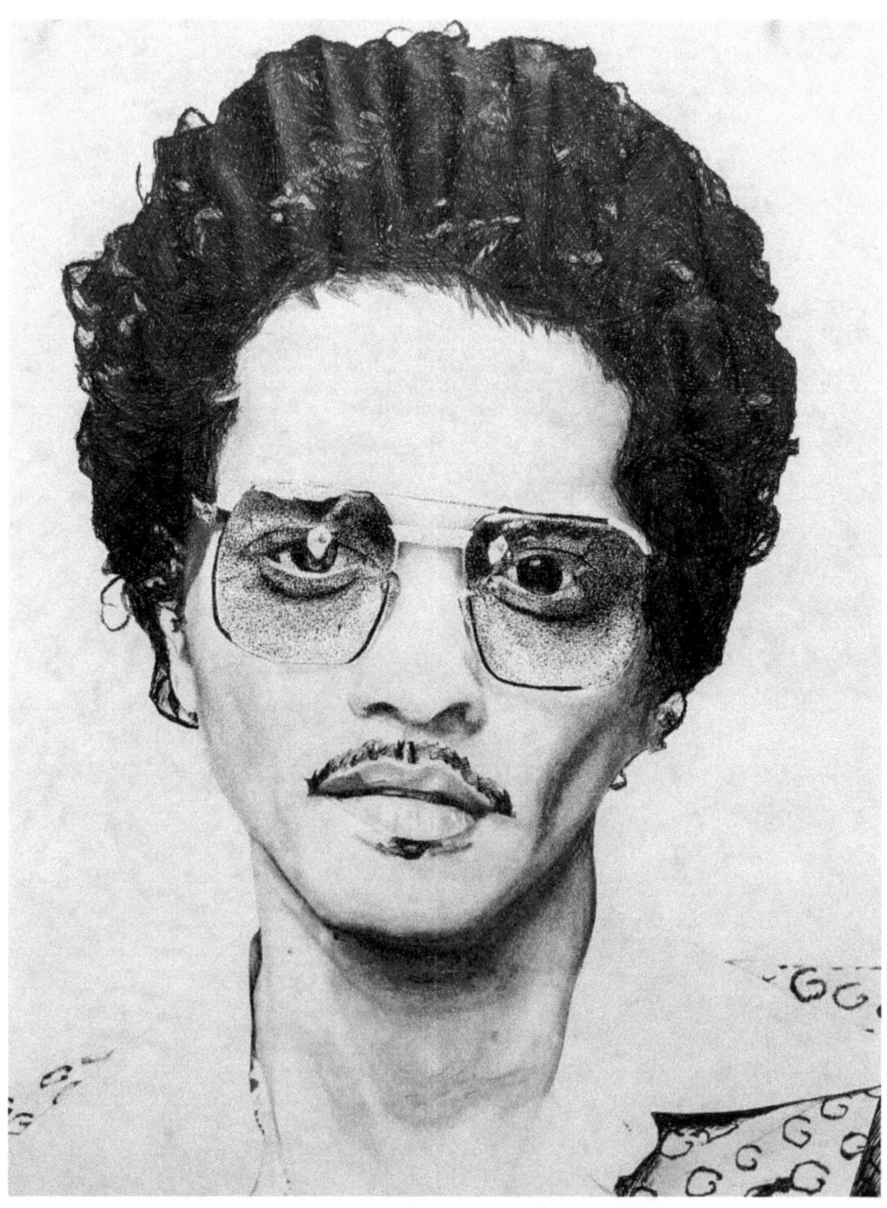

Ariana Ayala

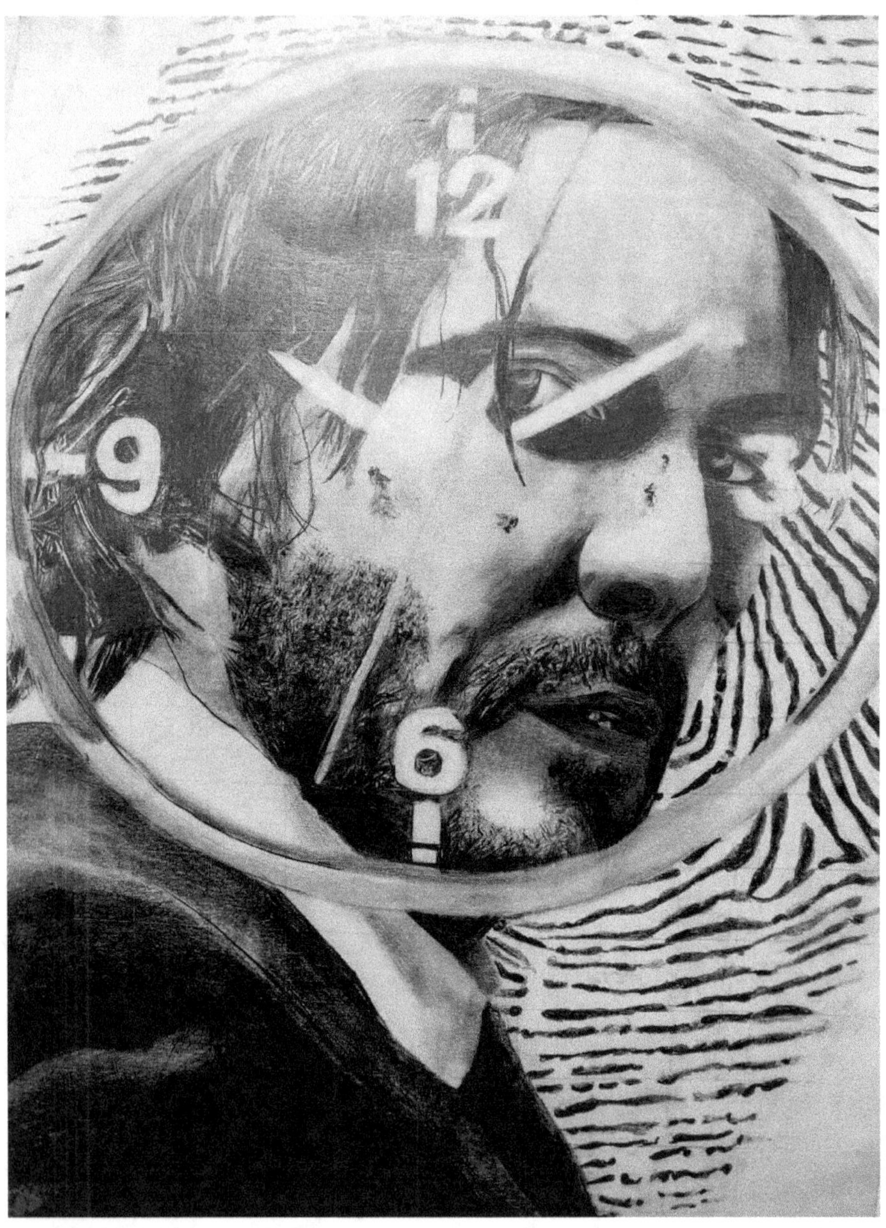

Isabella Munoz

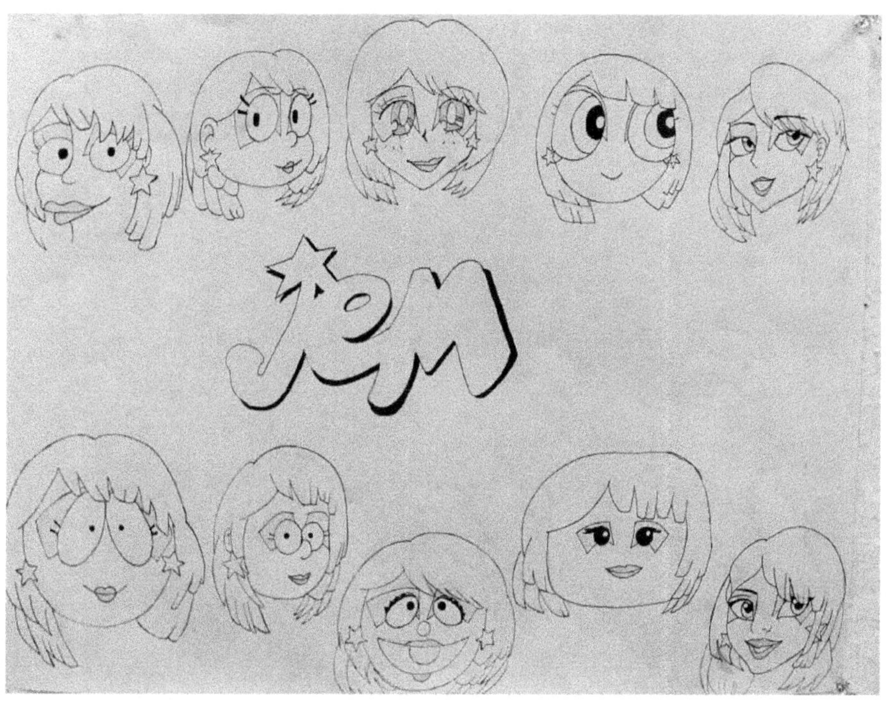

By: Amanda Escobedo

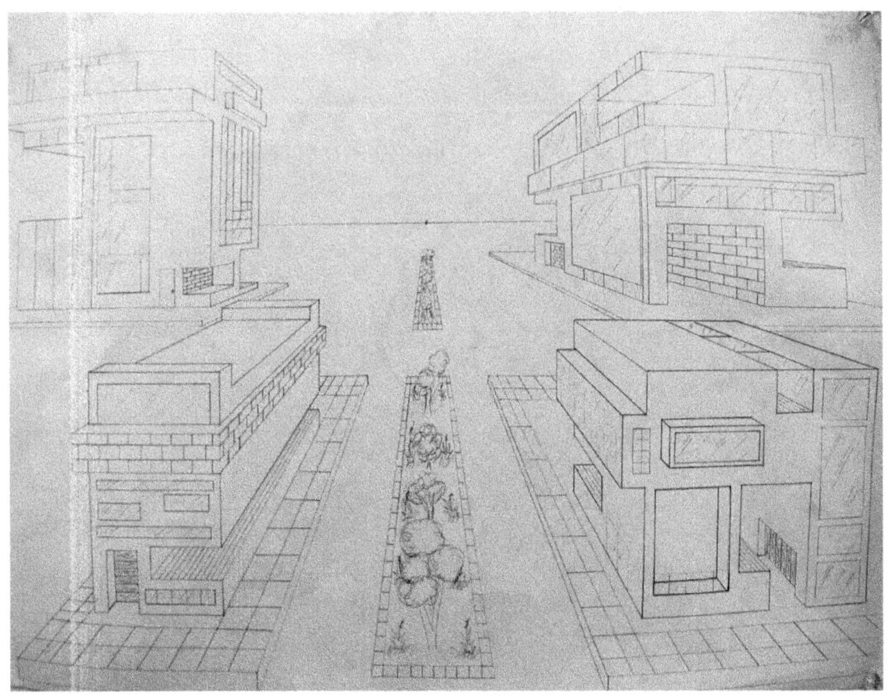

Rubee Gonzalez

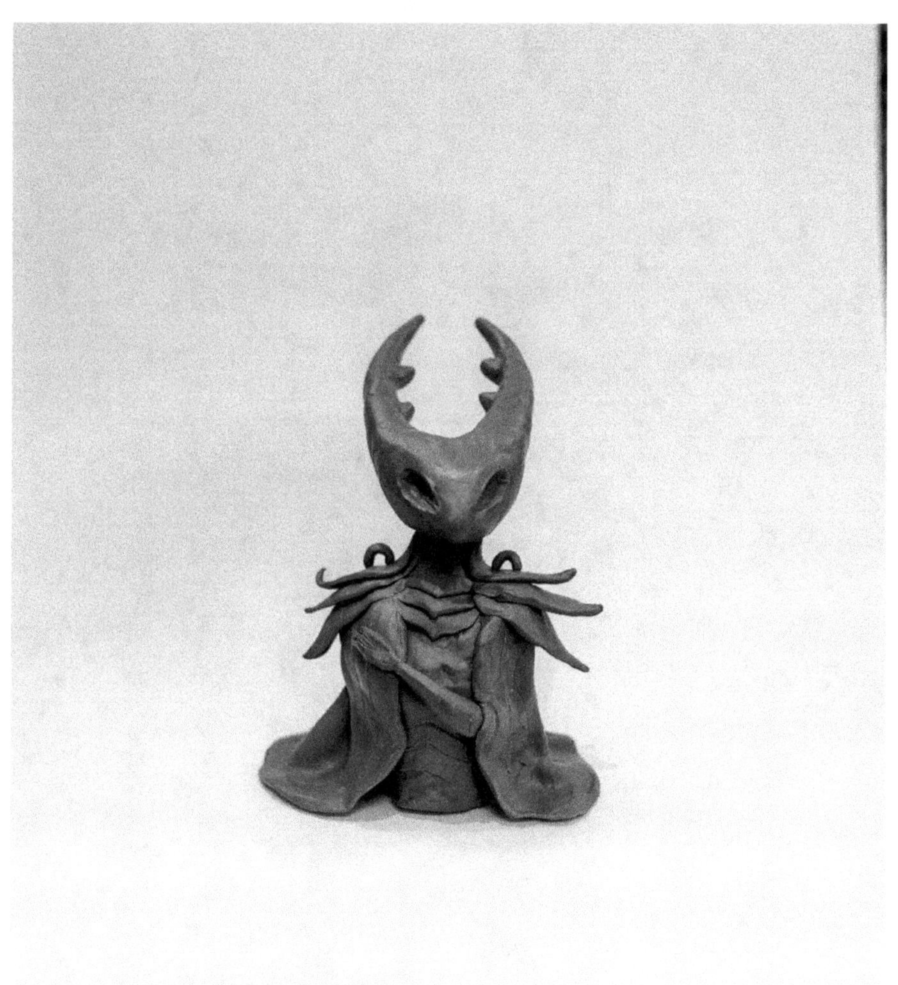

Evelyn Cruz

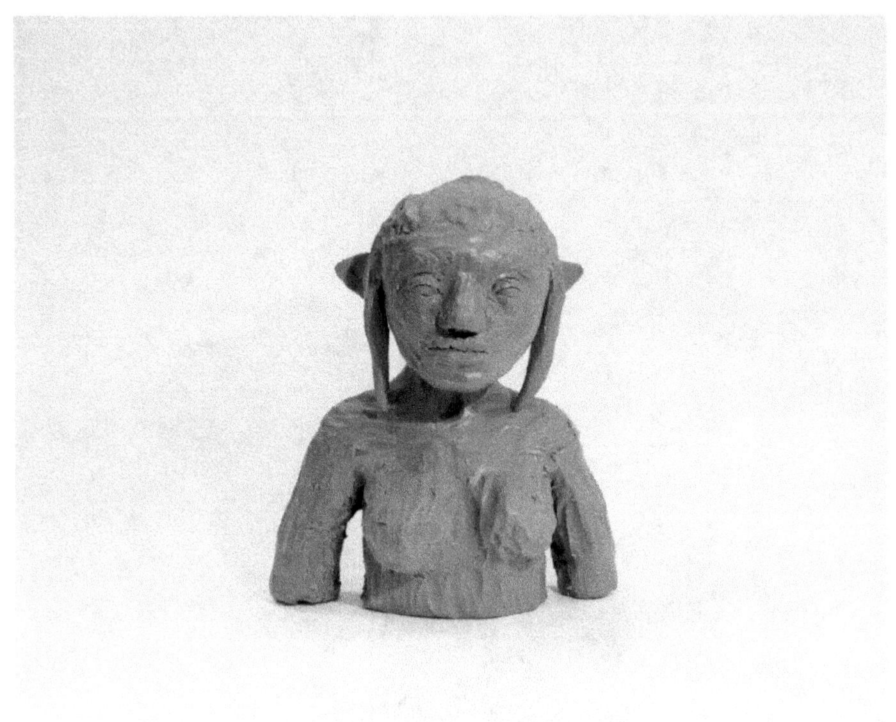

Salem Breneman

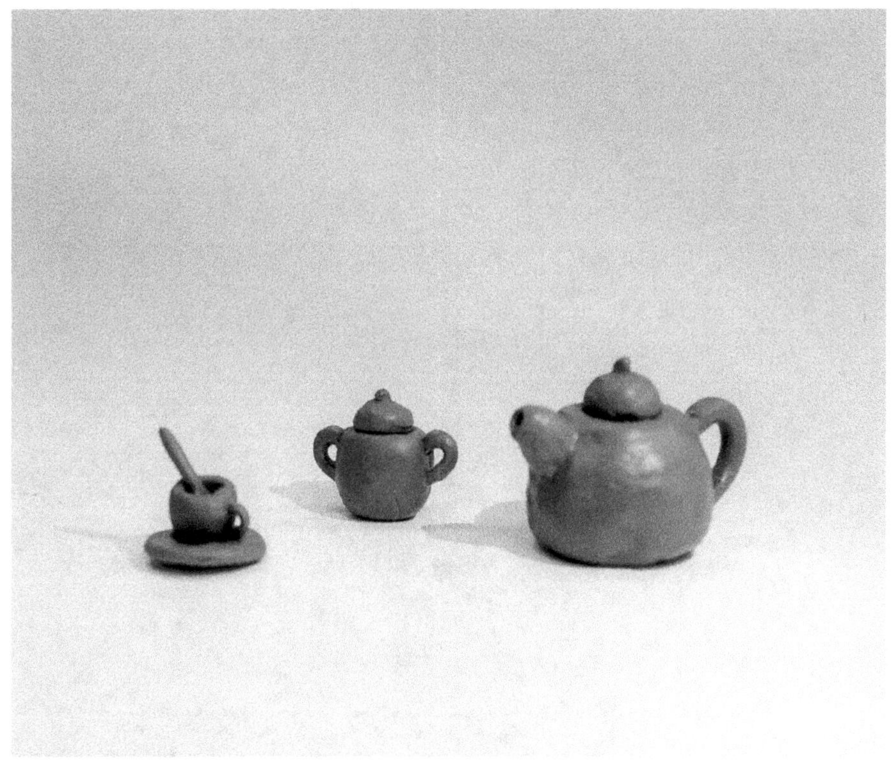

Salem Breneman

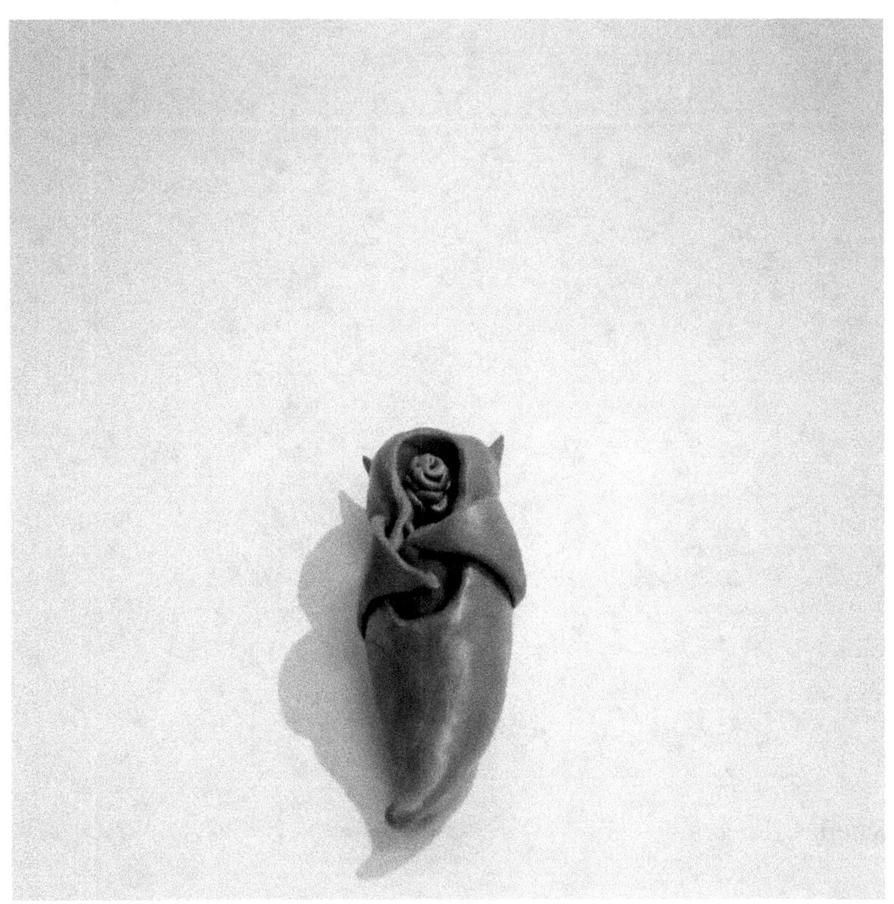

Evelyn Cruz

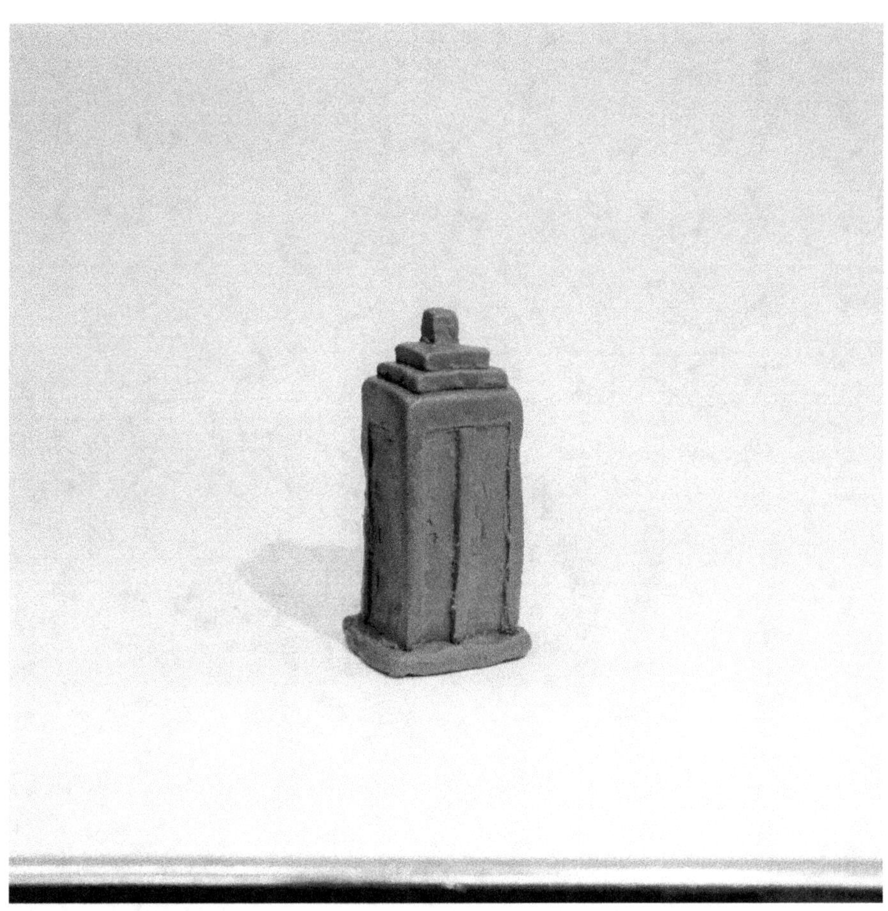

Salem Breneman

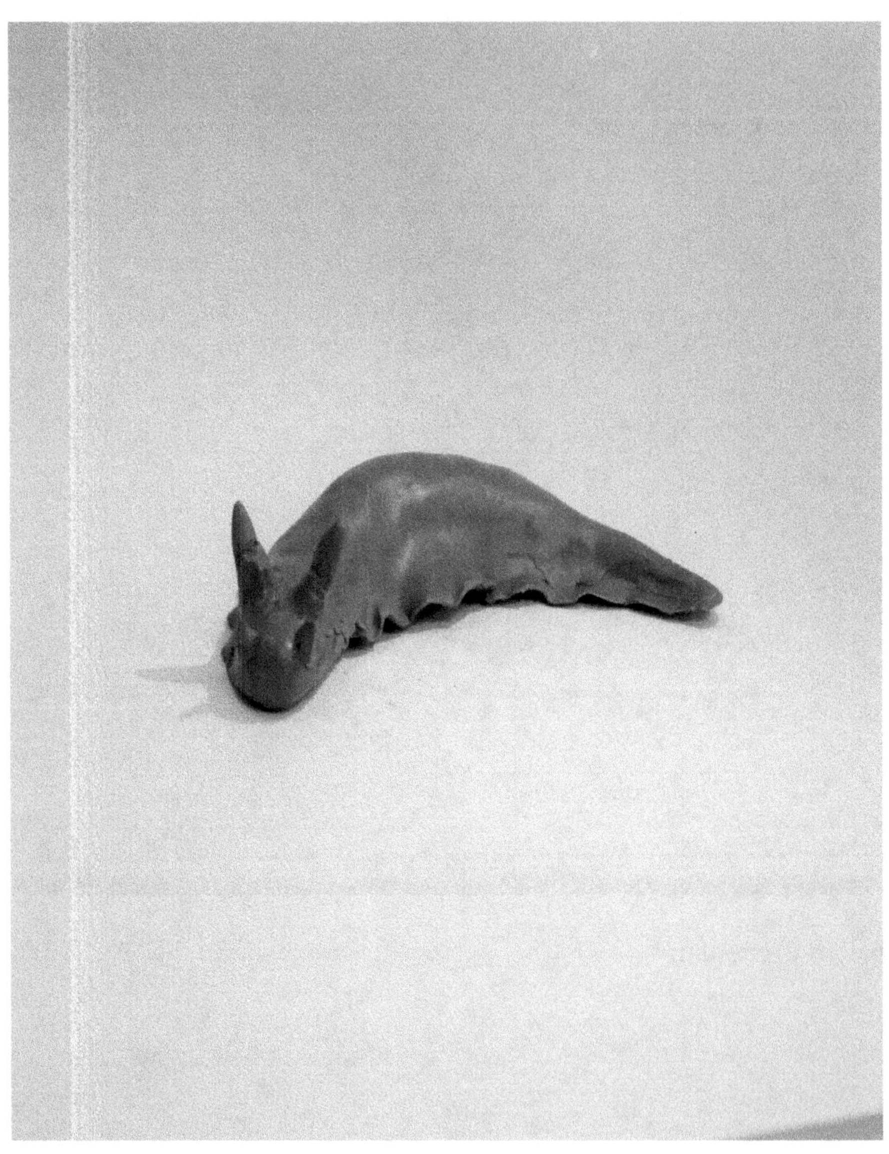

Andryna Receno

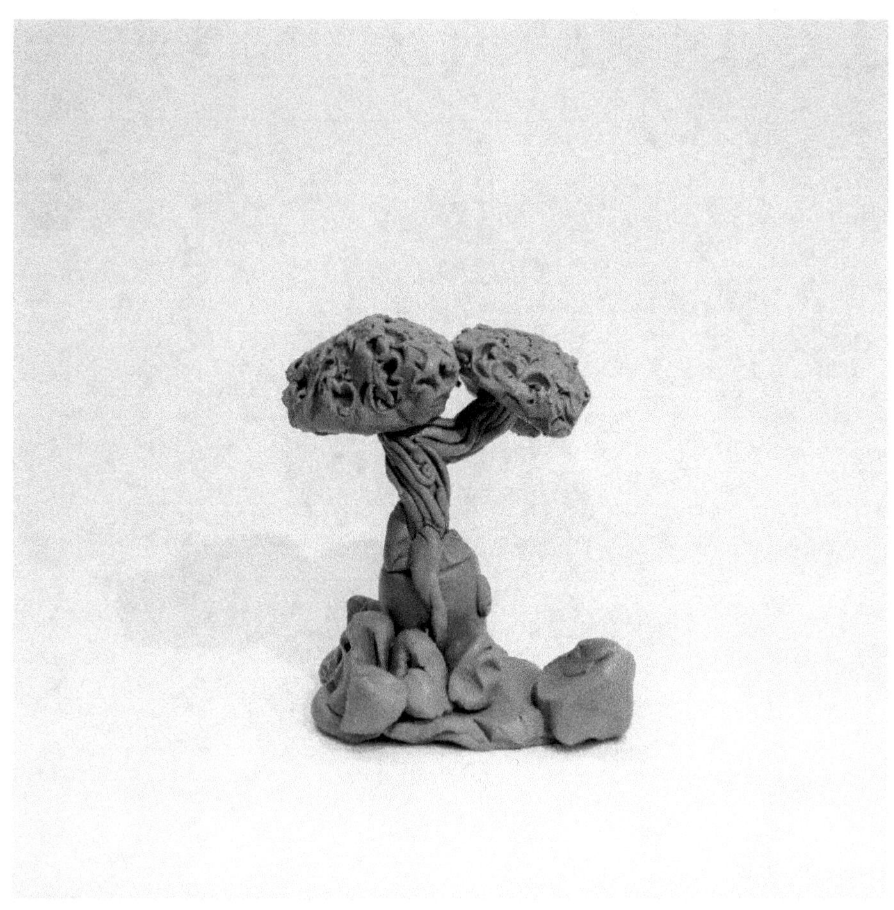

Vanessa Pantoja

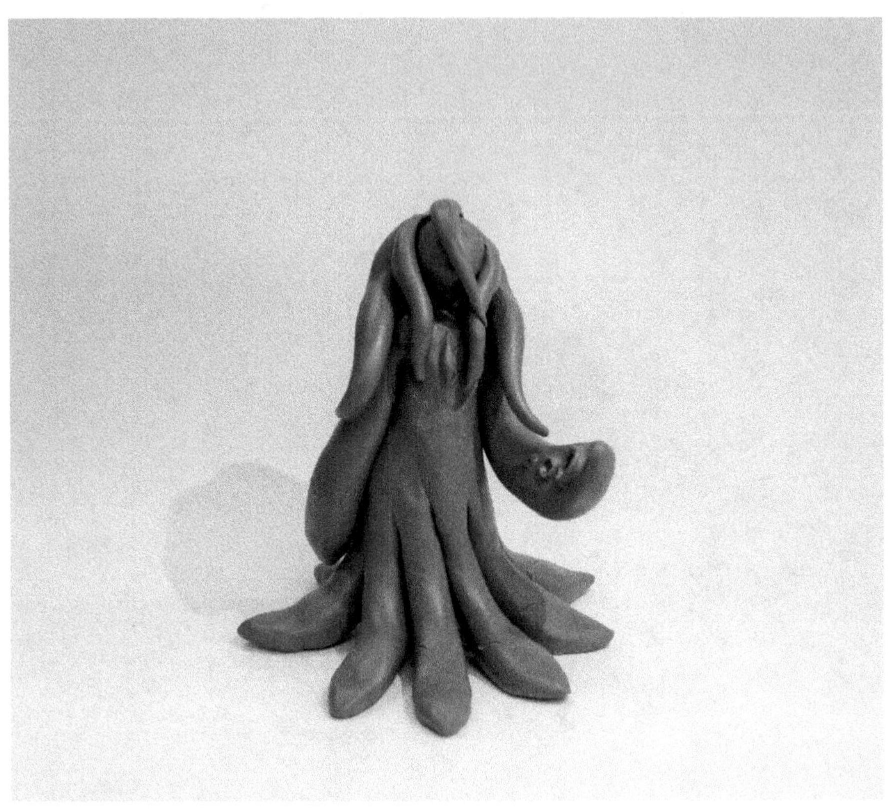

Evelyn Cruz

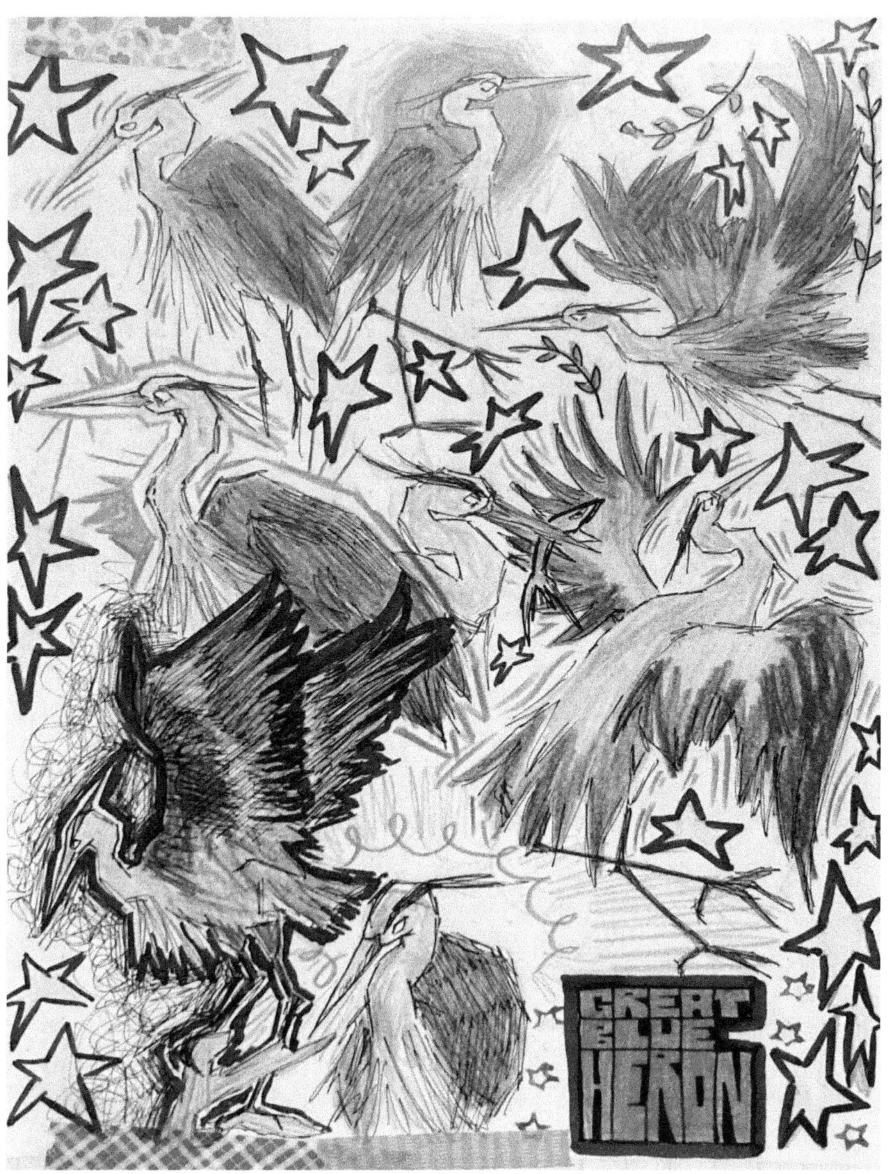

Michelle Lalla

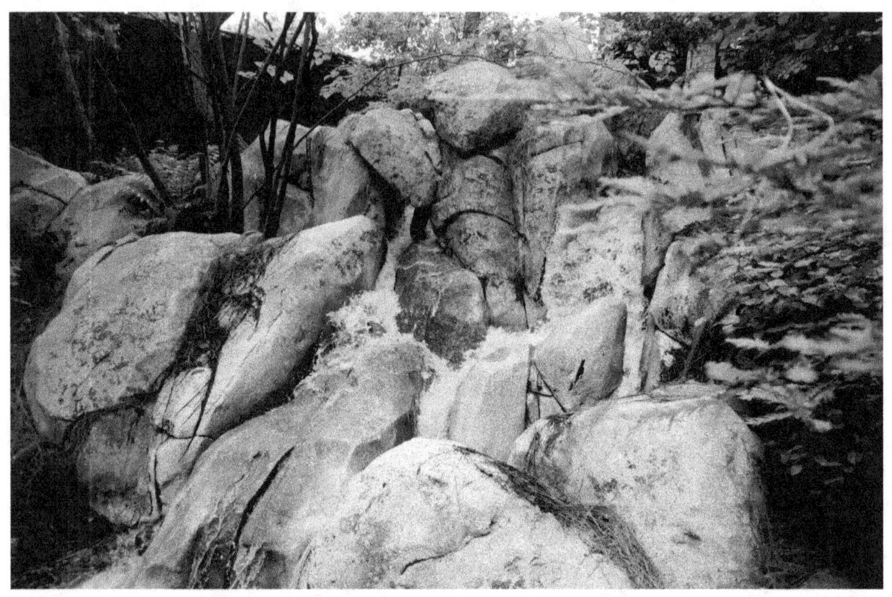

Ashley Lazo-Ruiz

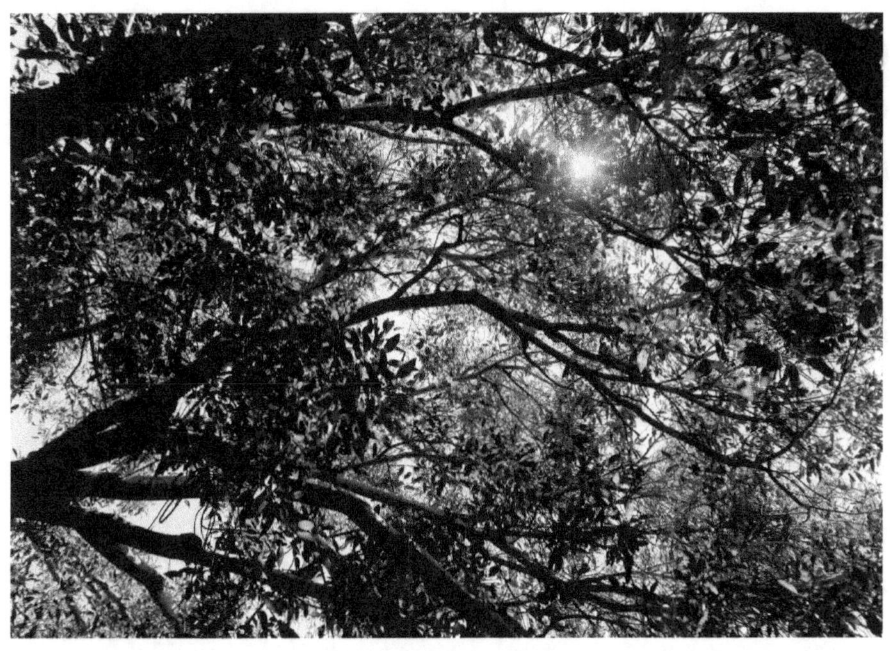

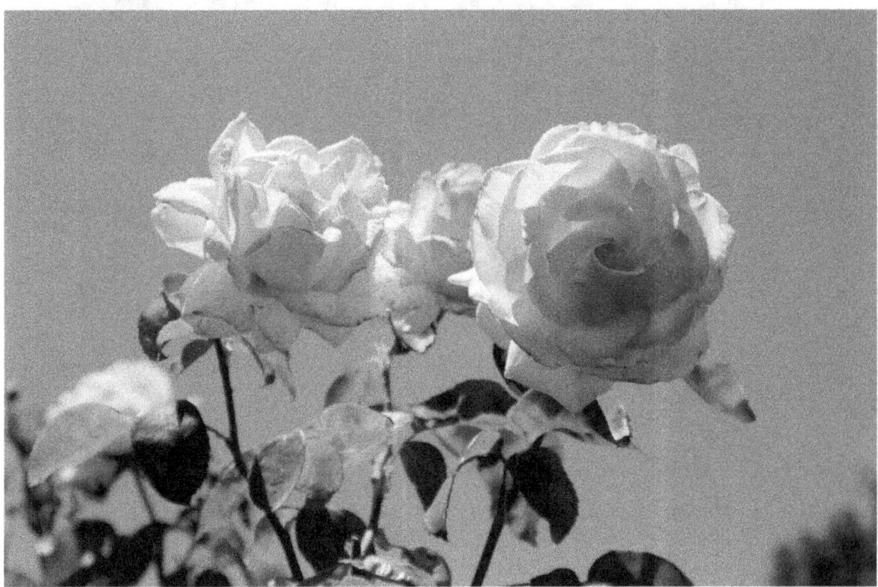

Ashley Lazo-Ruiz

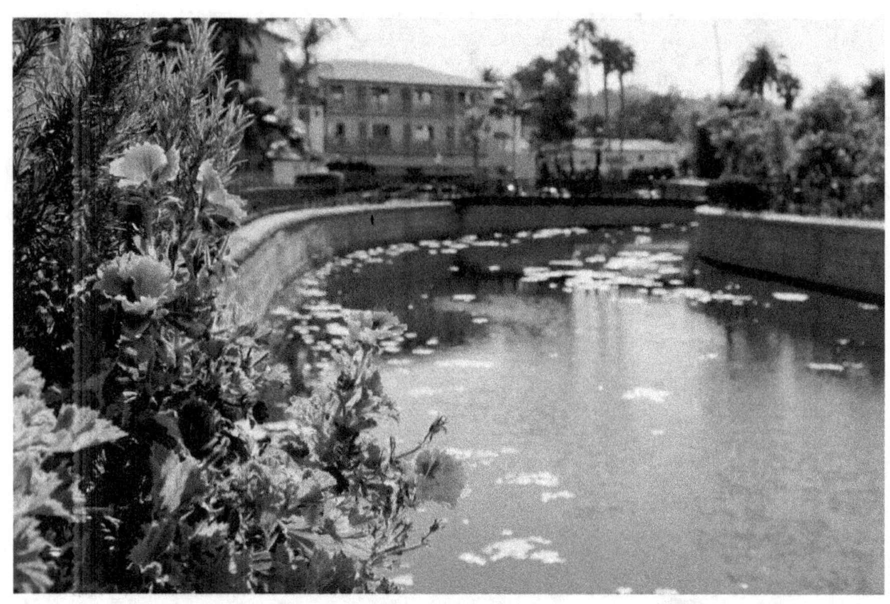

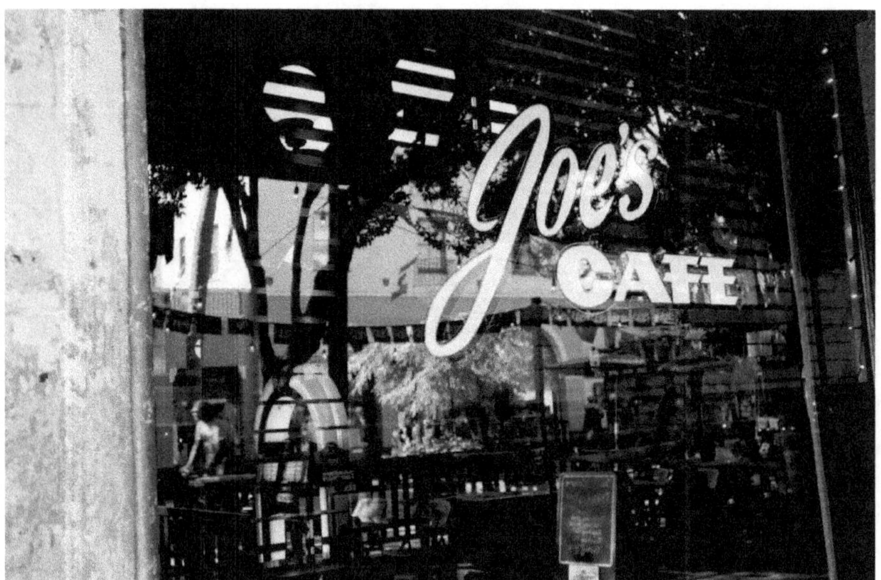

Ashley Lazo-Ruiz

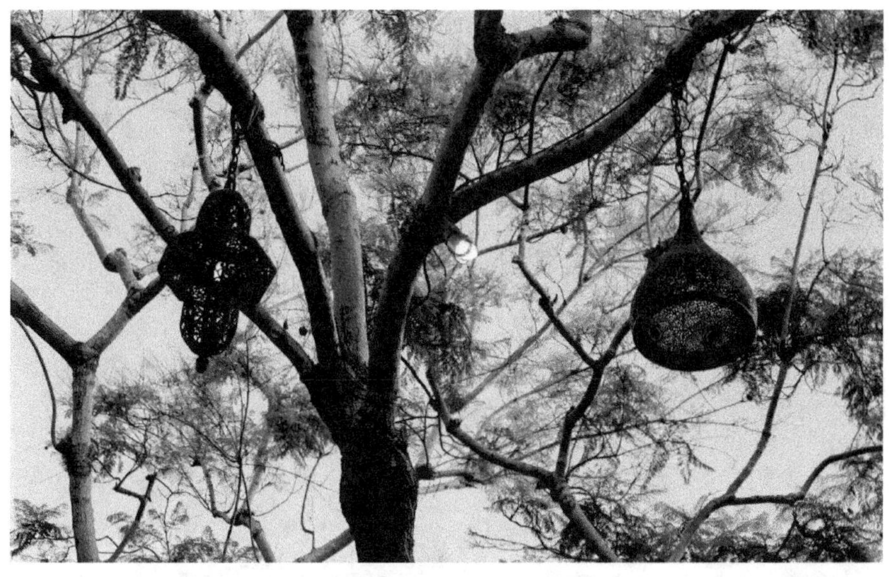

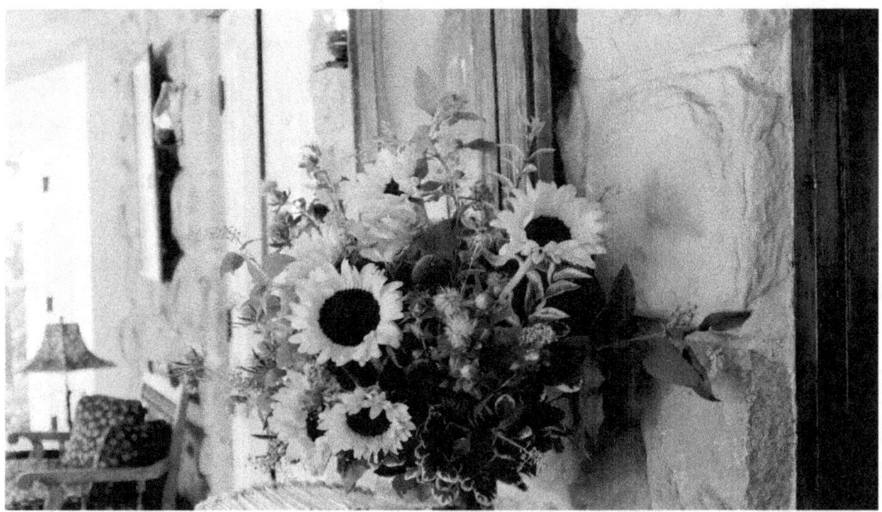

Ashley Lazo-Ruiz

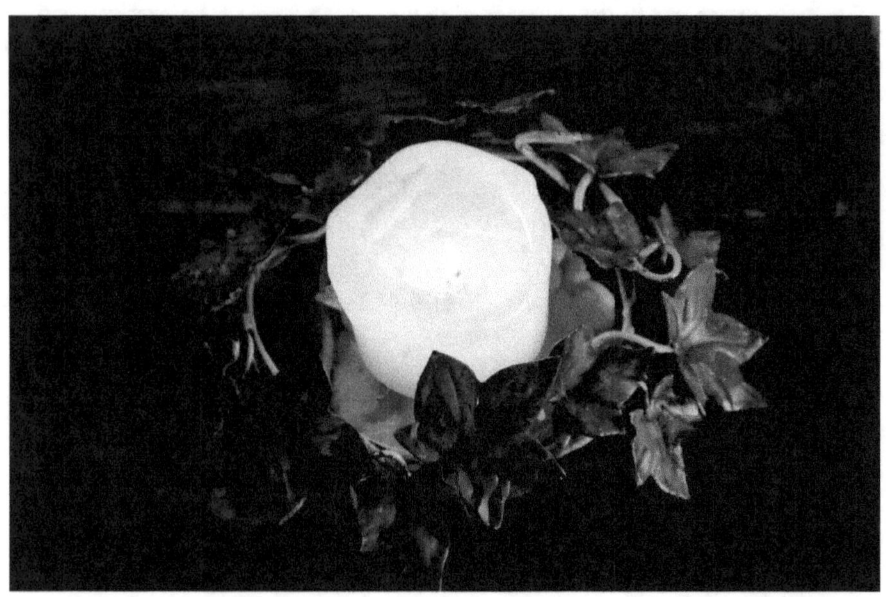

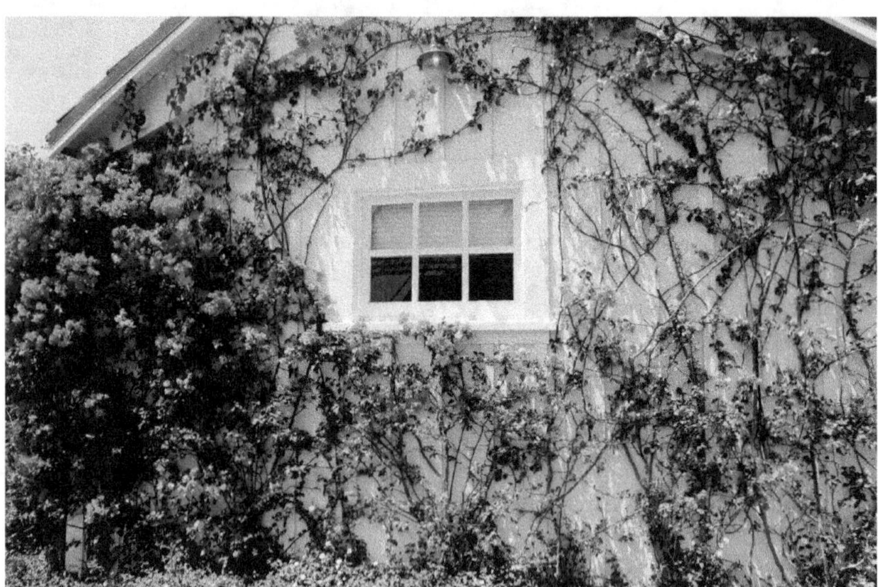

Ashley Lazo-Ruiz

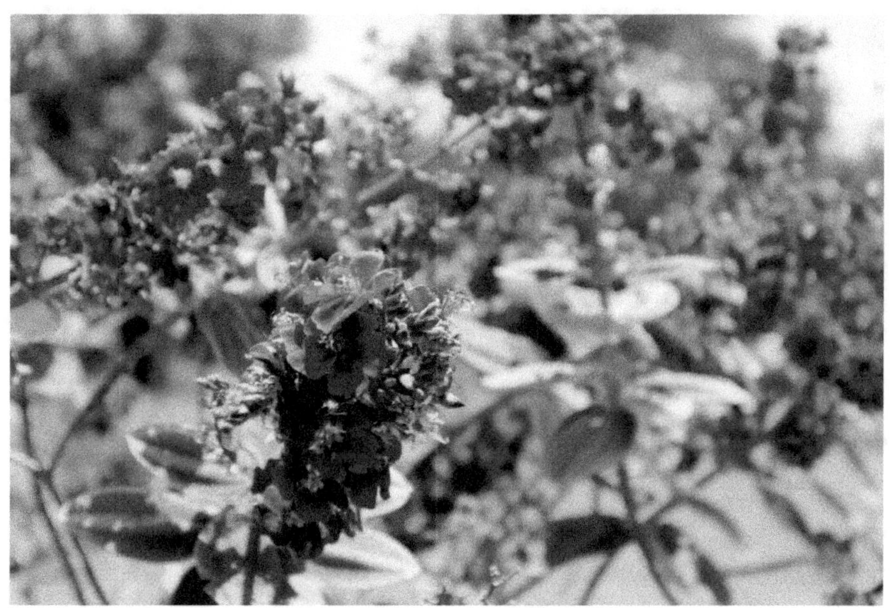

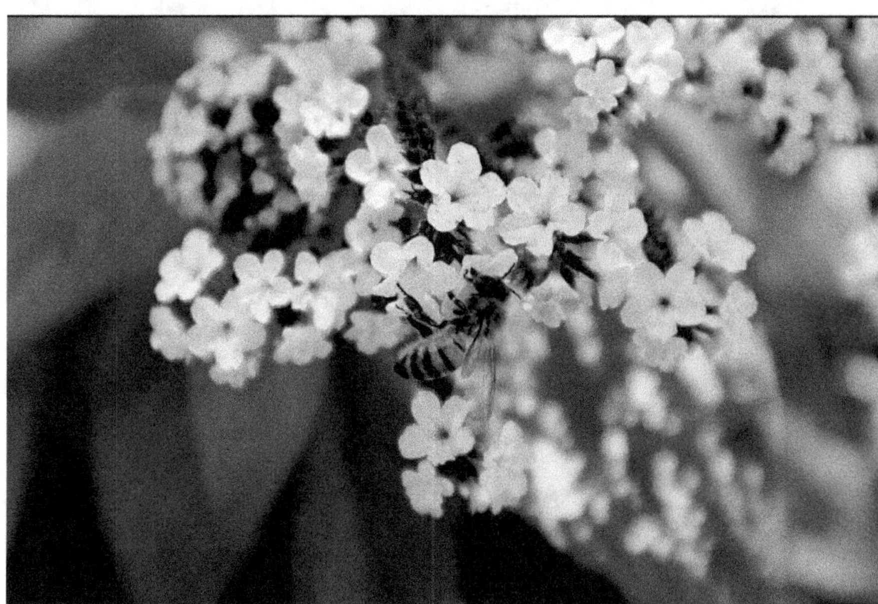

Ashley Lazo-Ruiz

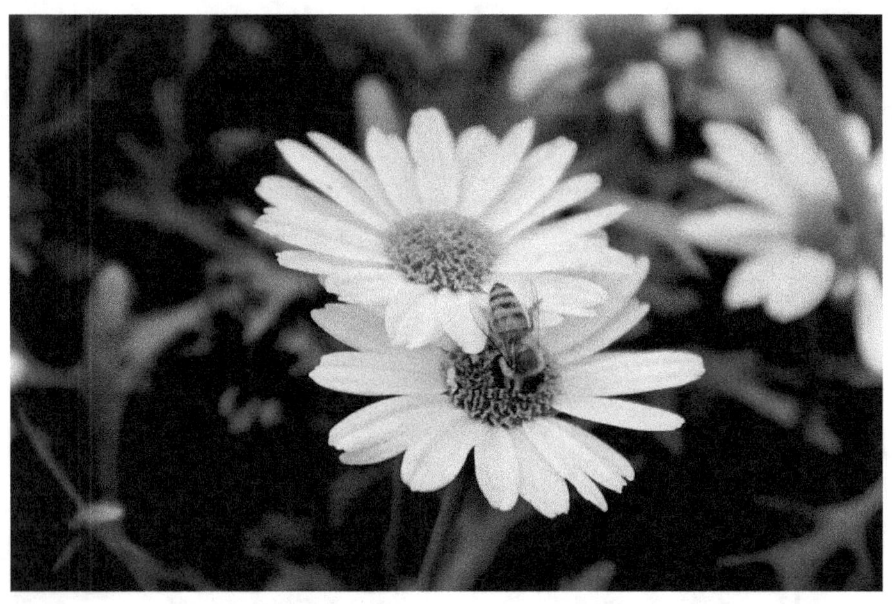

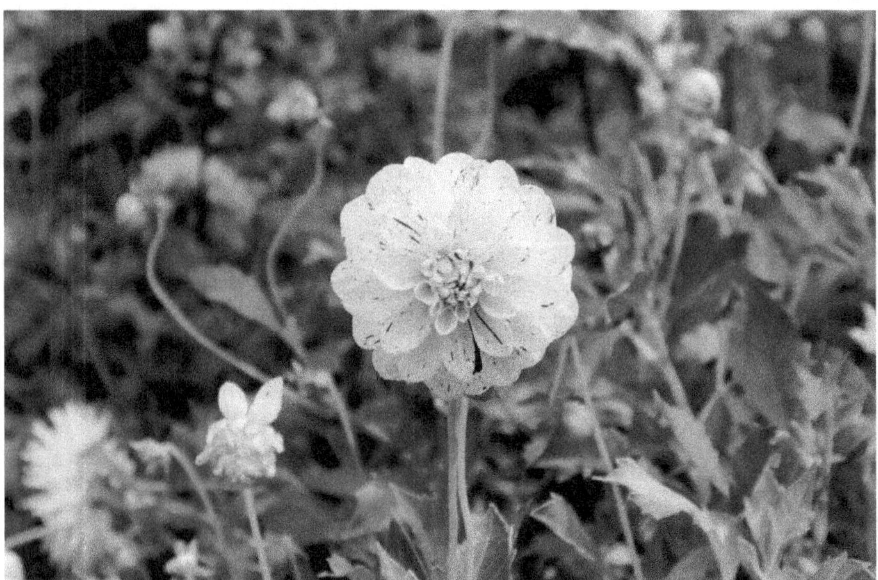

Ashley Lazo-Ruiz

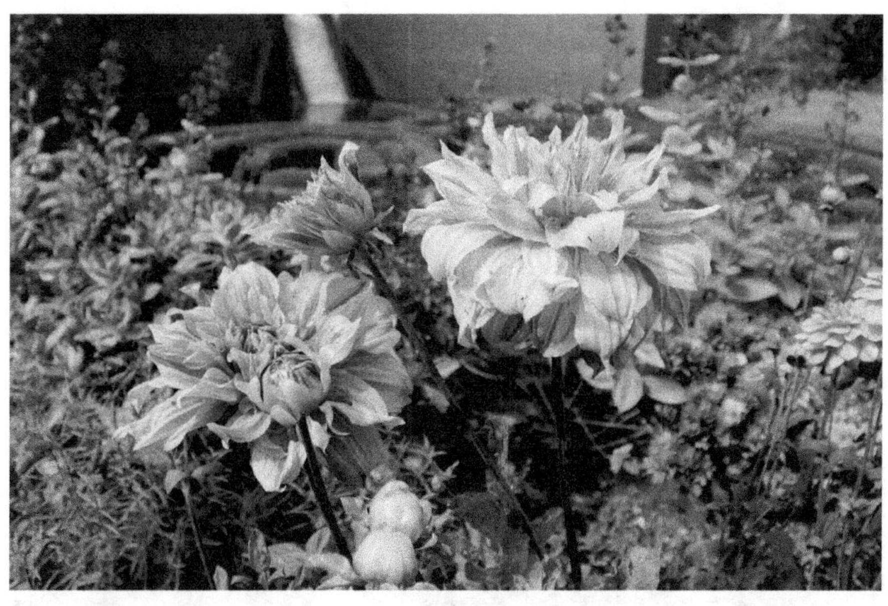

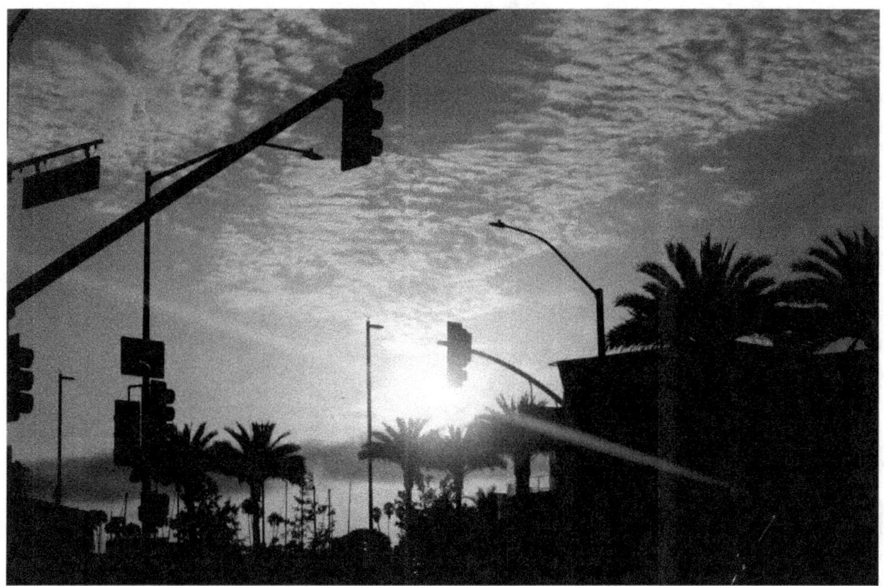

Ashley Lazo-Ruiz

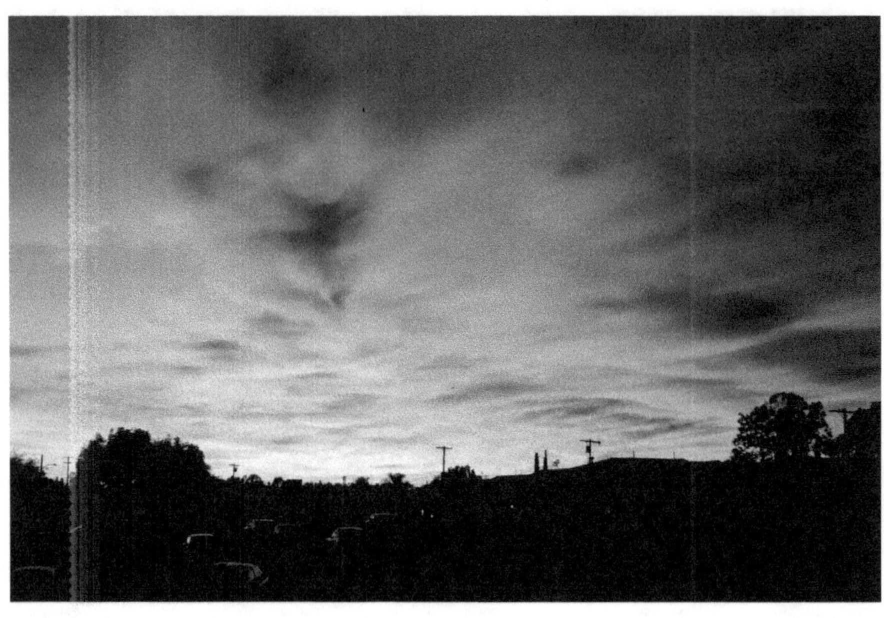

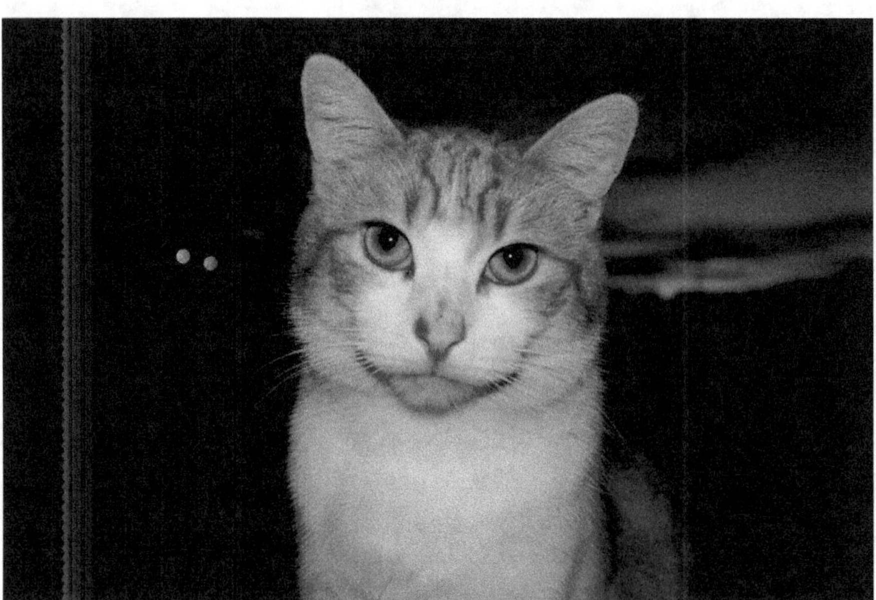

Ashley Lazo-Ruiz

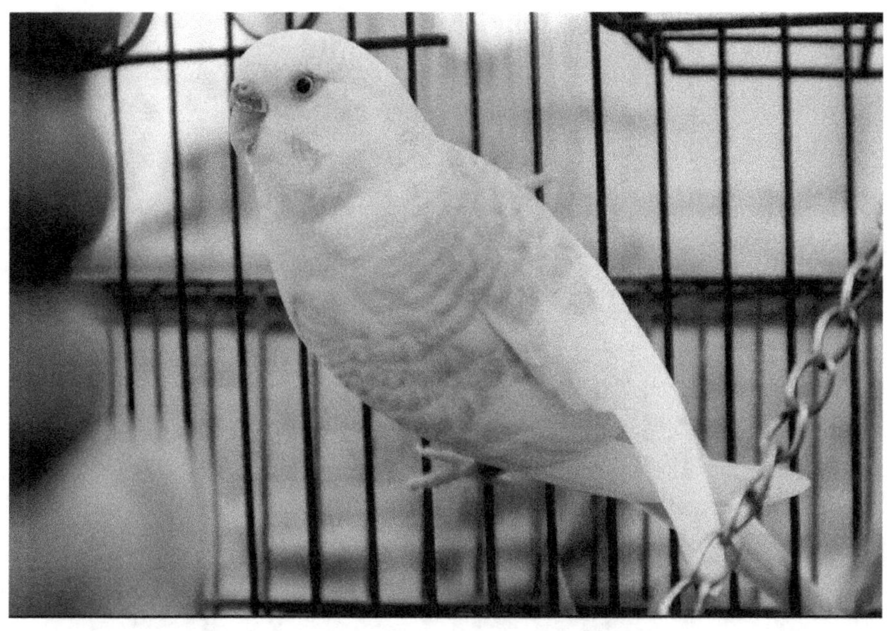

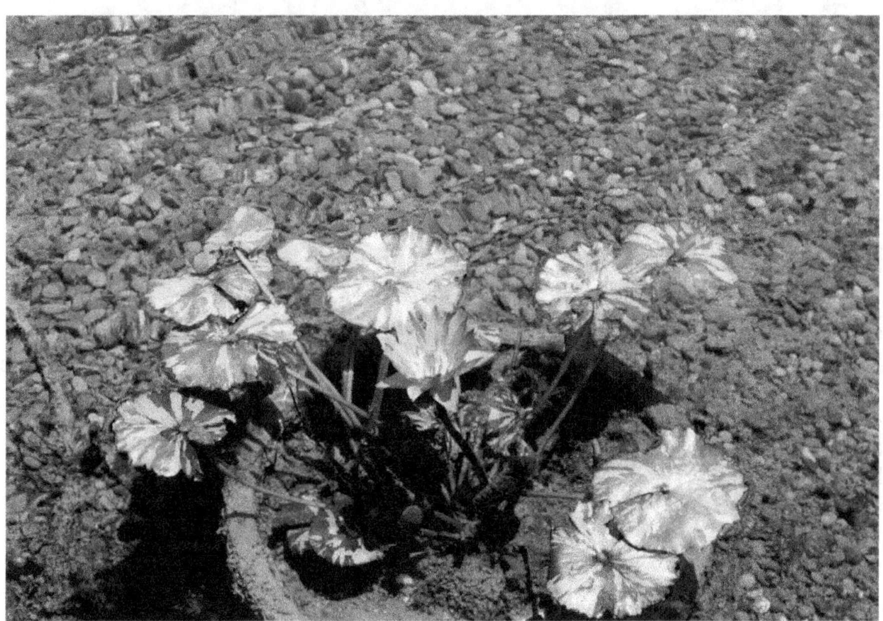

Ashley Lazo-Ruiz

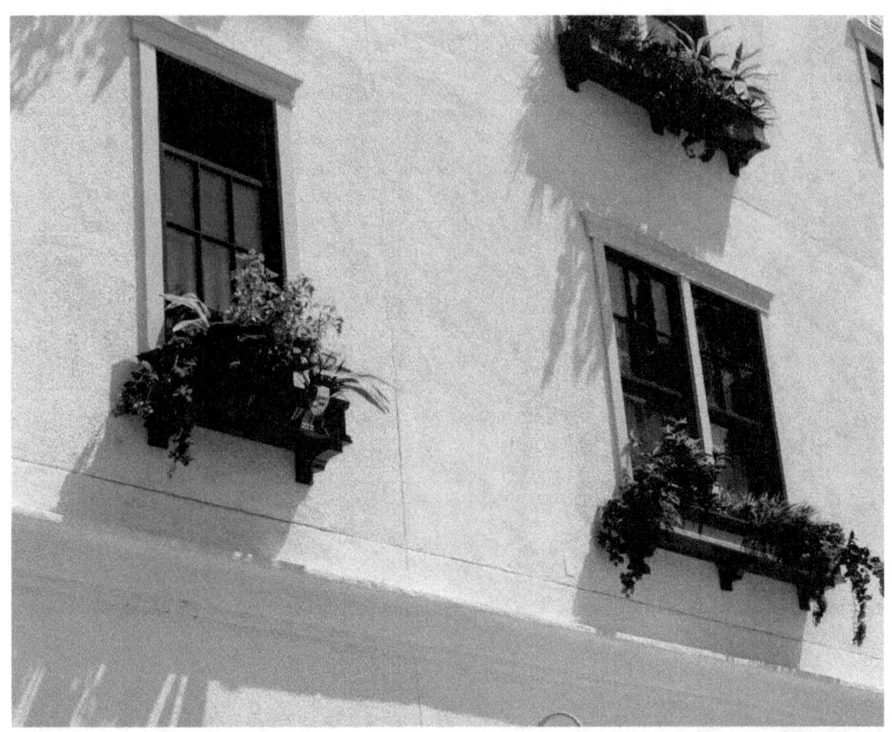

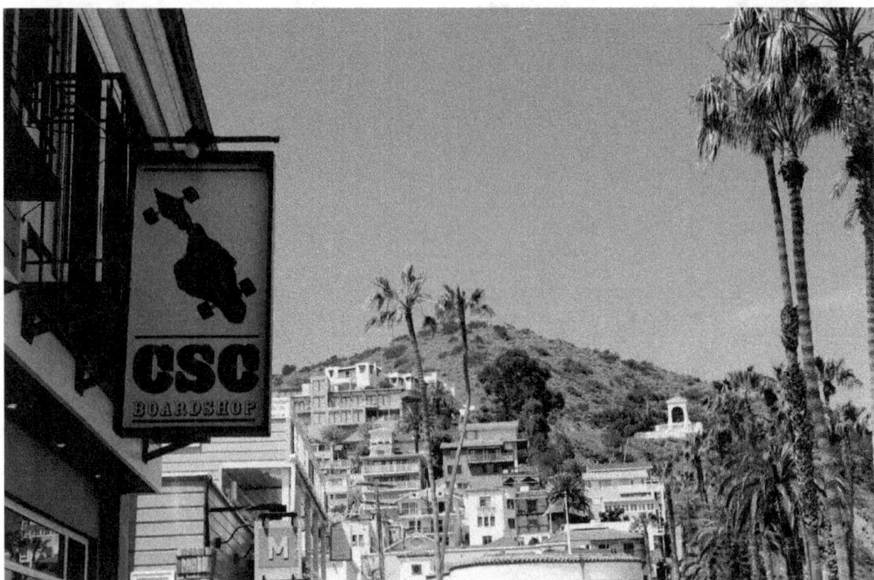

Ashley Lazo-Ruiz

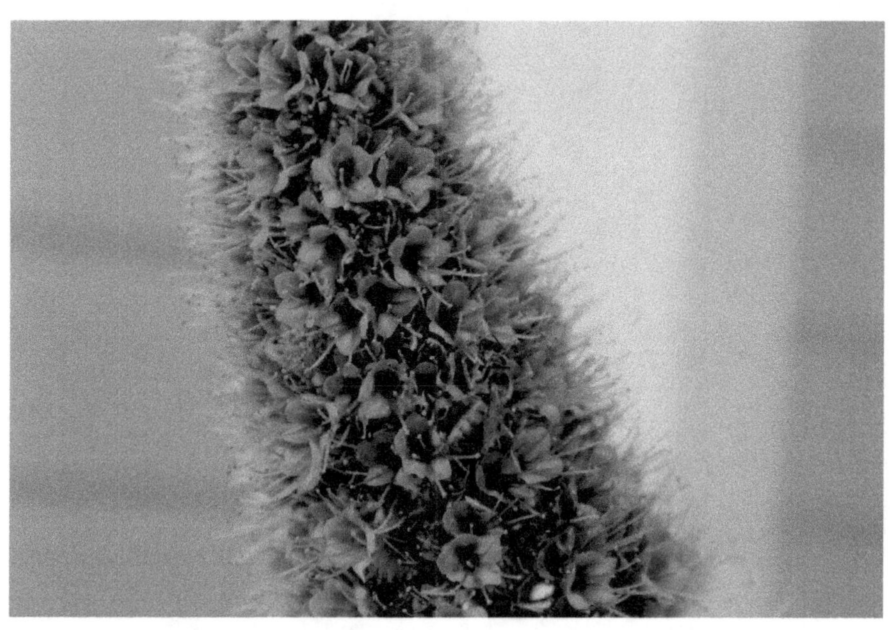

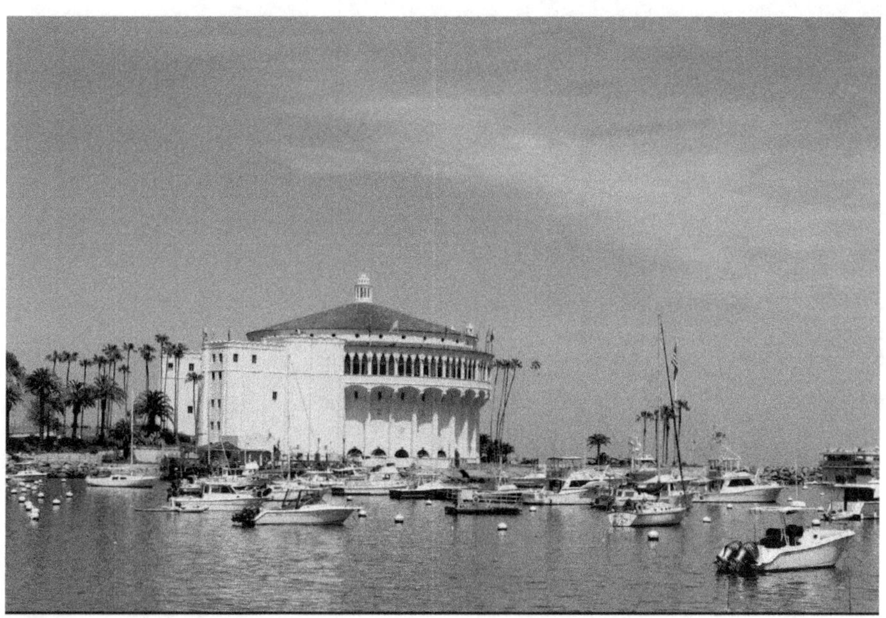

Ashley Lazo-Ruiz

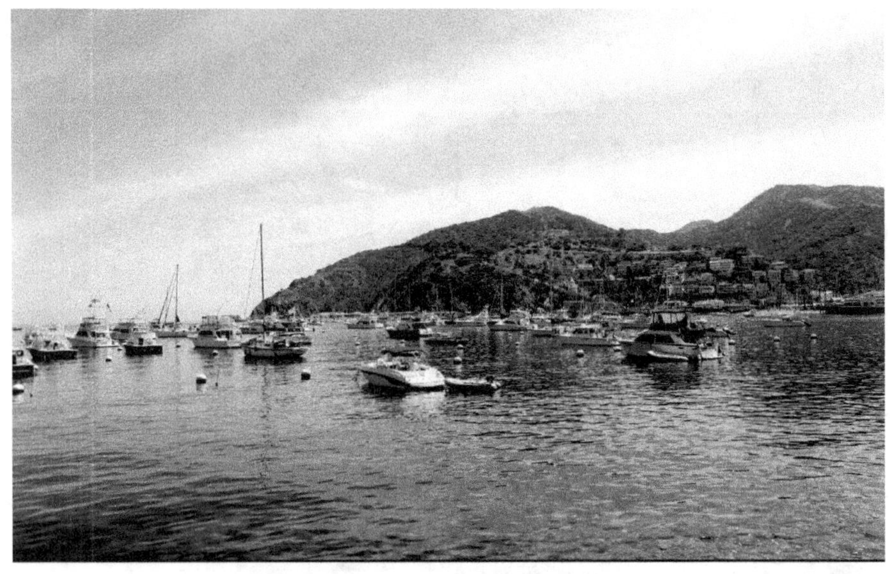

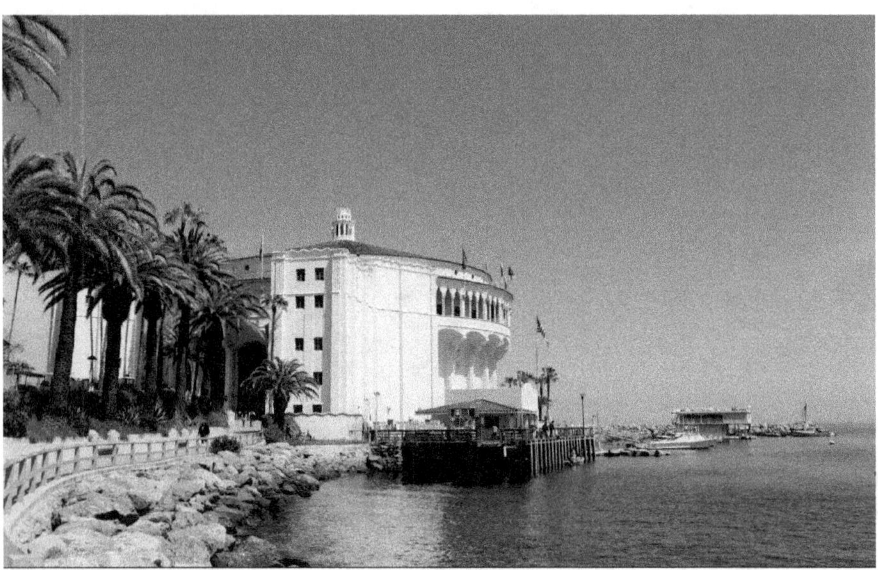

Ashley Lazo-Ruiz

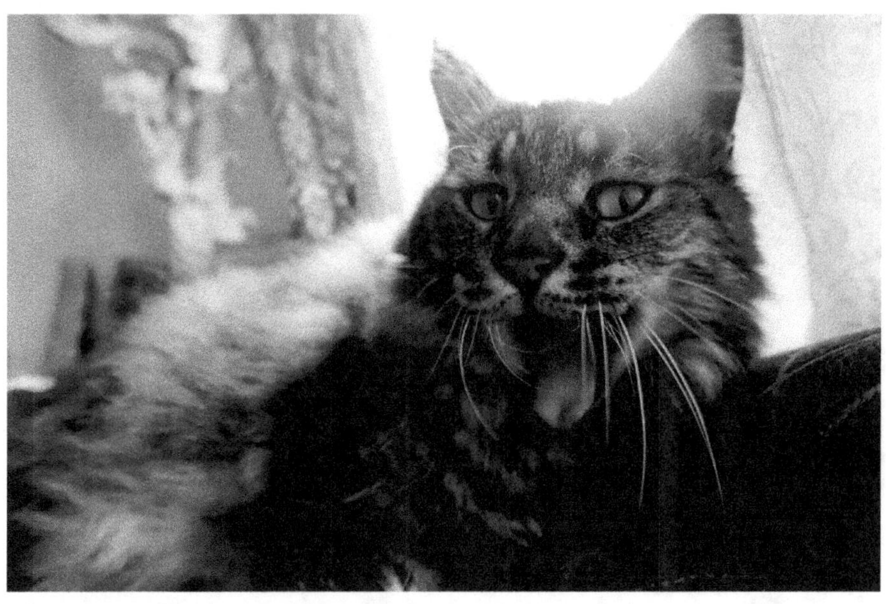

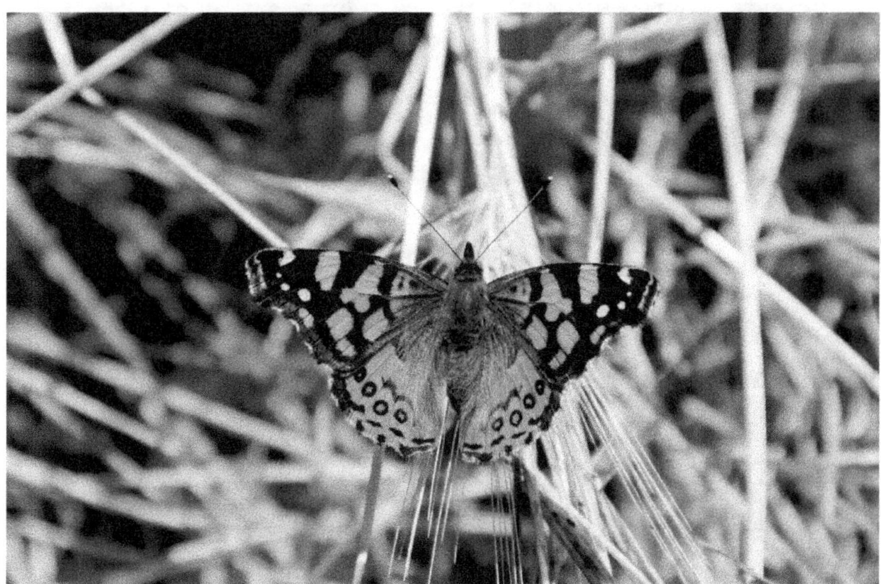

Ashley Lazo-Ruiz

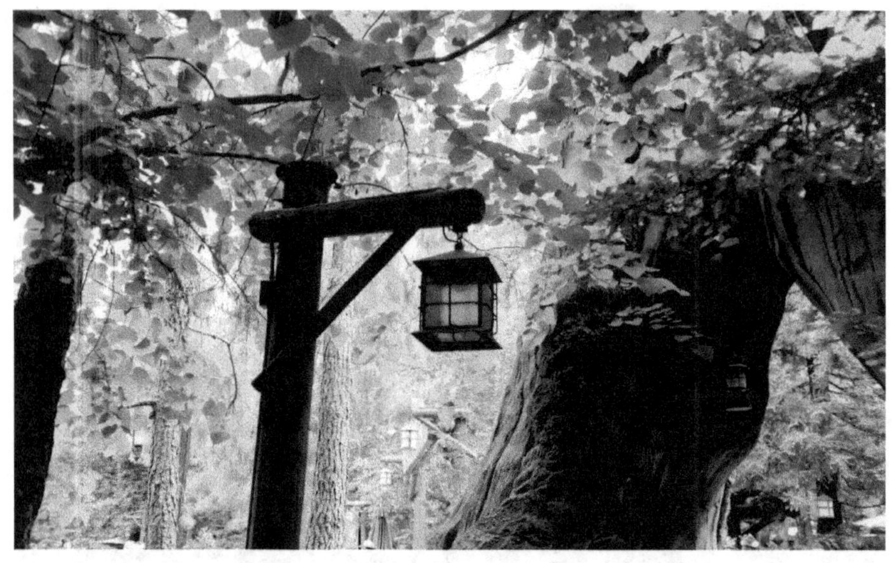

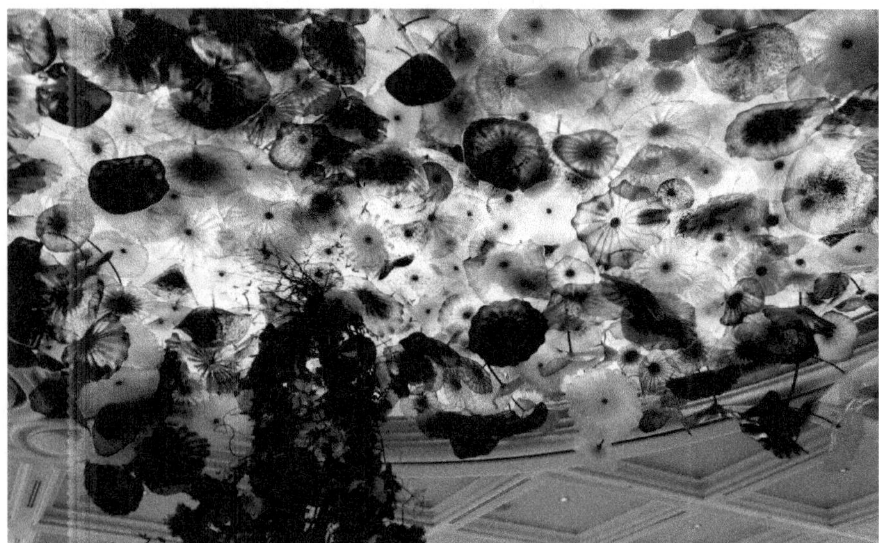

Ashley Lazo-Ruiz

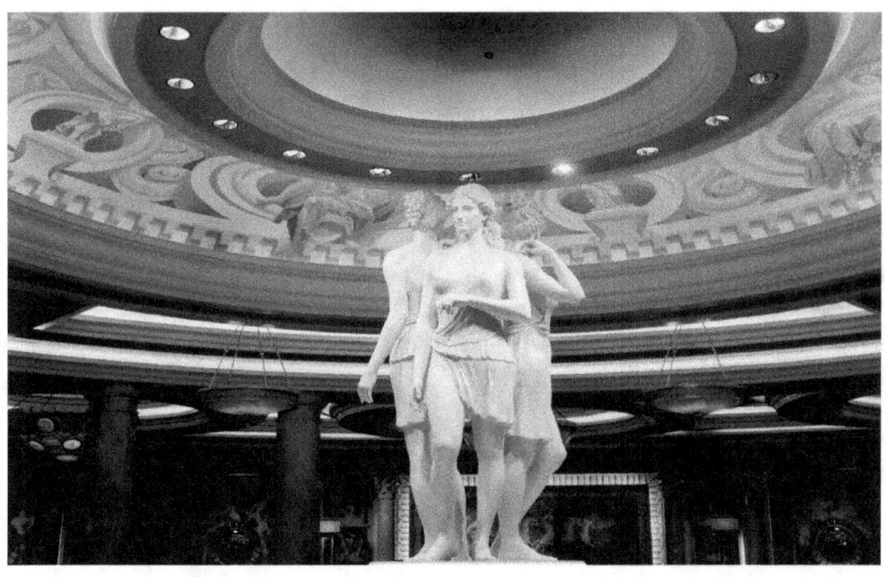

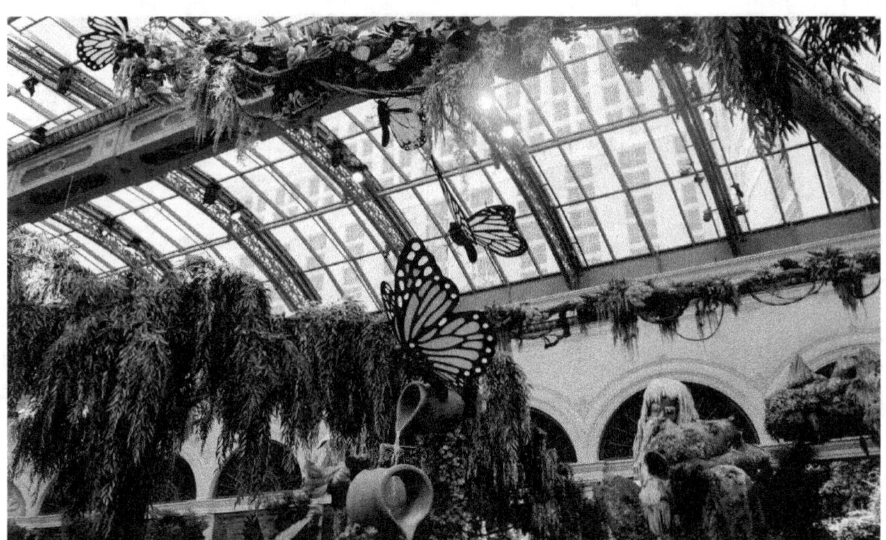

Ashley Lazo-Ruiz

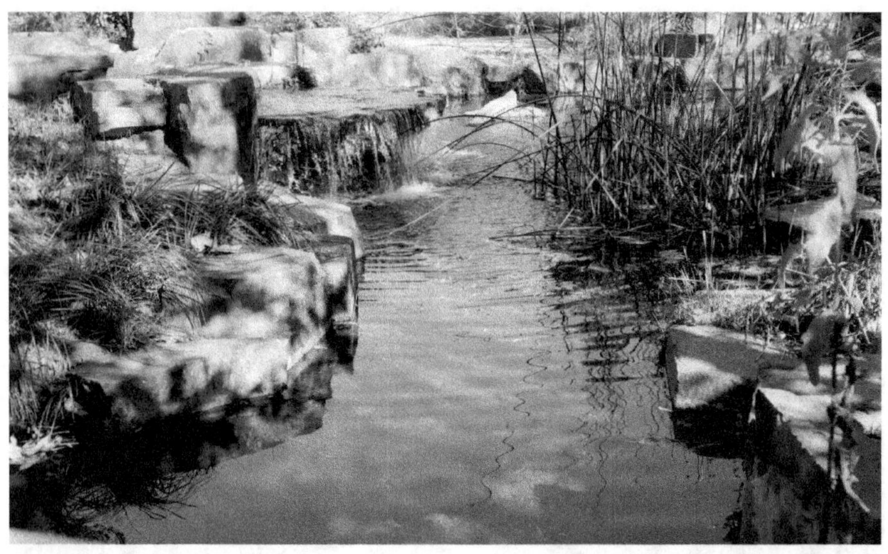

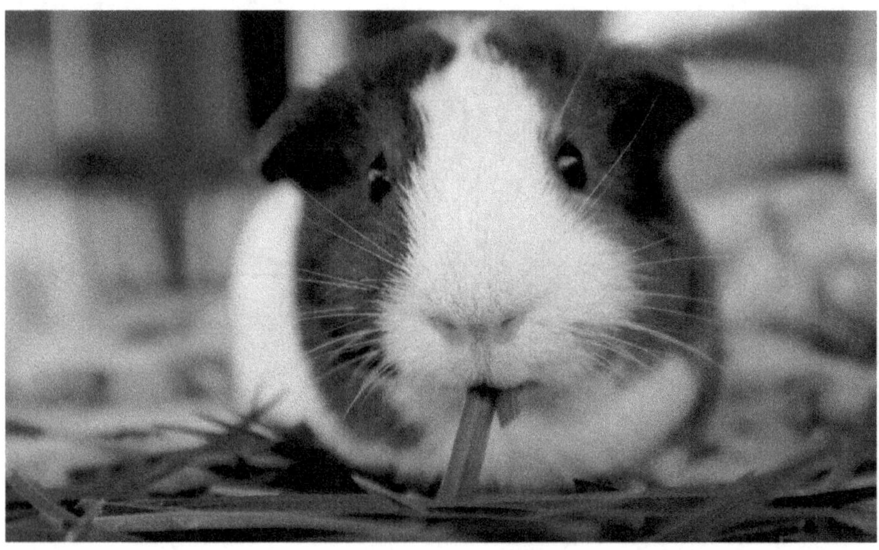

Ashley Lazo-Ruiz

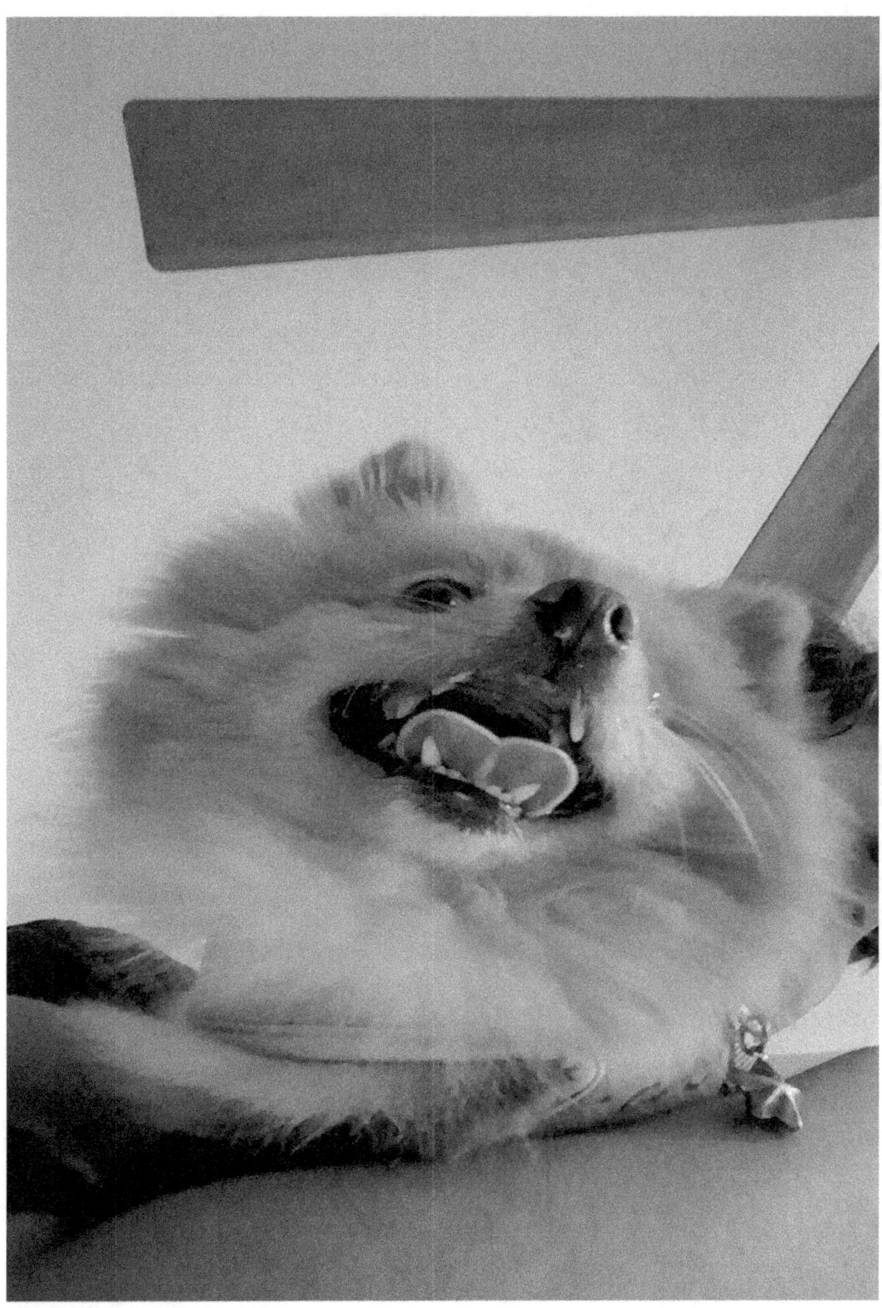

Brayan Sanchez

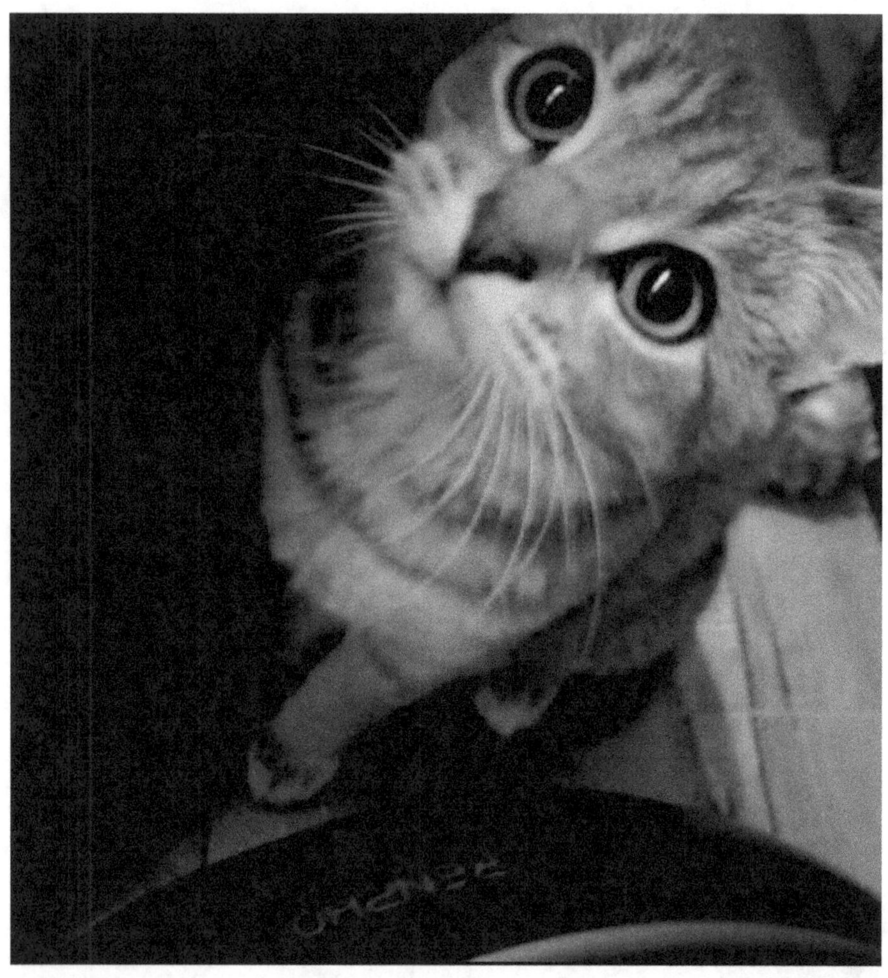

Brayan Sanchez

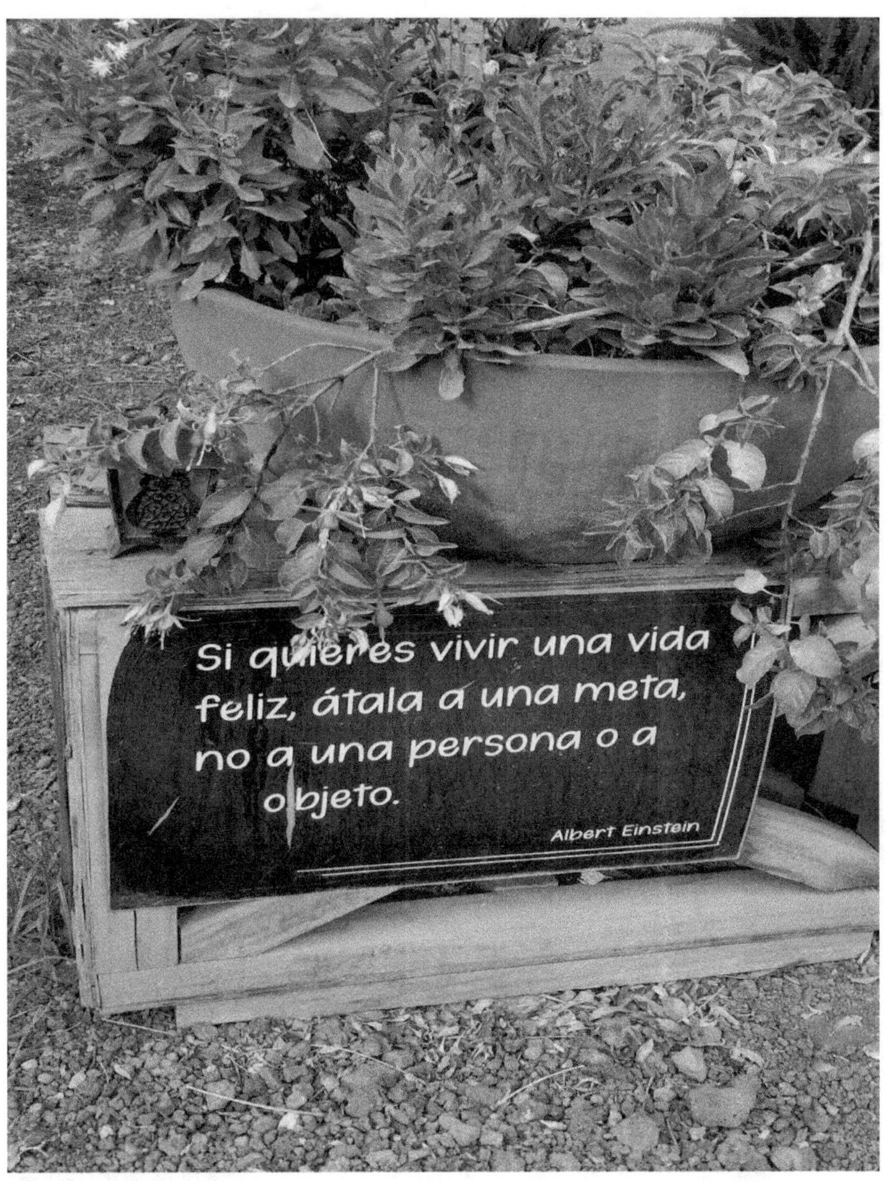

Brayan Sanchez

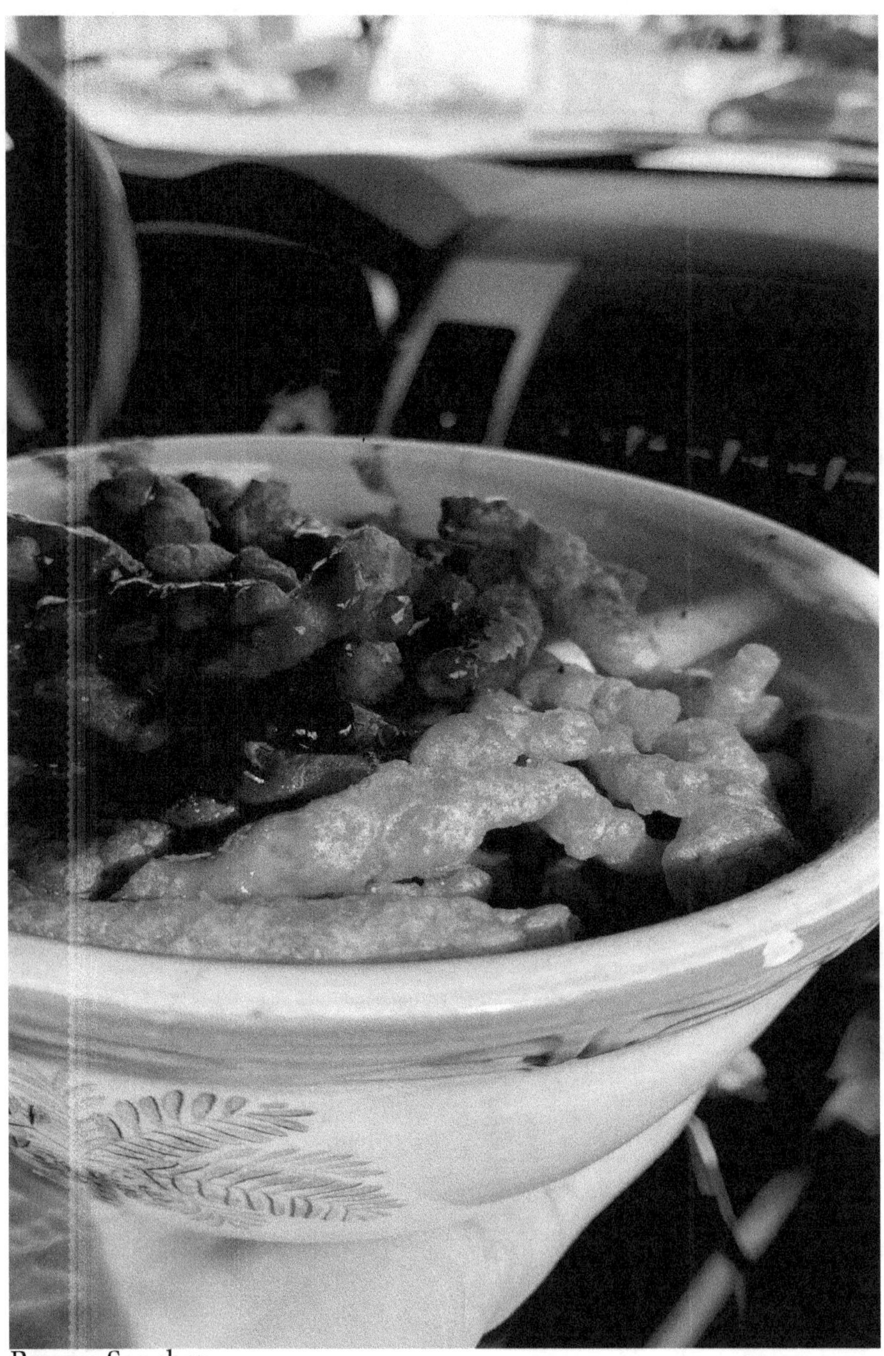

Brayan Sanchez

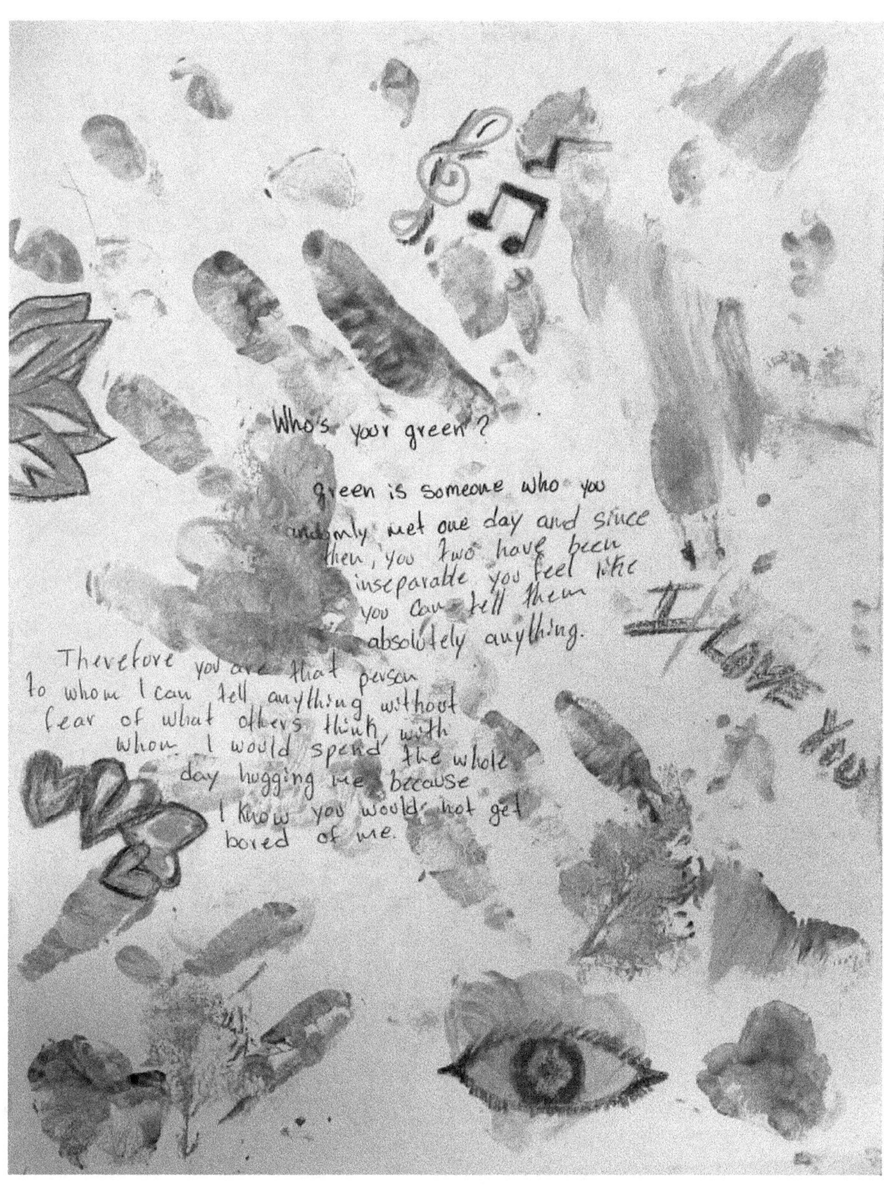

Brayan Sanchez

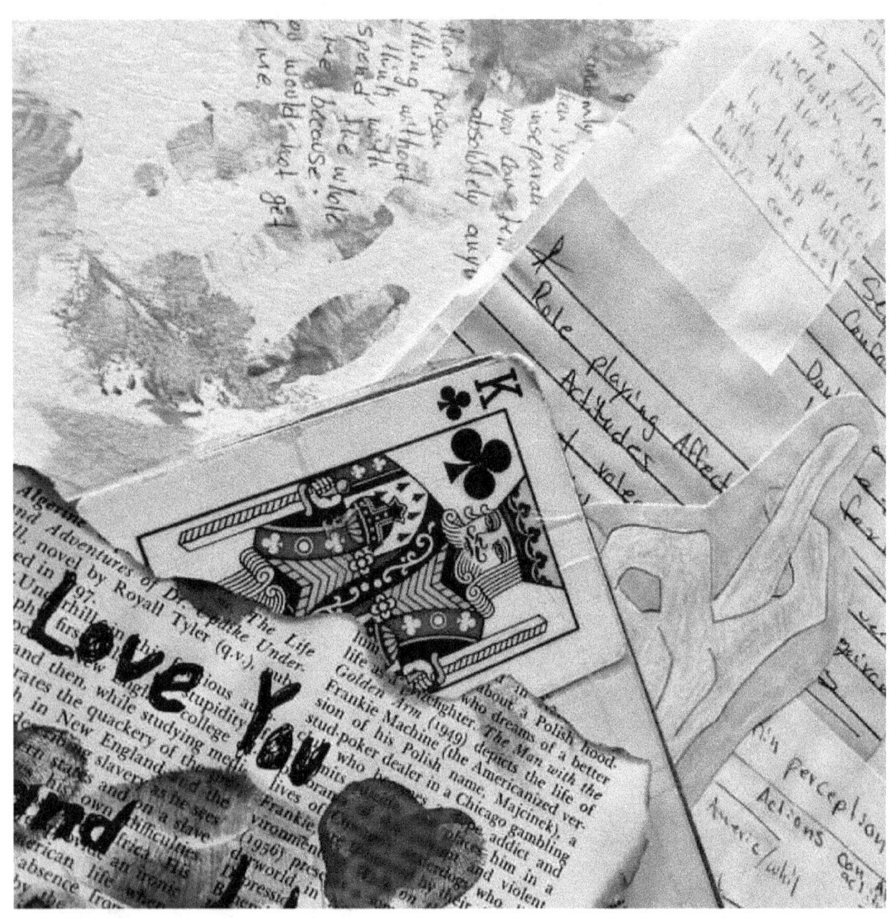

Brayan Sanchez

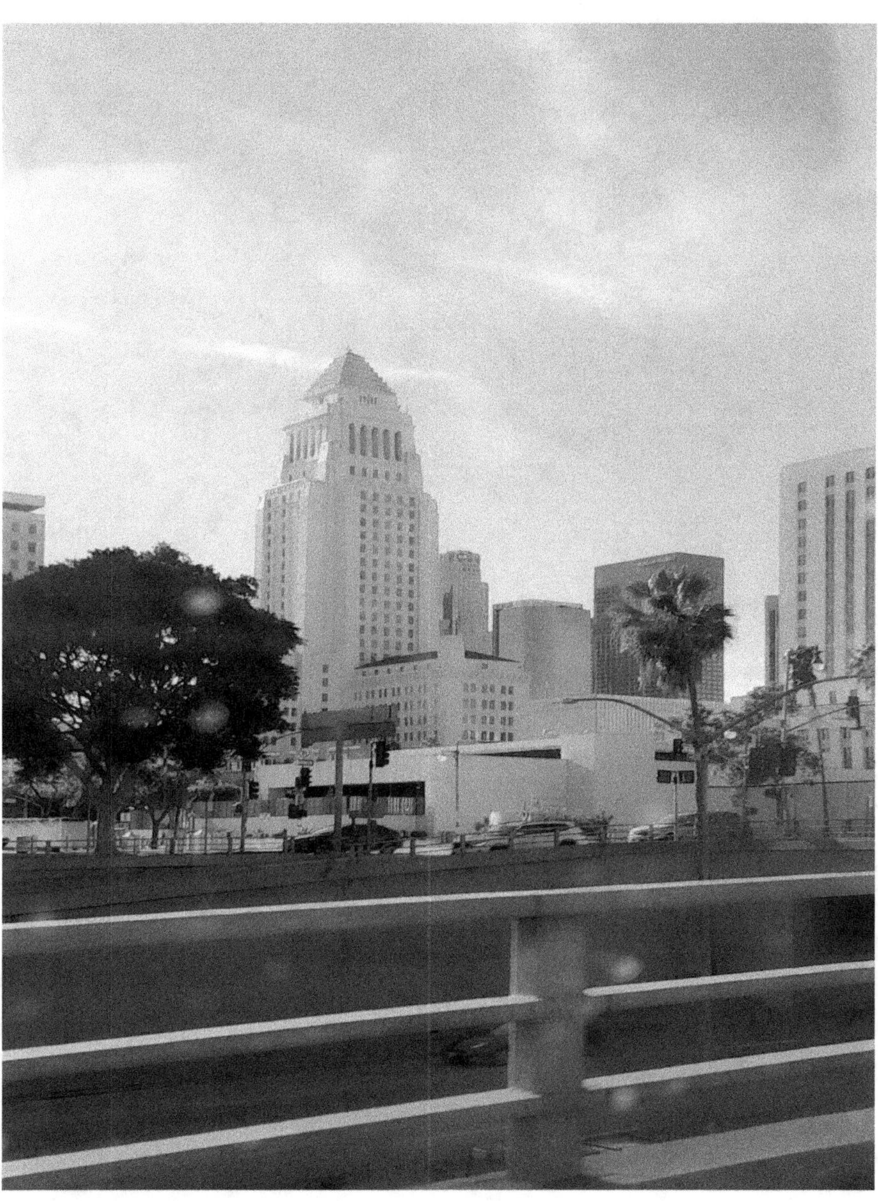

Brayan Sanchez

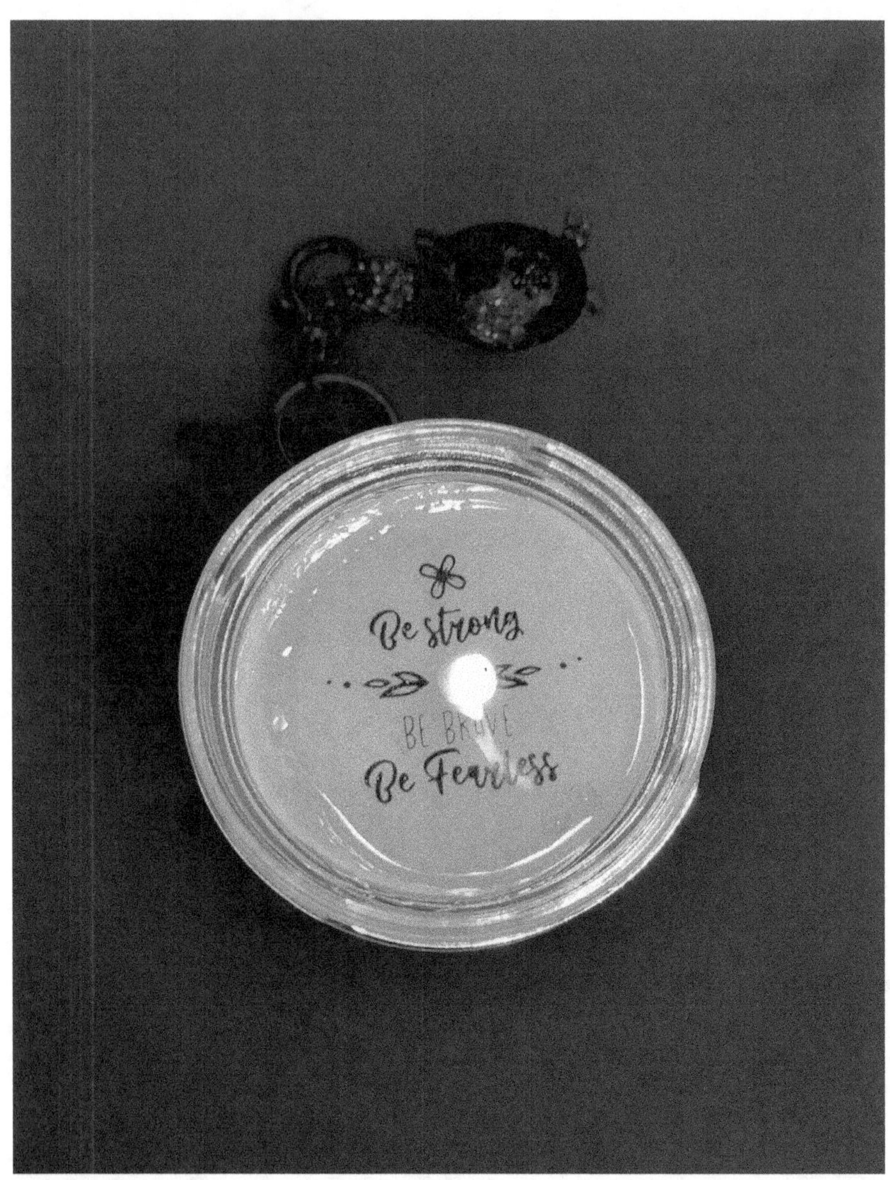

Brayan Sanchez

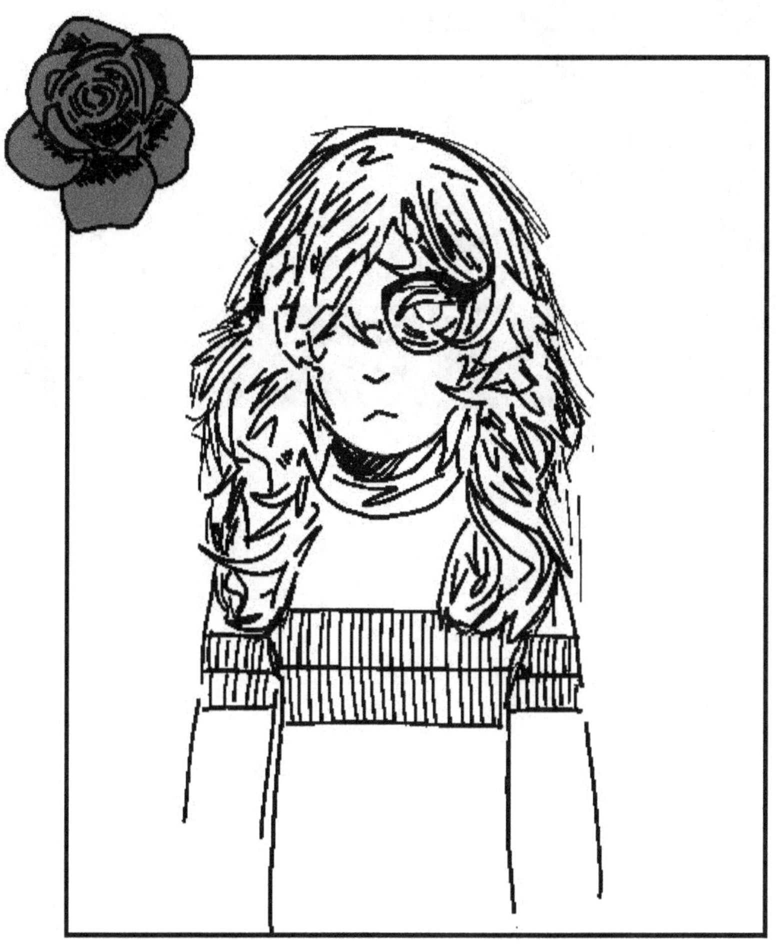

Nicholas Hinton

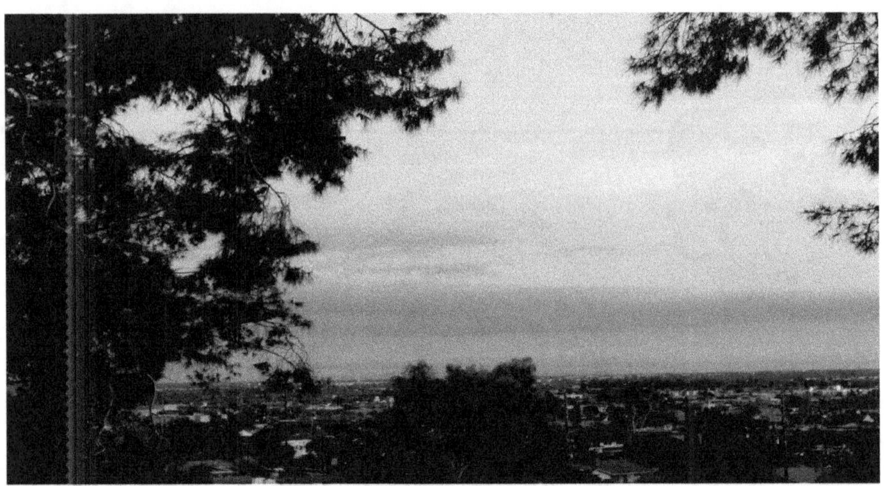

Kathy Tinoco

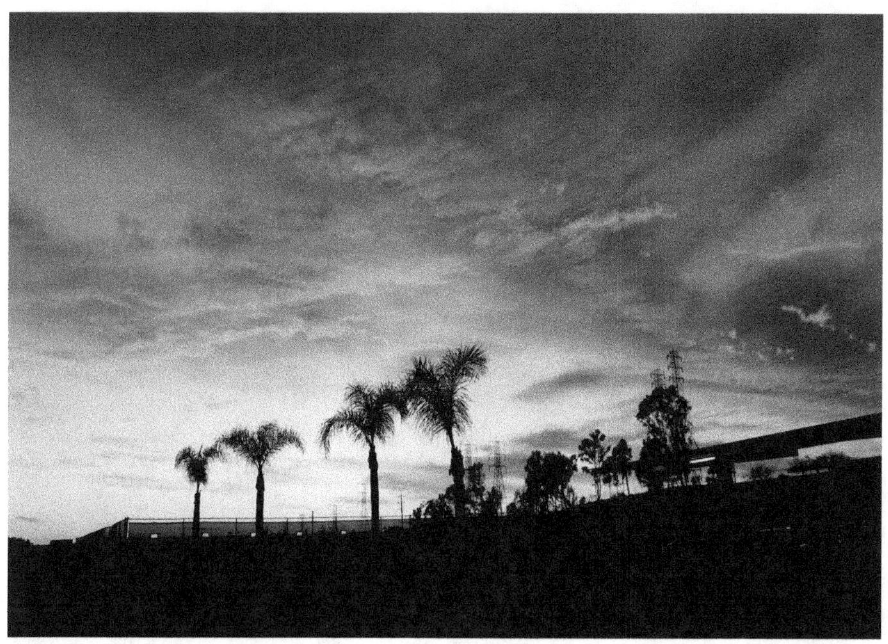

Kathy Tinoco

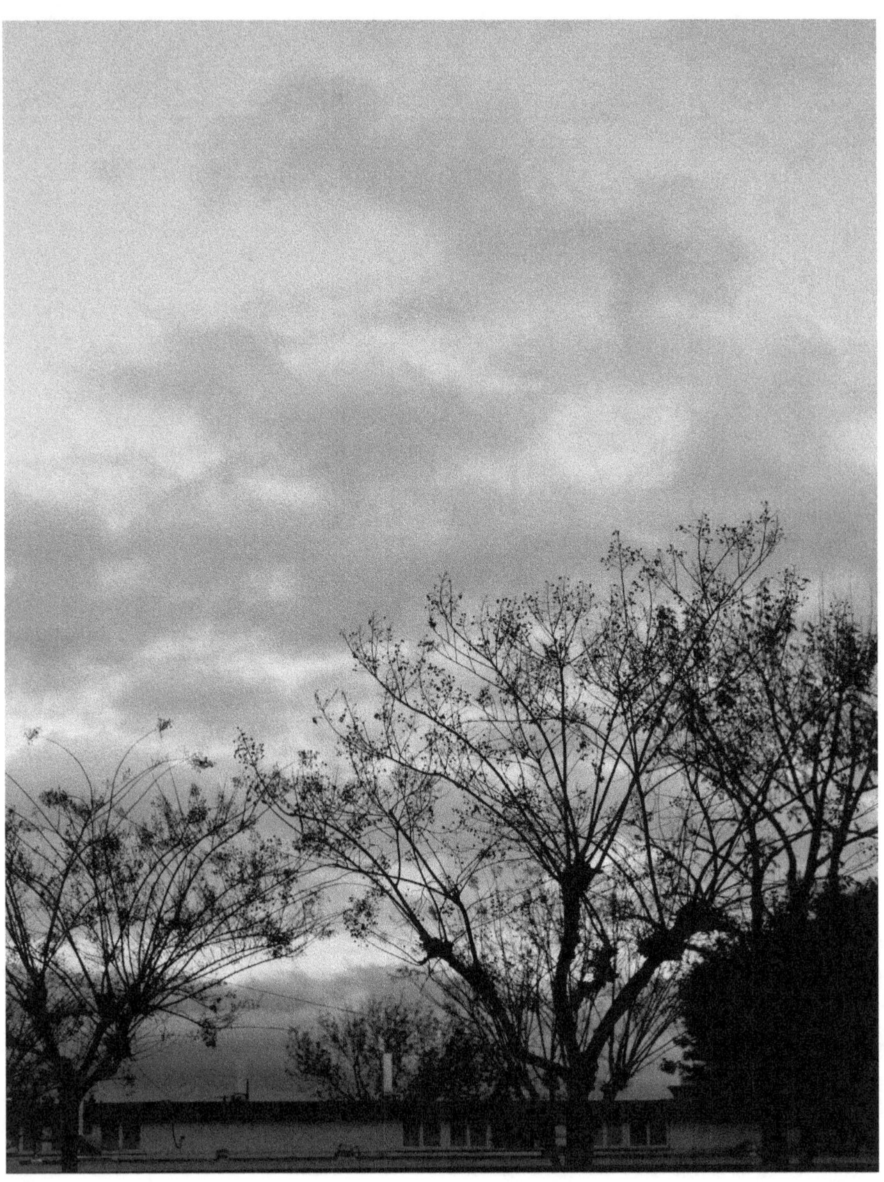

Kathy Tinoco

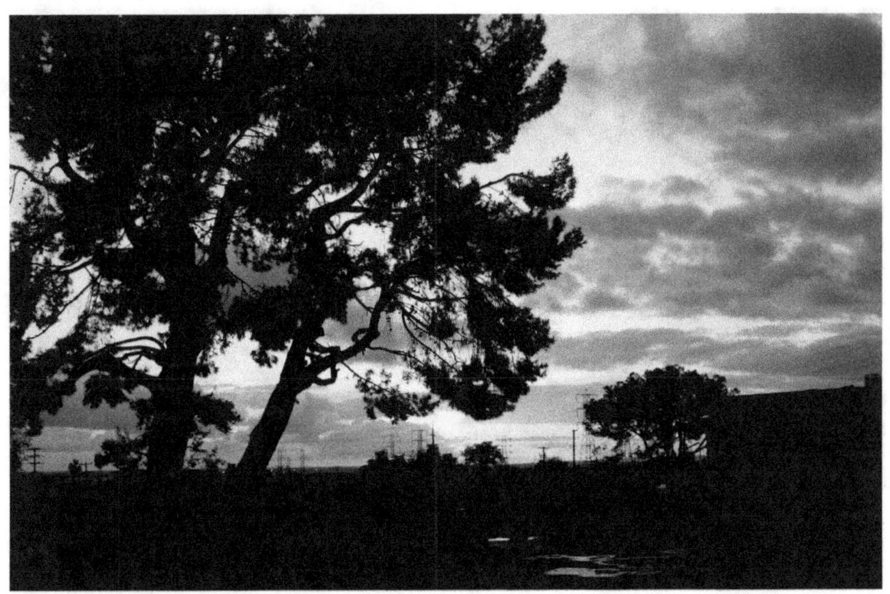

Kathy Tinoco

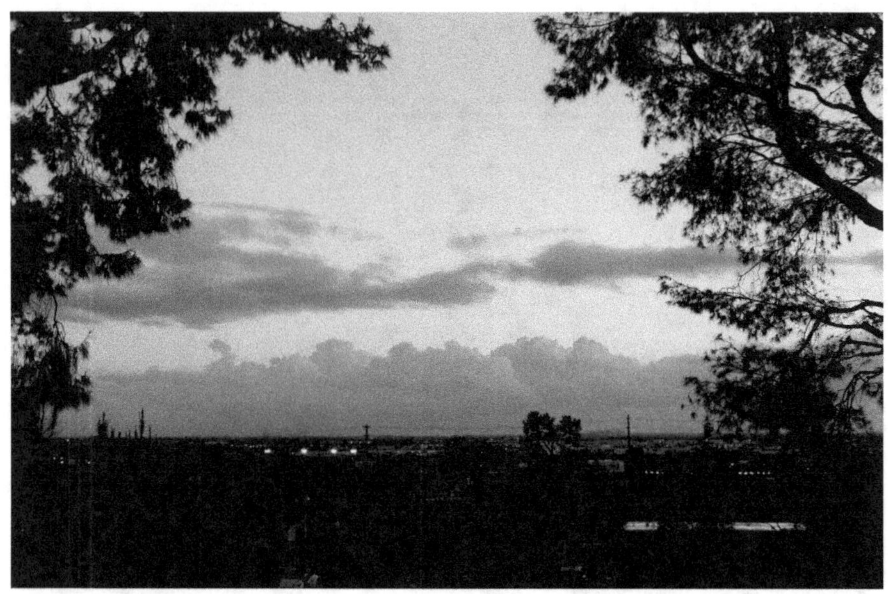

Kathy Tinoco

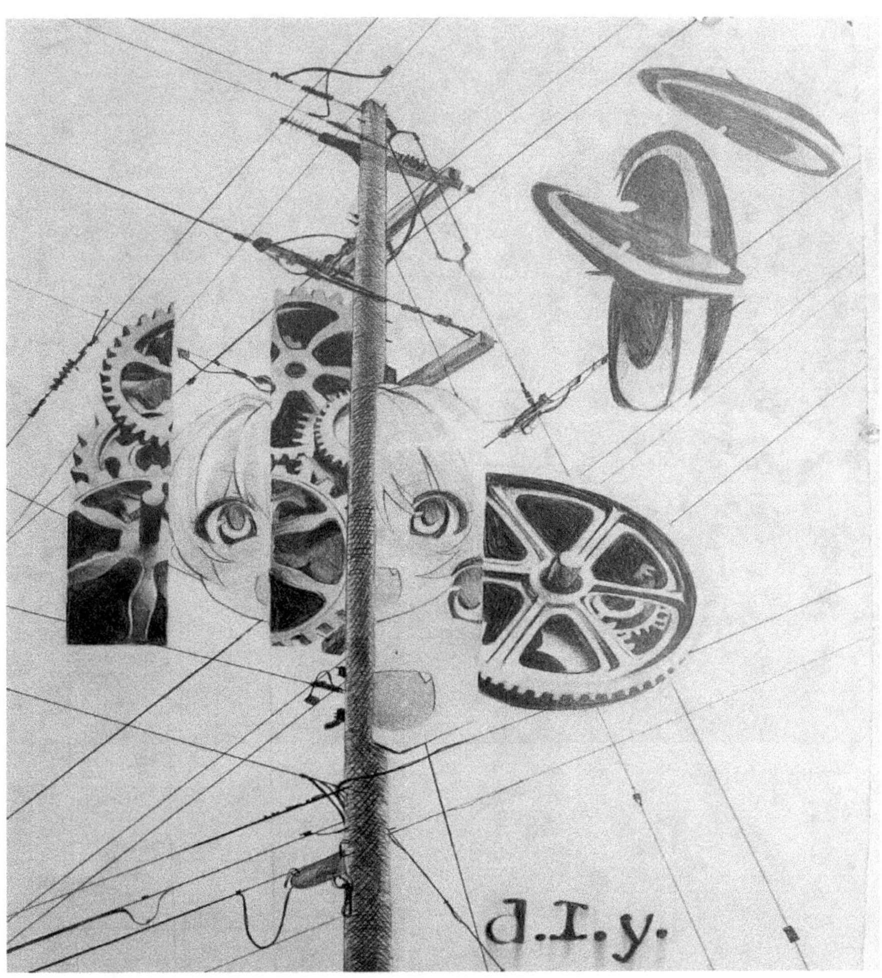

Delilah Bringas

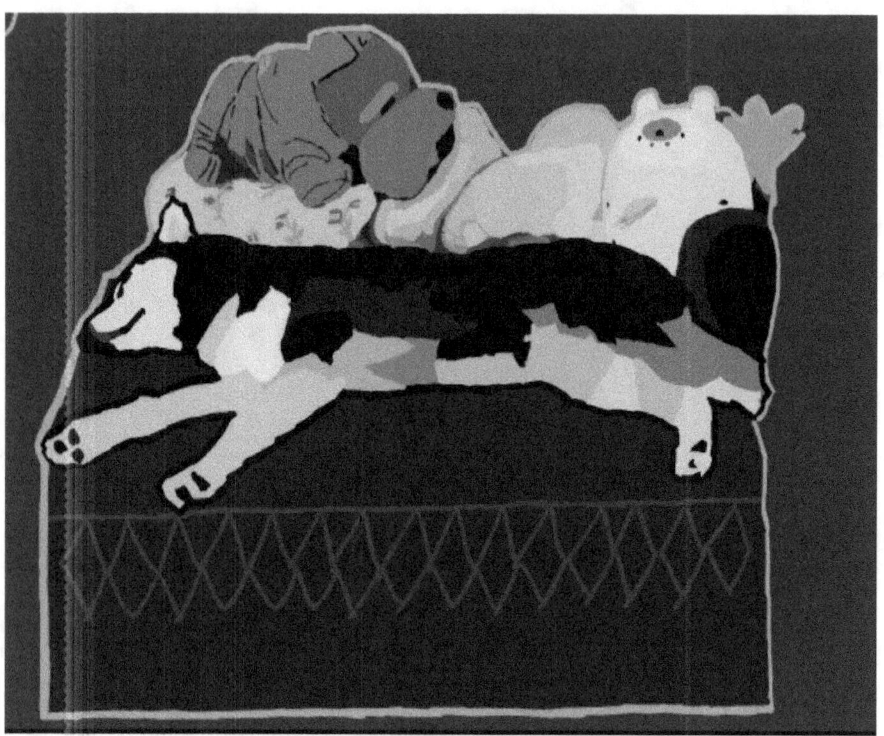

Patrick Ortiz

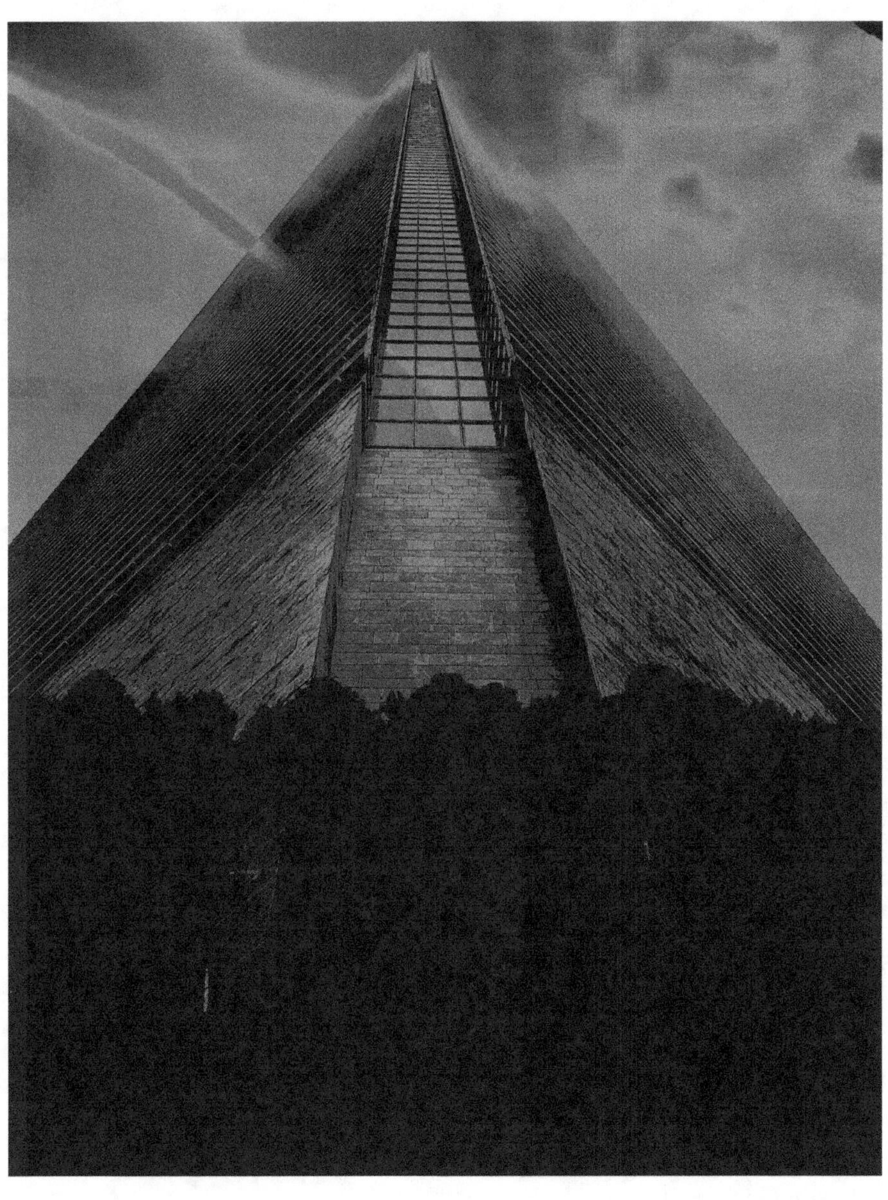

Christopher Acosta

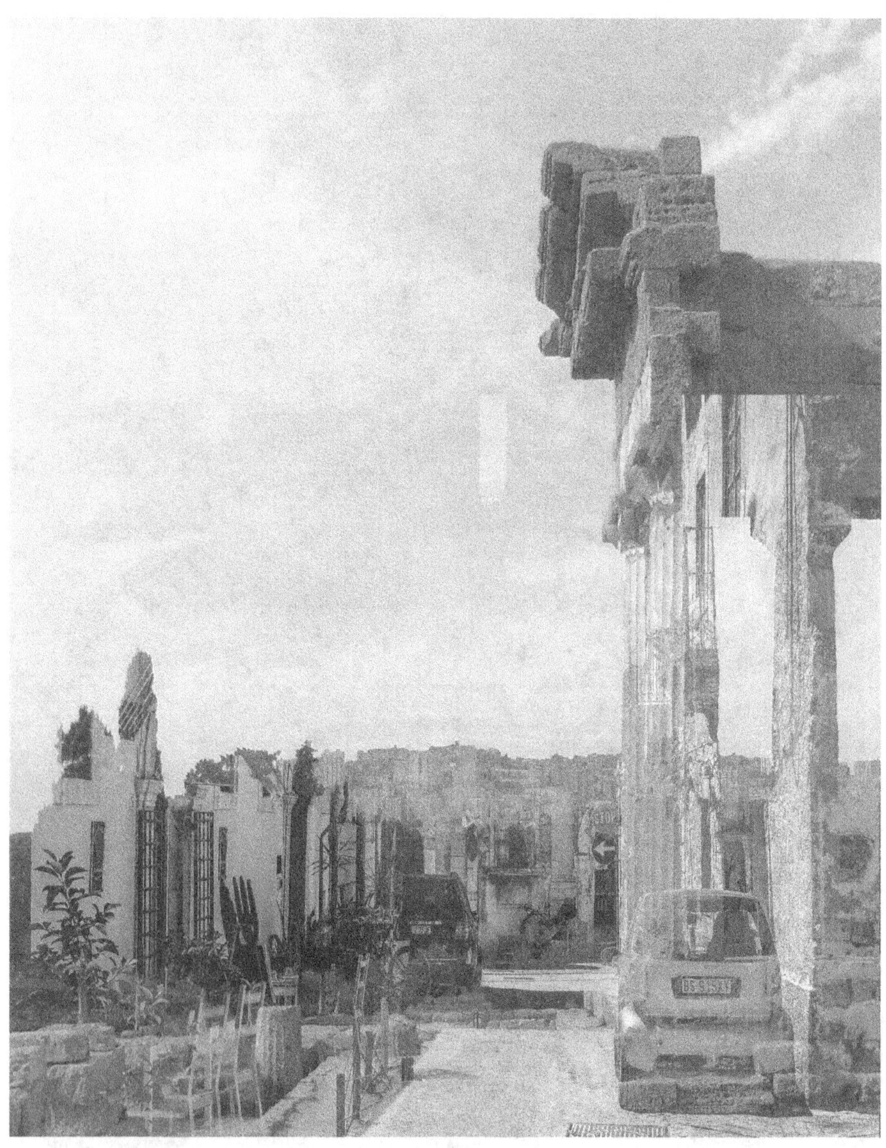

Leslie Castaneda

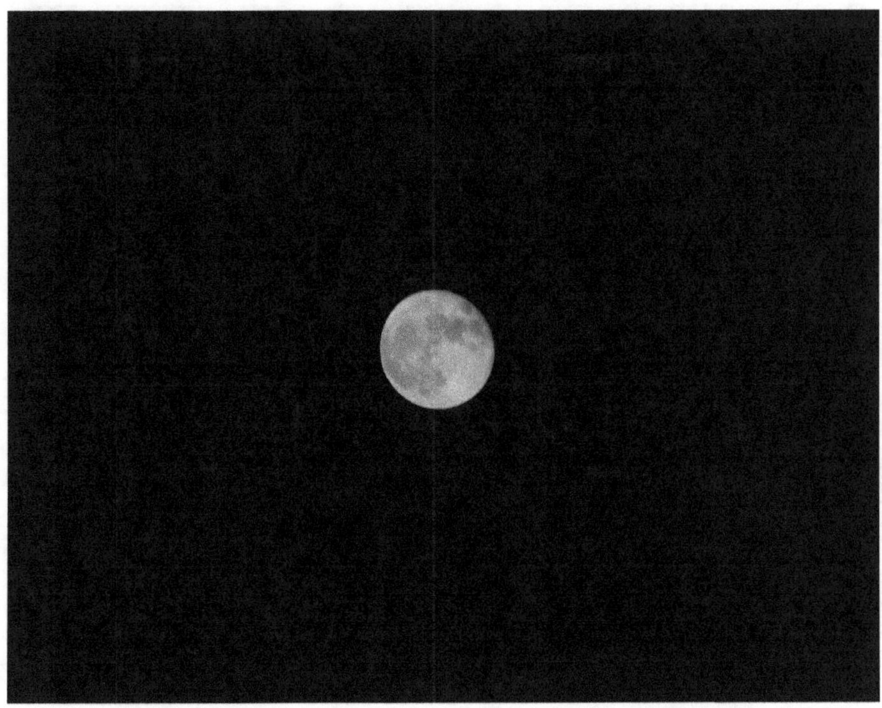

Dannielynn Escobar

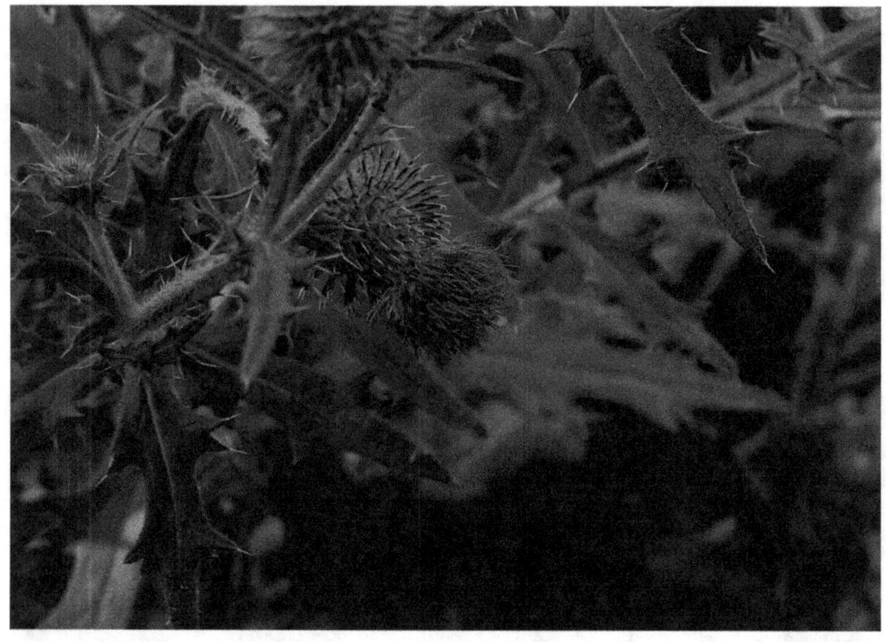

Dannielynn Escobar

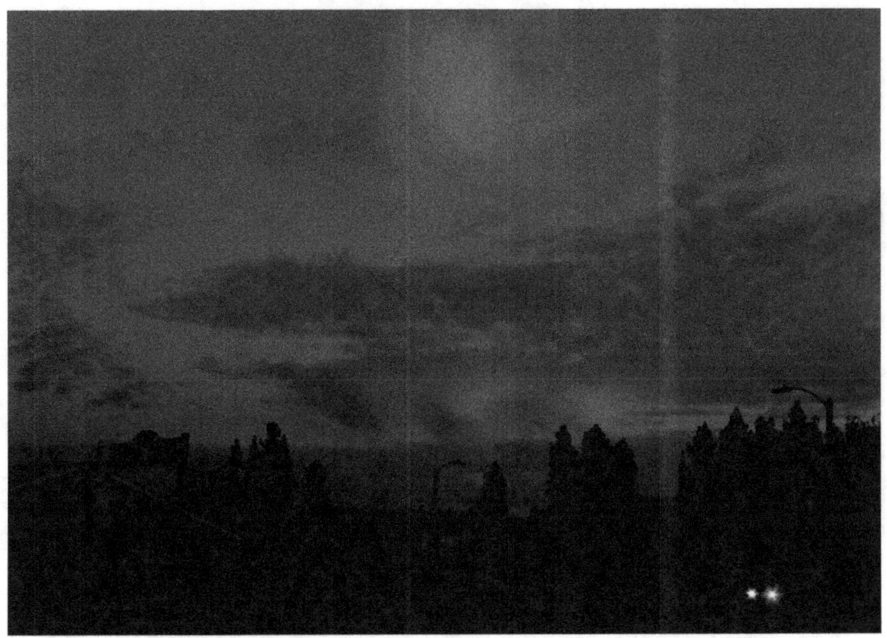

Dannielynn Escobar

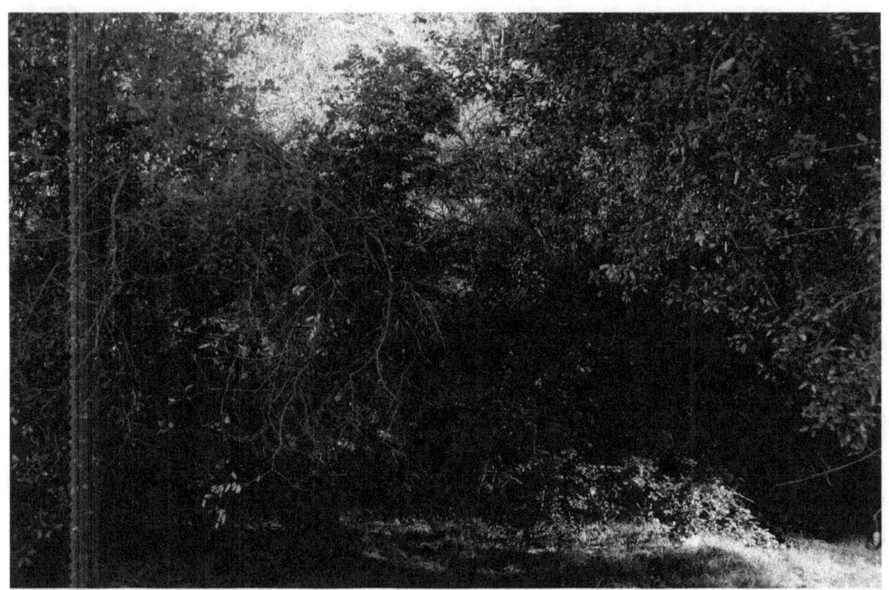

Dannielynn Escobar

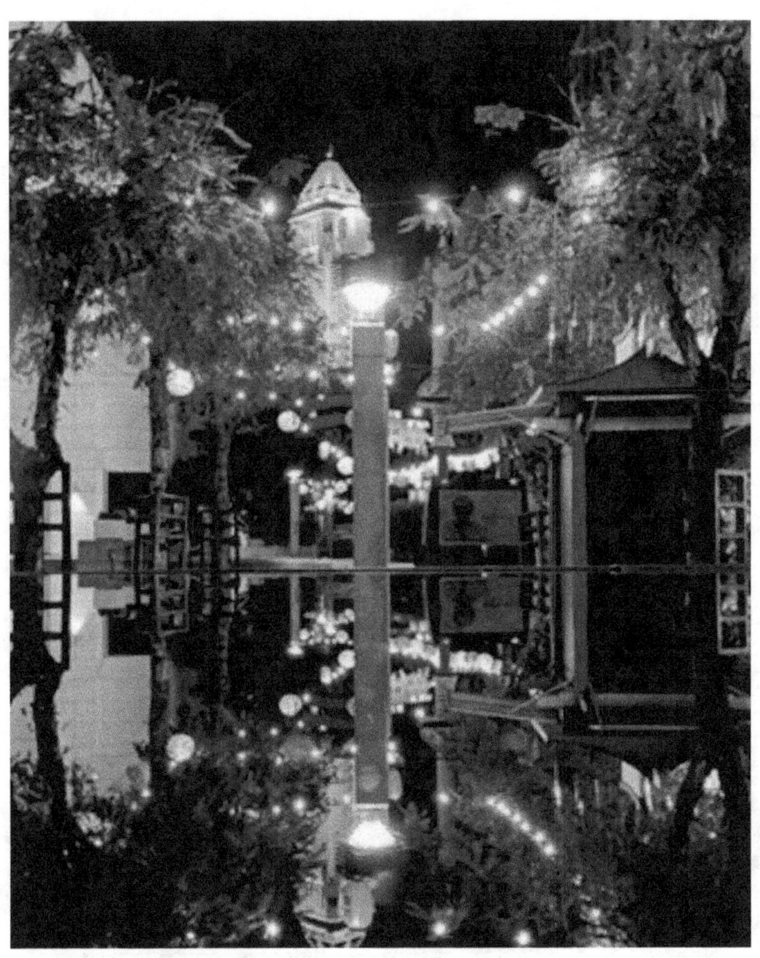

Esmeralda Ambrocio

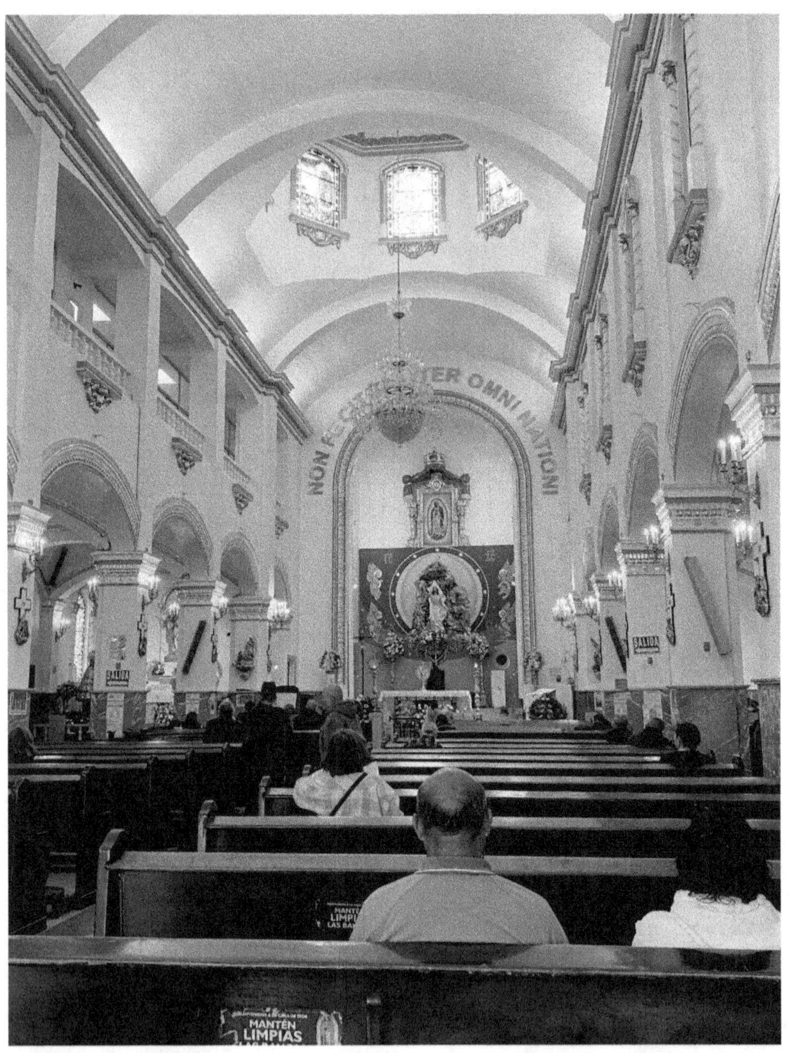

Esmeralda Ambrocio

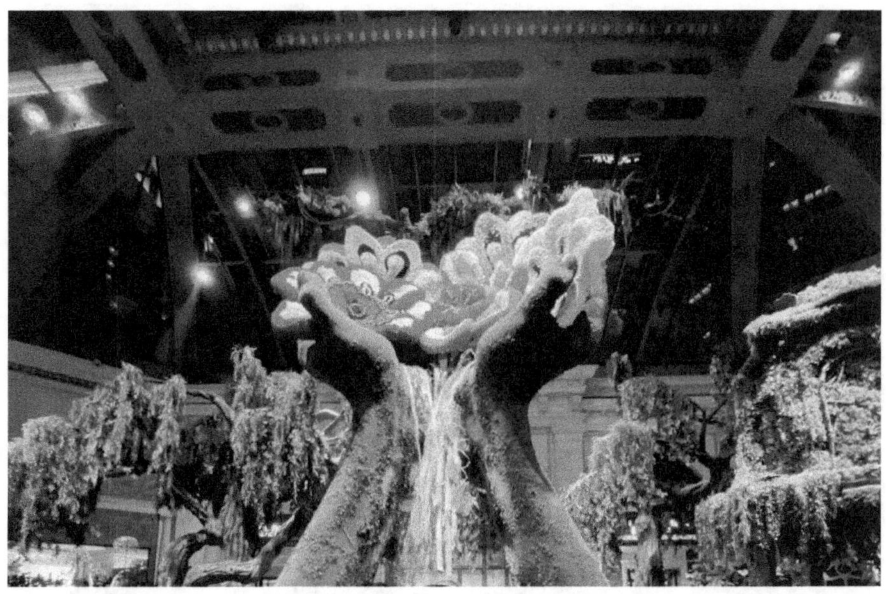

Esmeralda Ambrocio

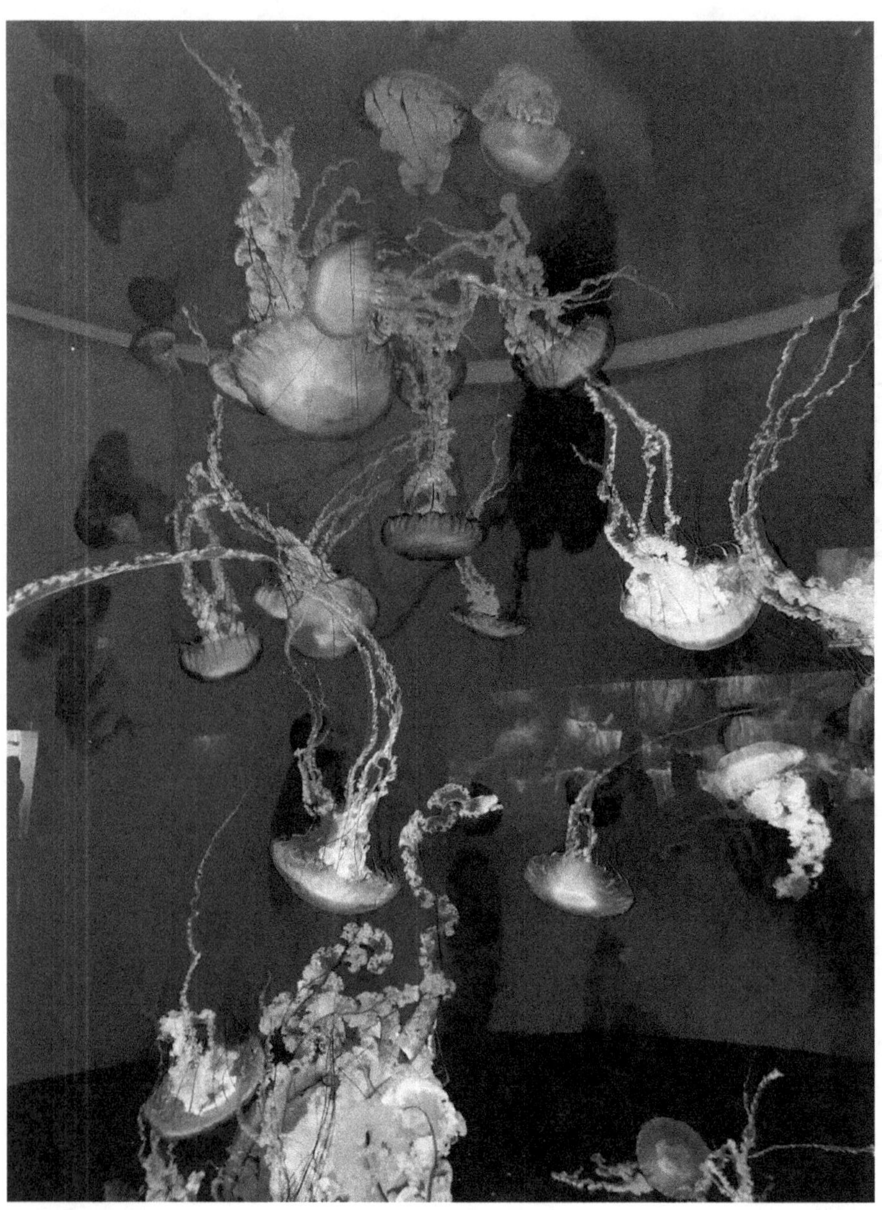

Esmeralda Ambrocio

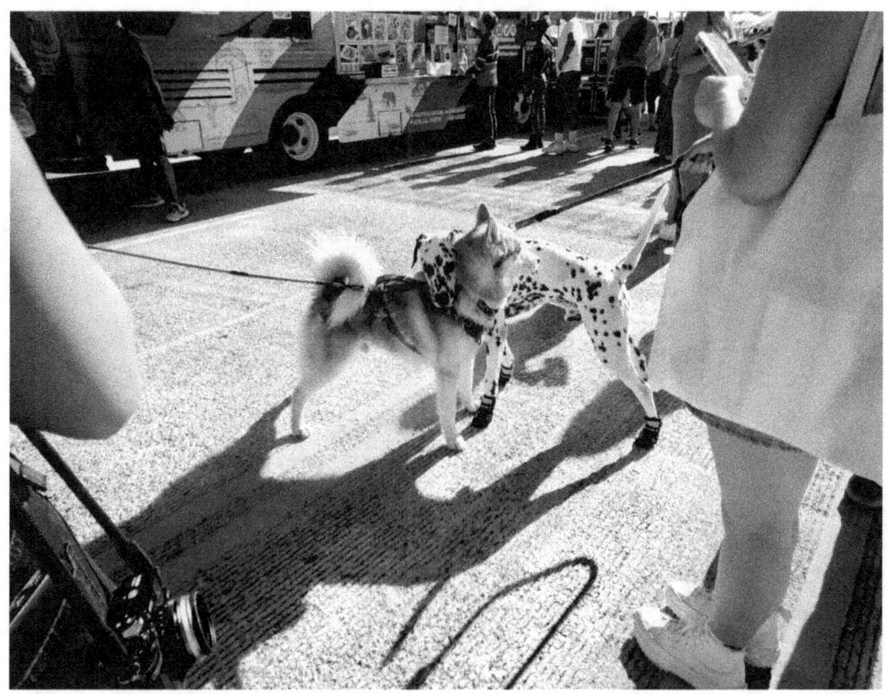

Valerie Castillo

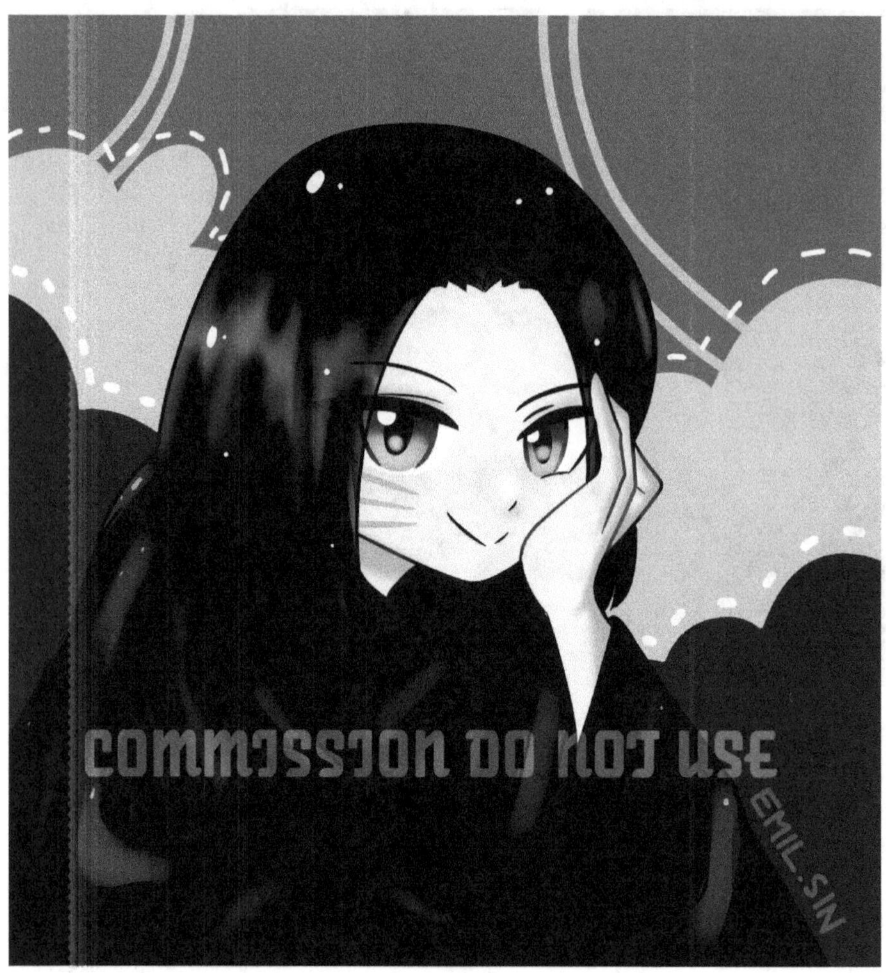

Emil Bae

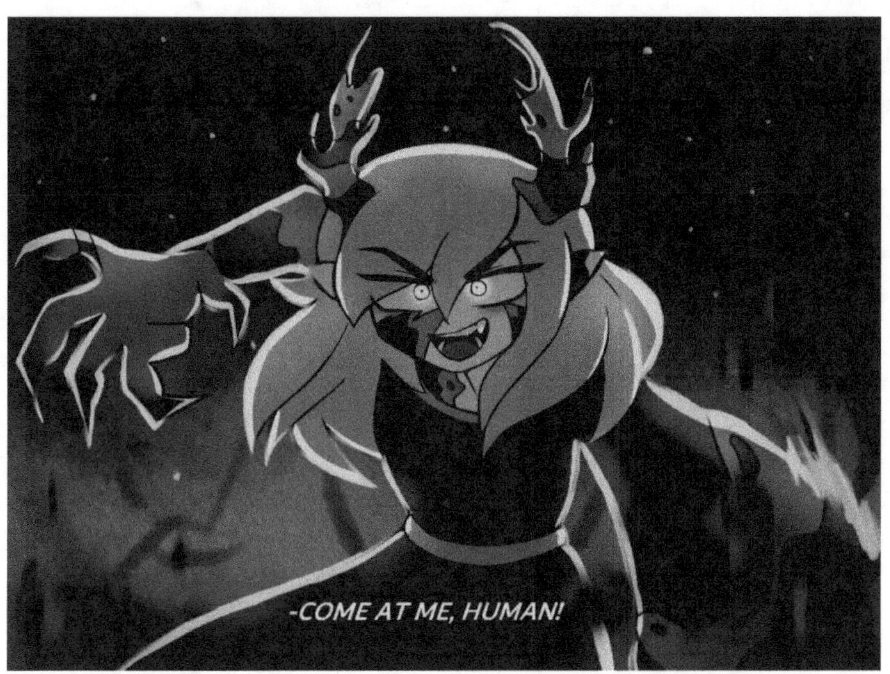

Emil Bae

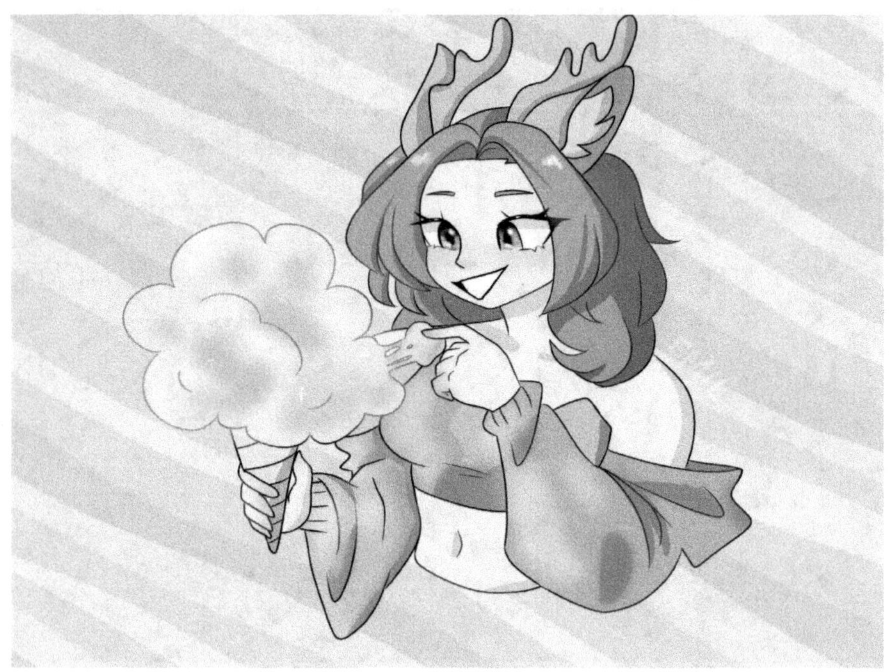

Emil Bae

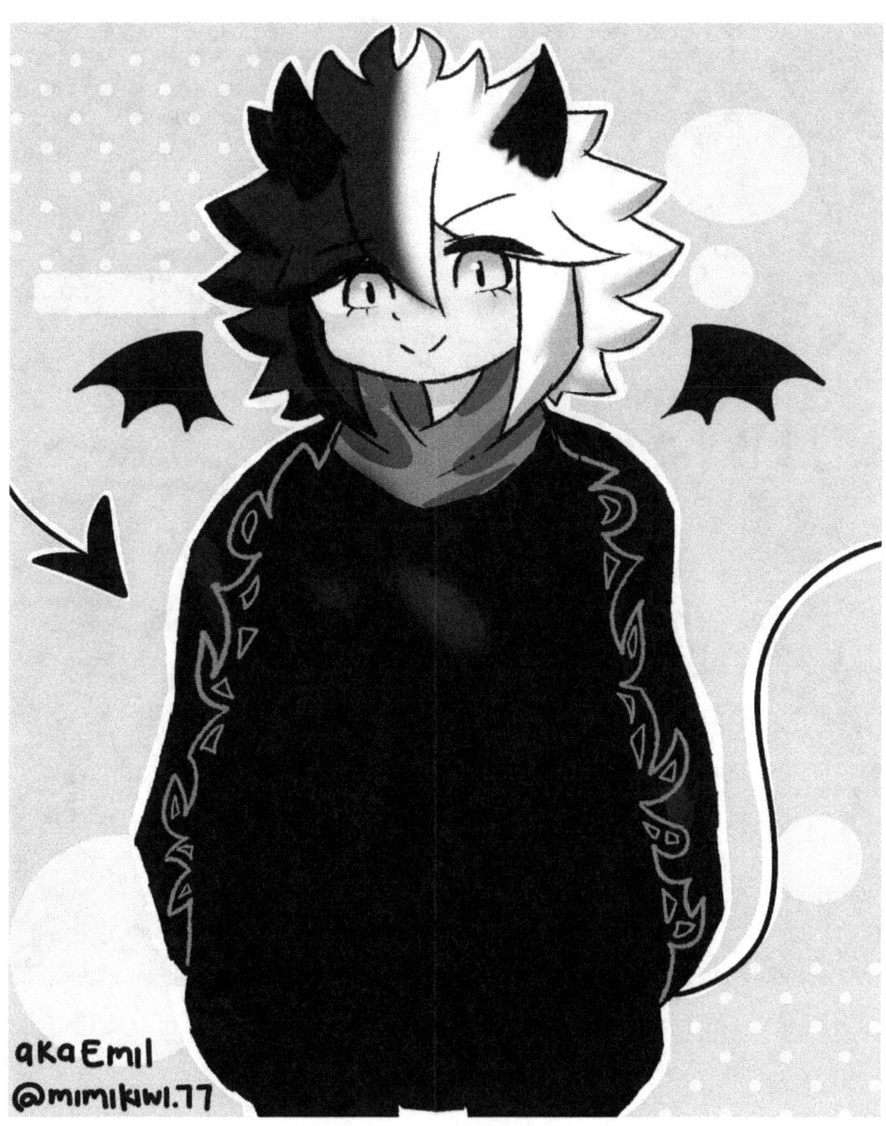

Emil Bae

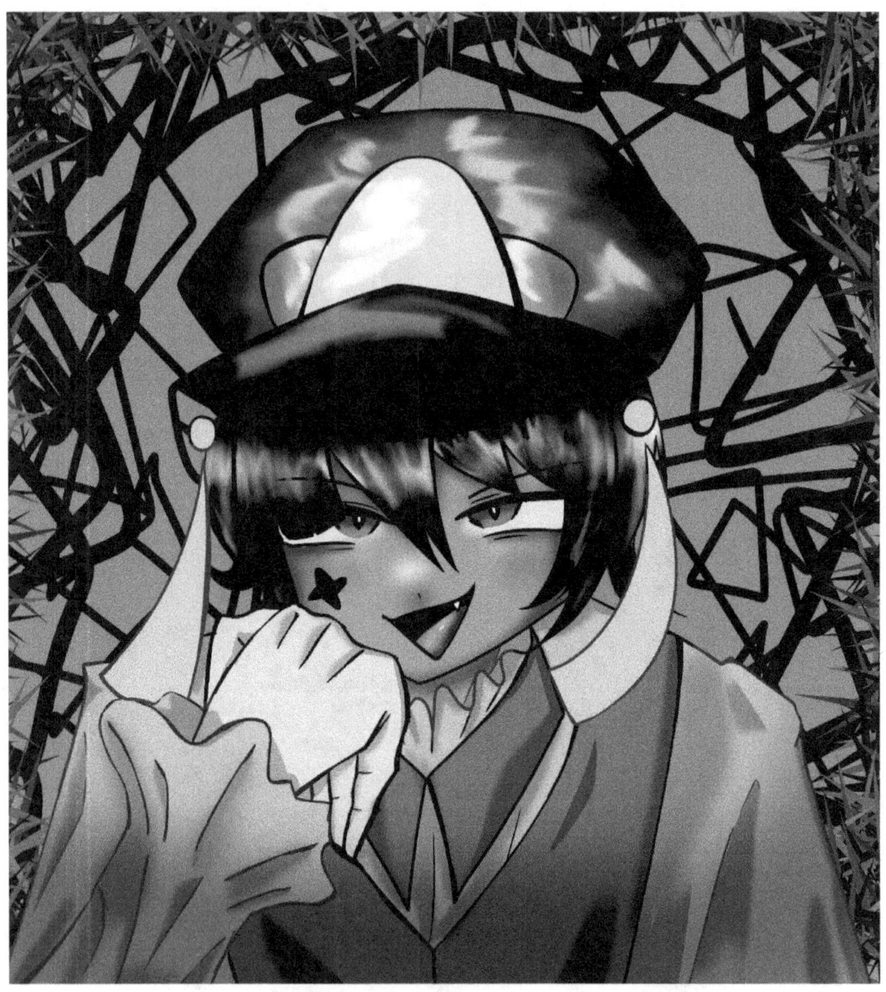

Emil Bae

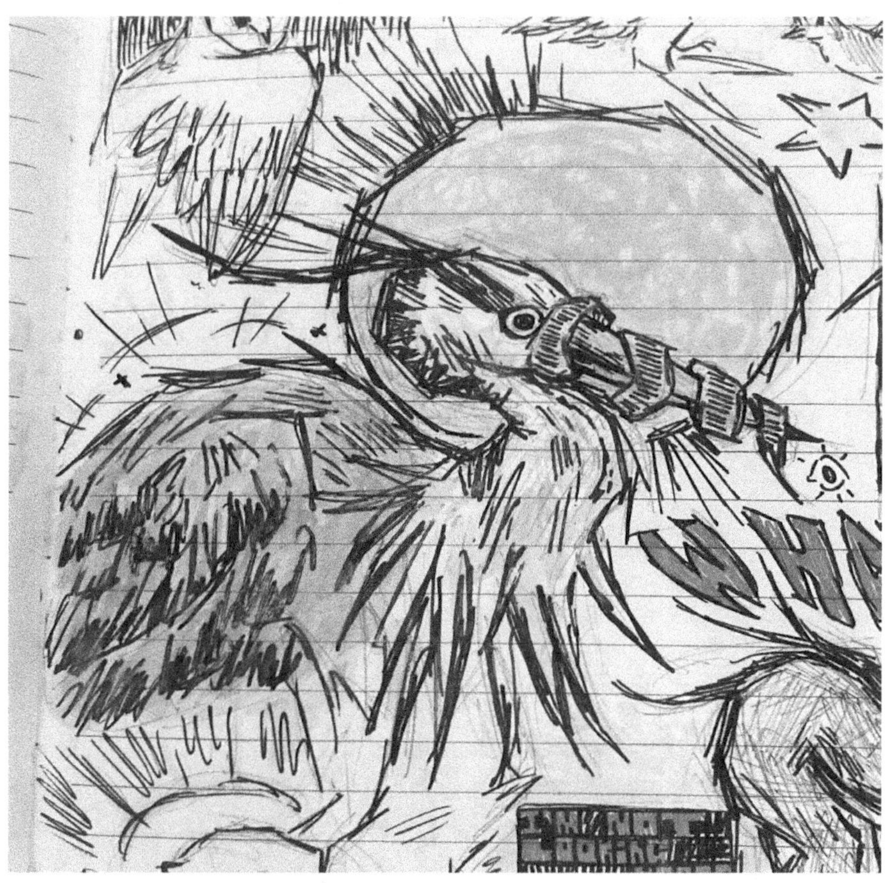

Michelle Lalla

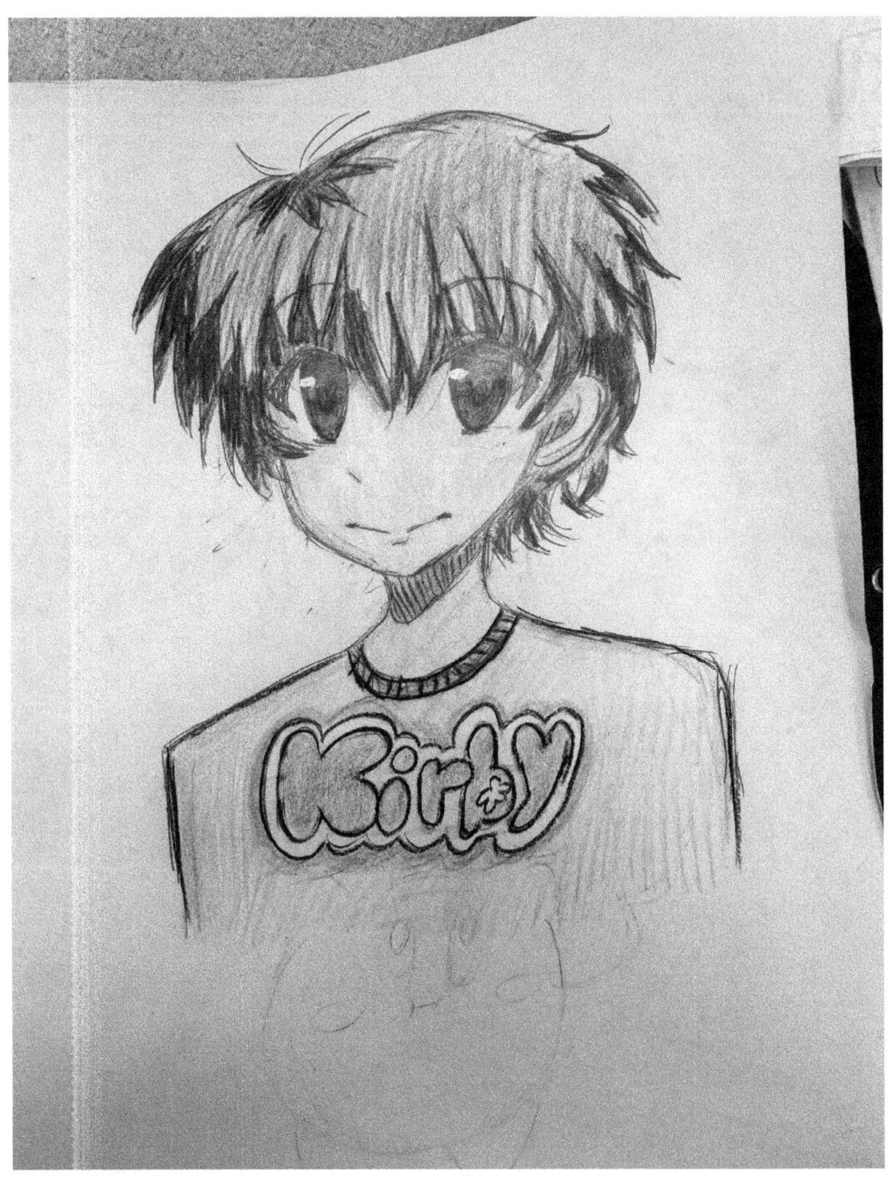

Itzil Quinones

215

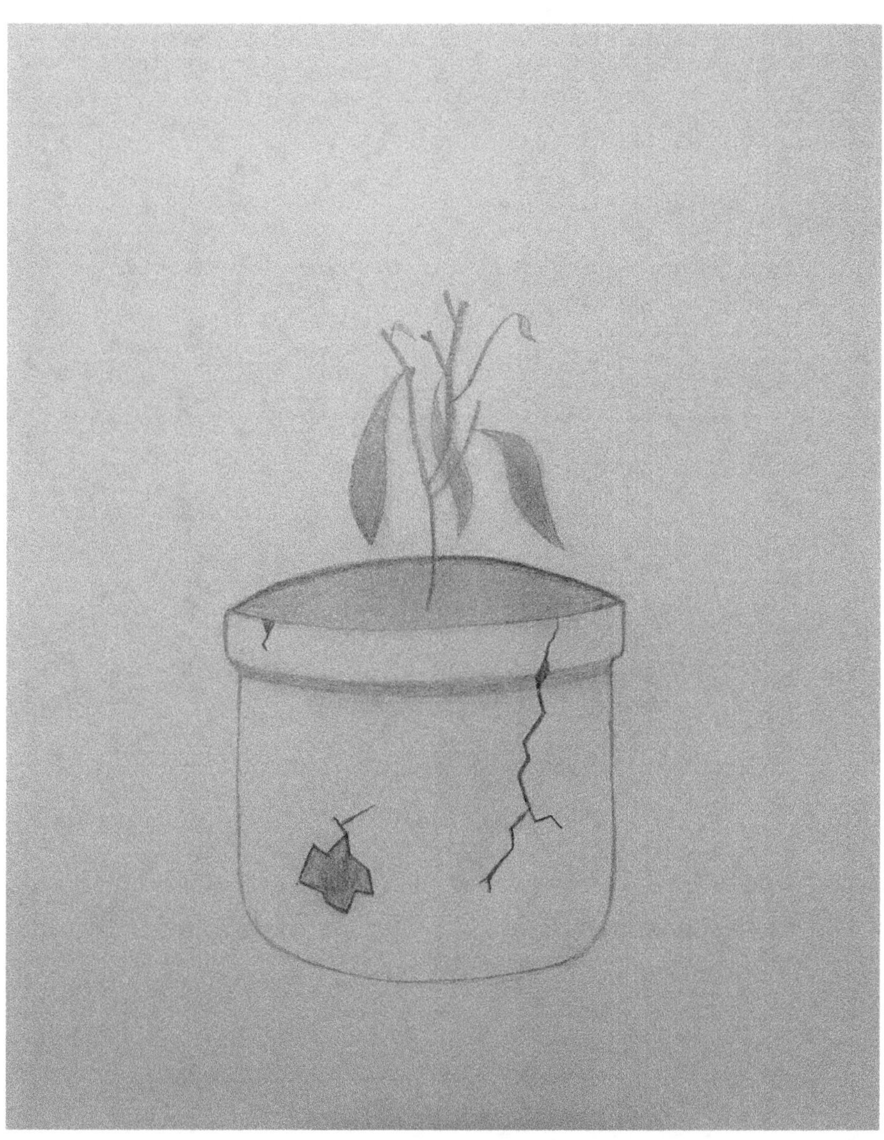

Katie Romero

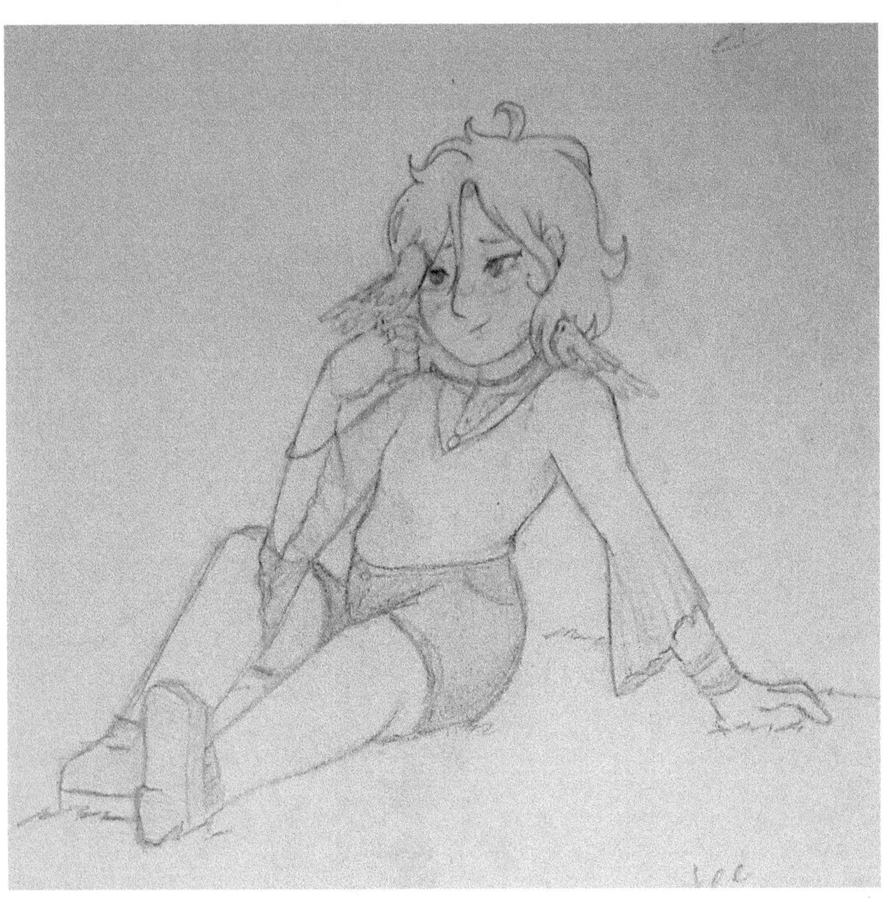

By: Adanesne Montano

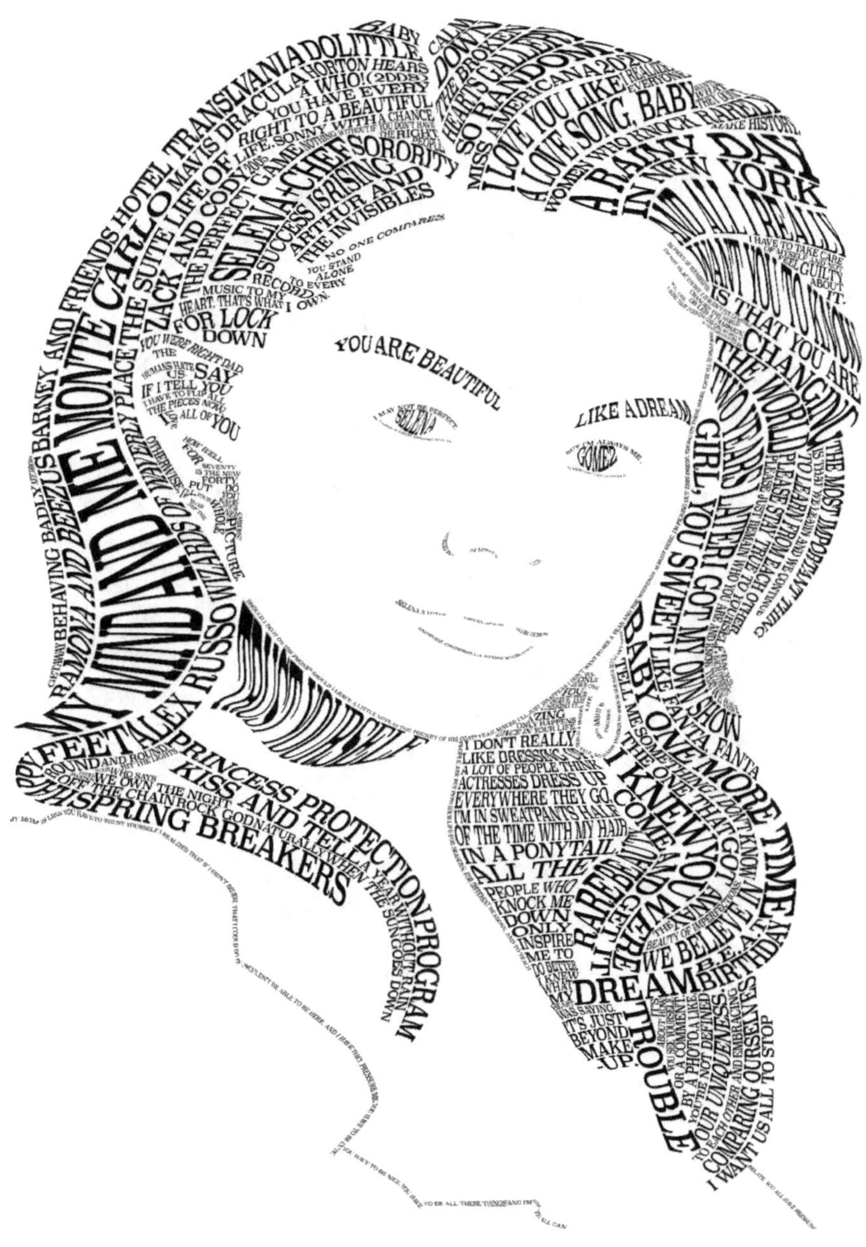

Heidi Valenzuela

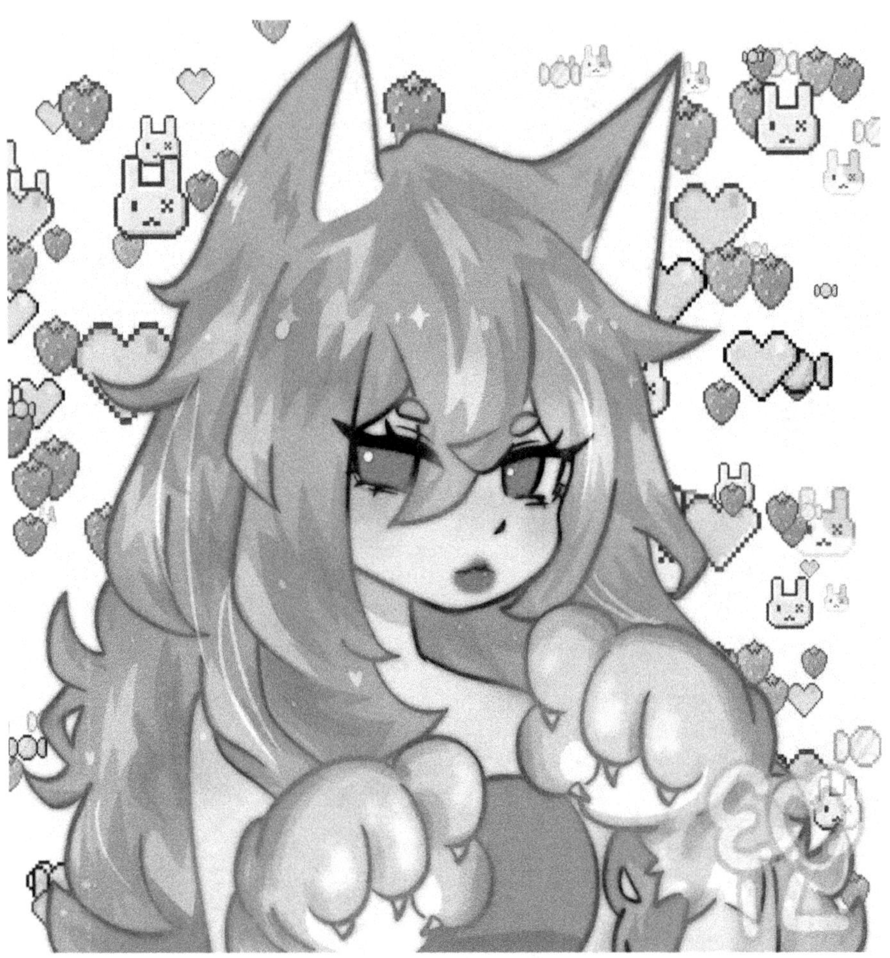

Emil Bae

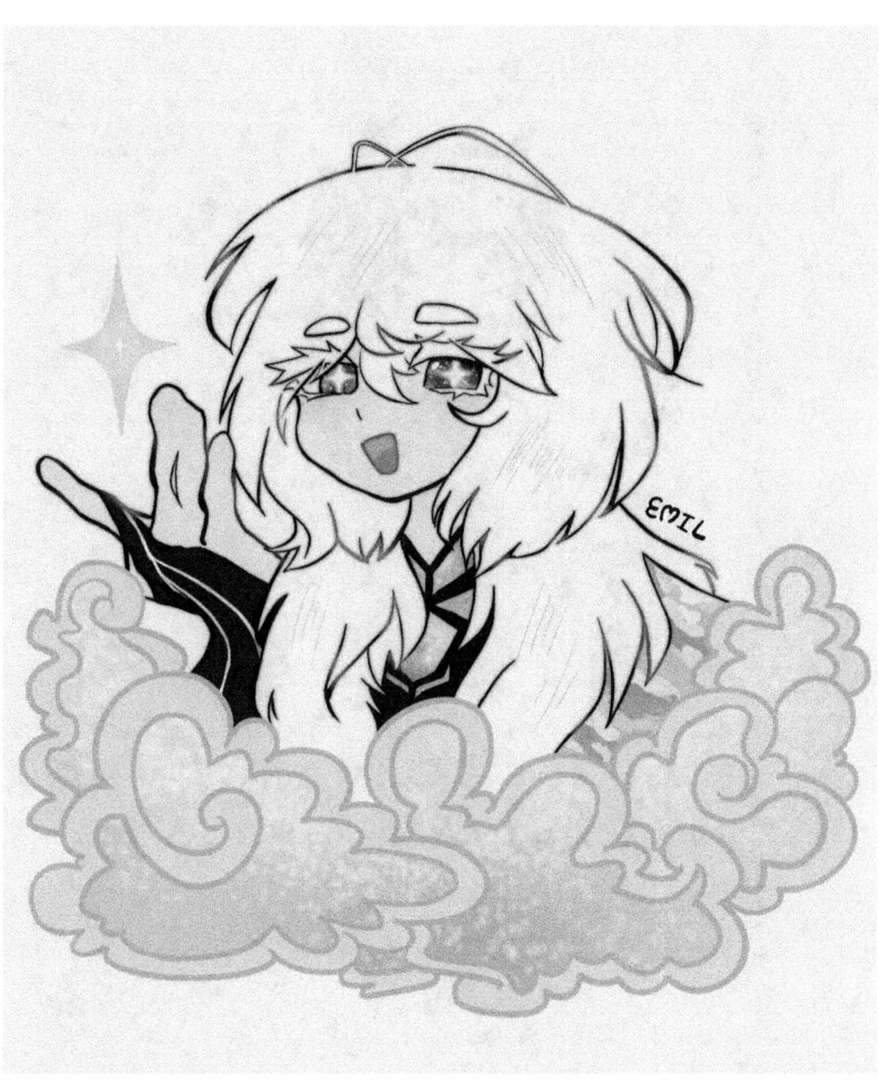

Emil Bae

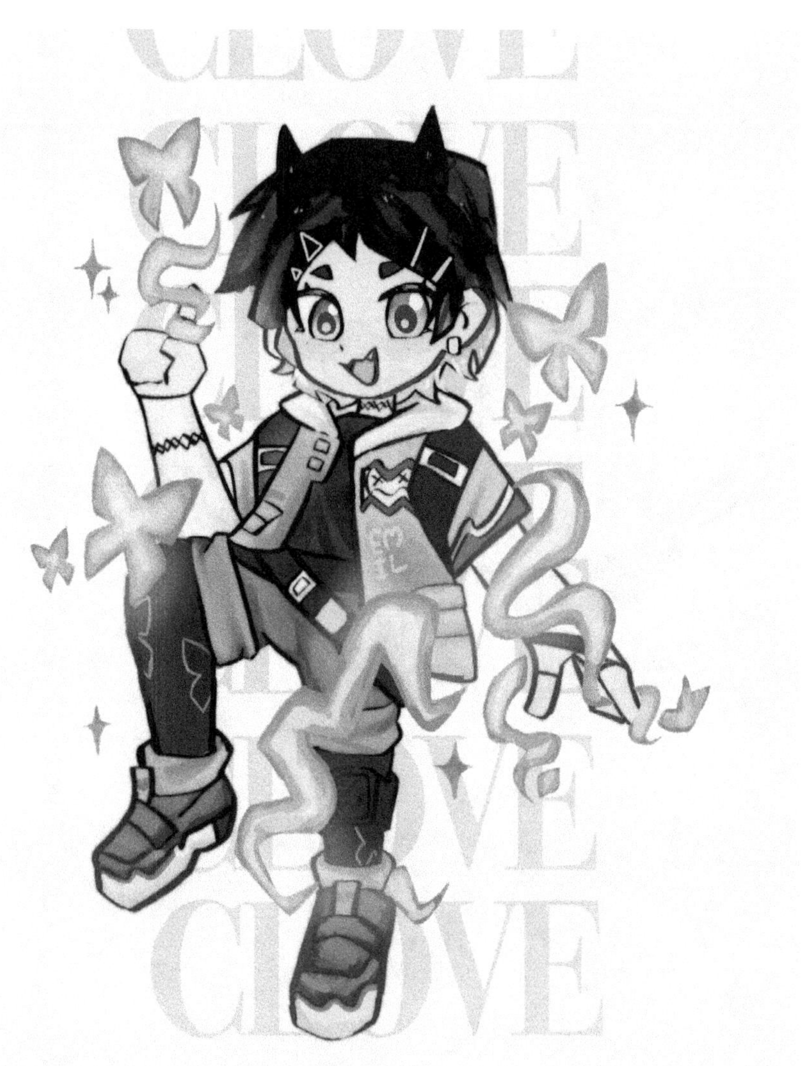

Emil Bae

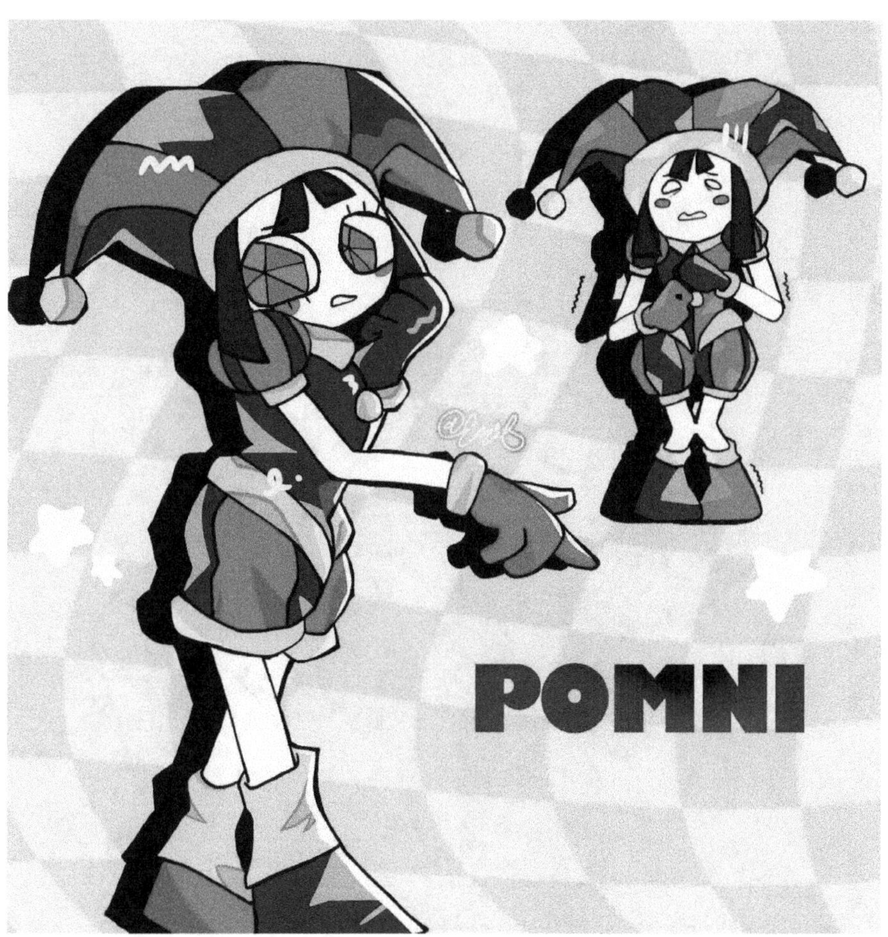

Emil Bae

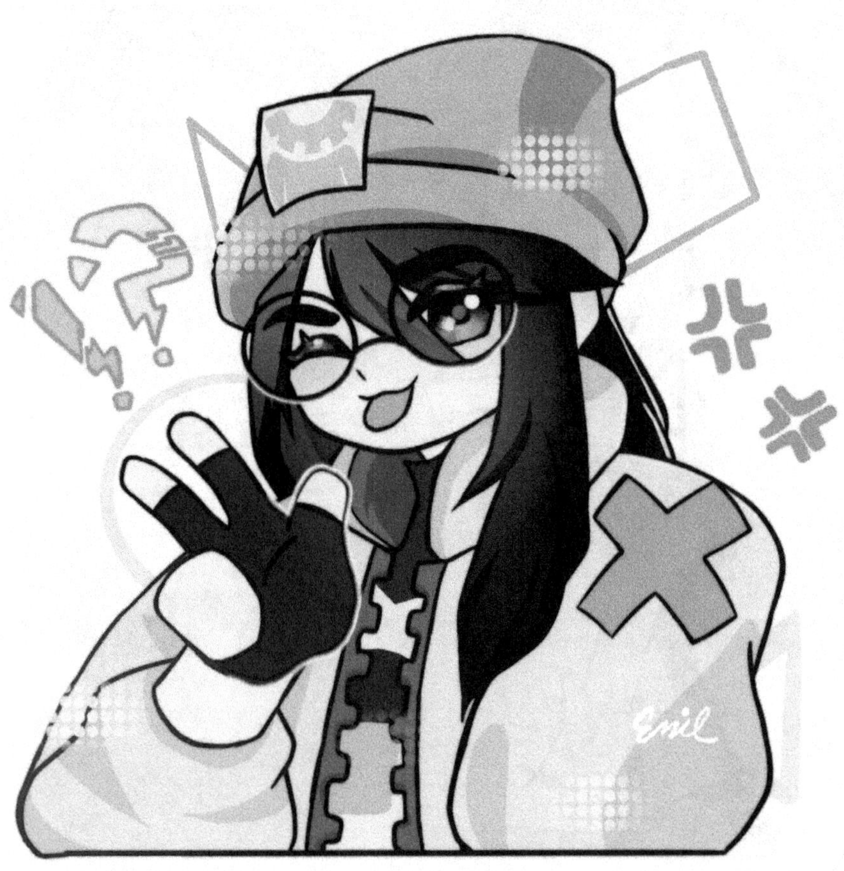

Emil Bae

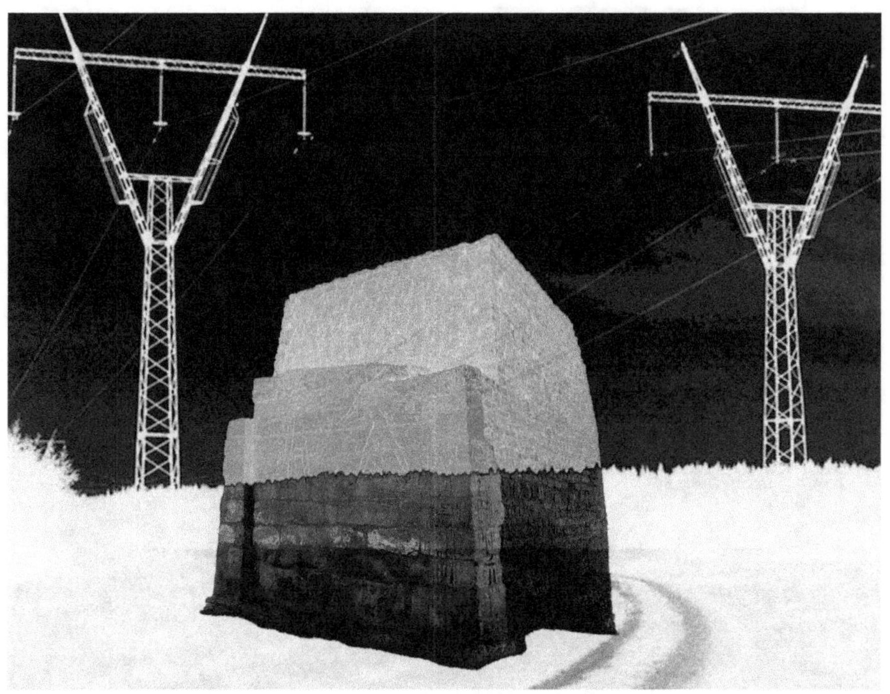

Andre Villareal

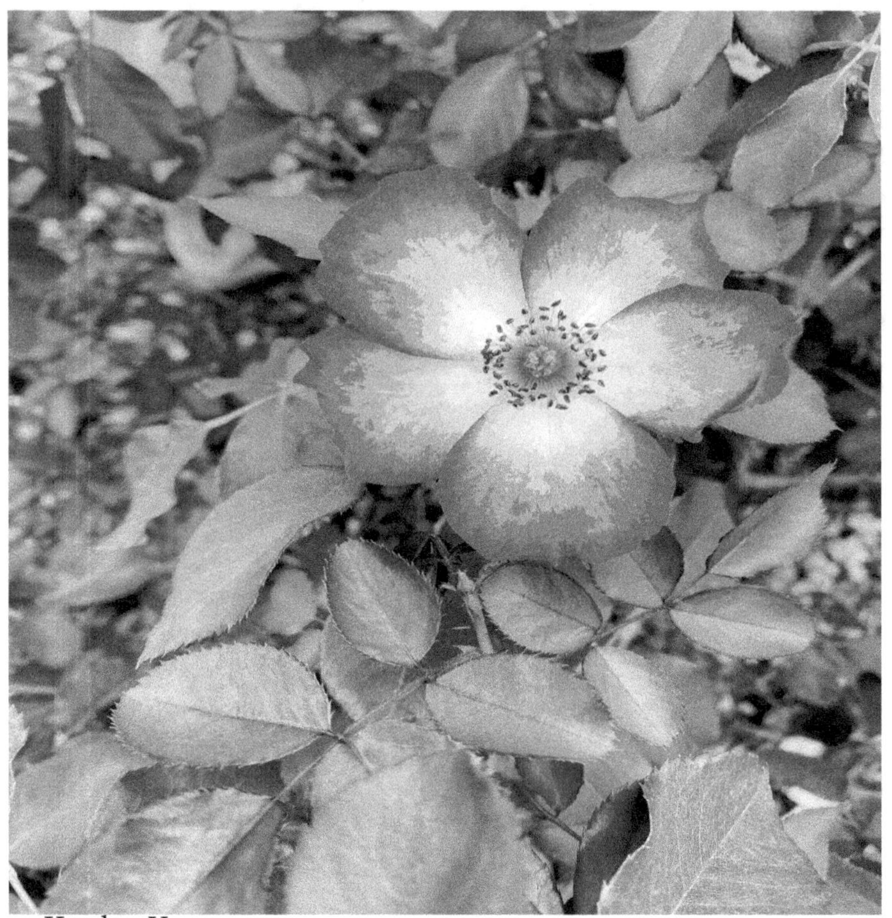

Katelyn Yang

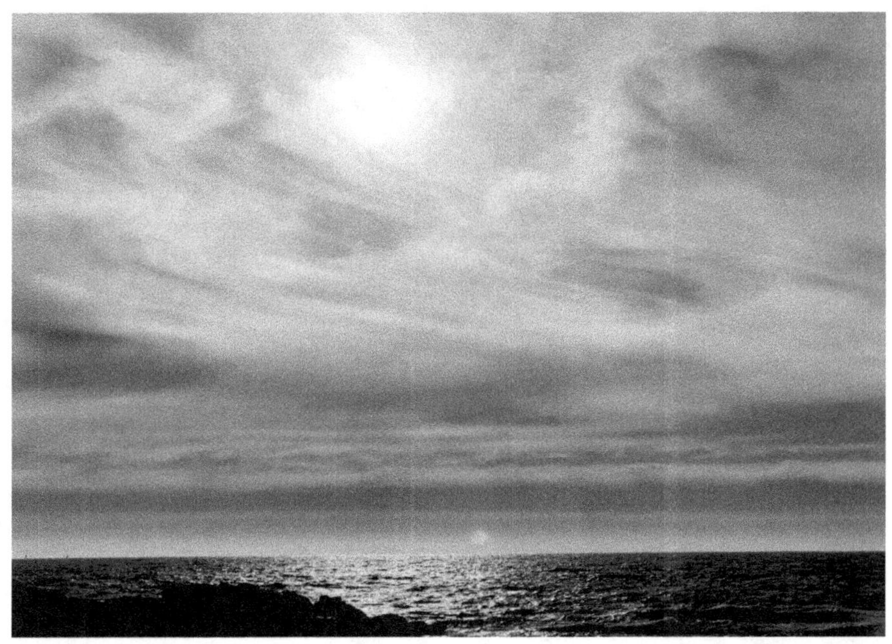

Alexa Mendoza

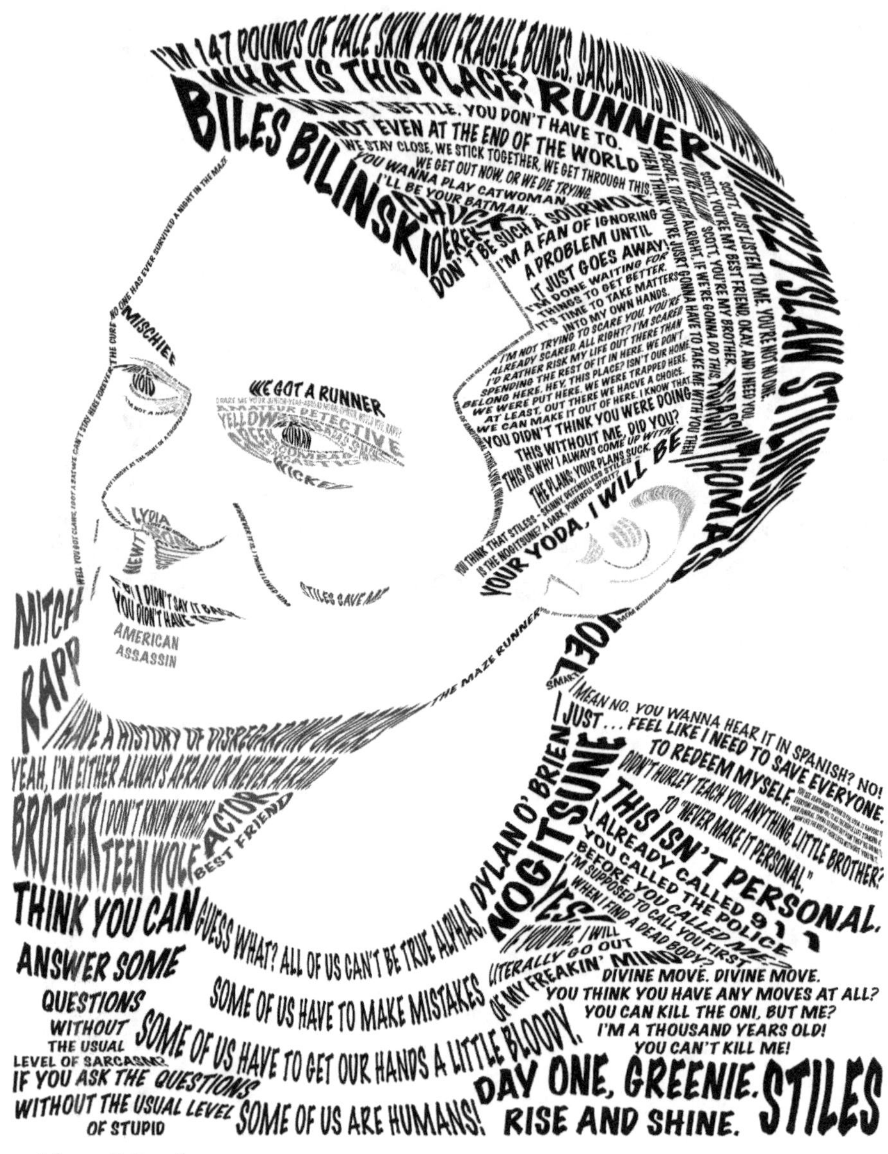

Alexa Mendoza

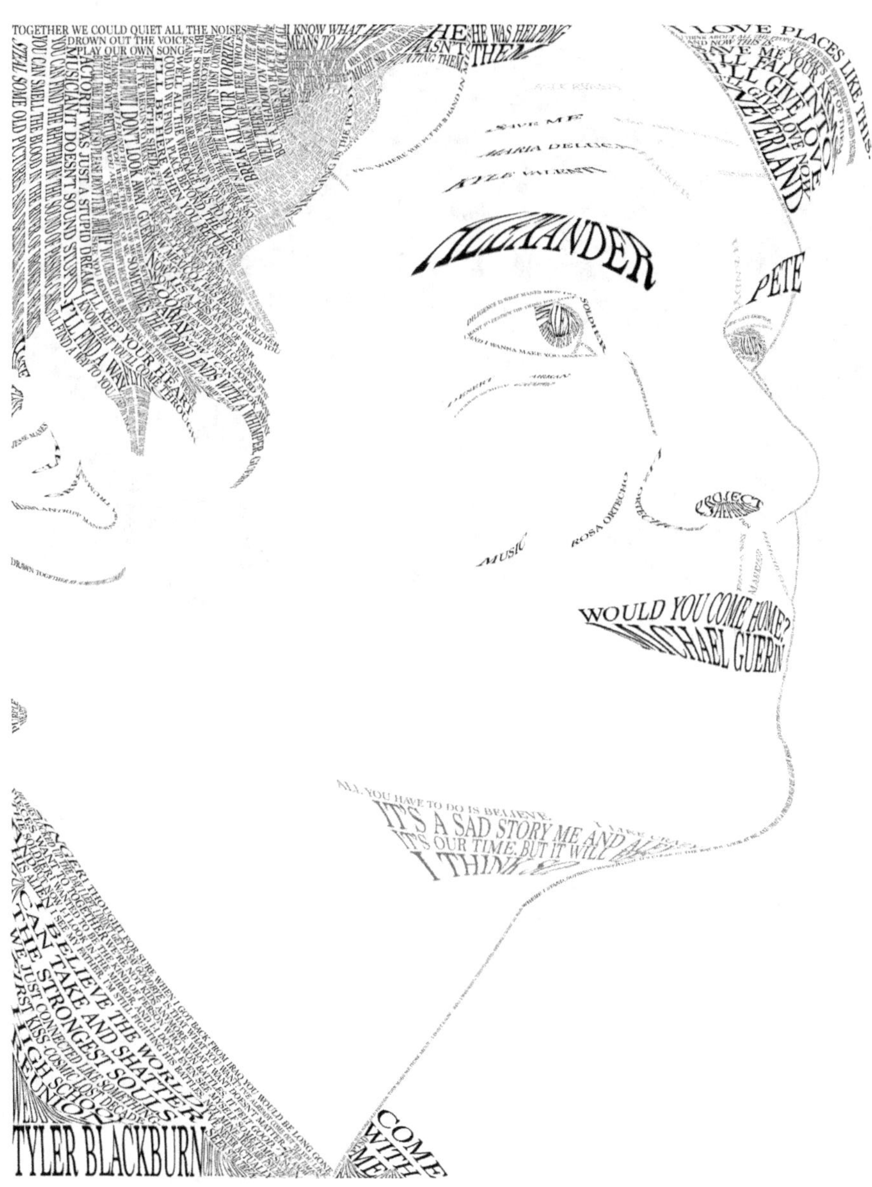

Alexa Mendoza

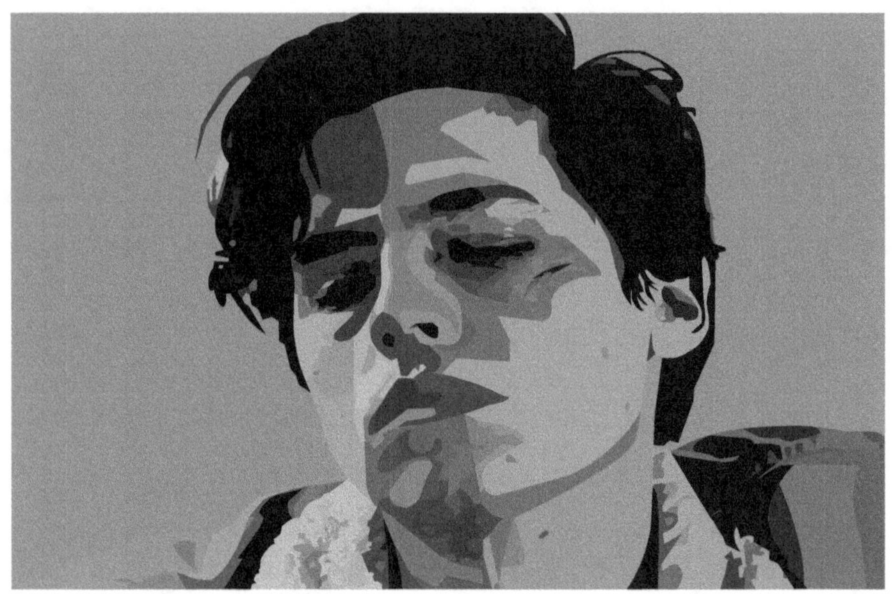

Alexa Mendoza

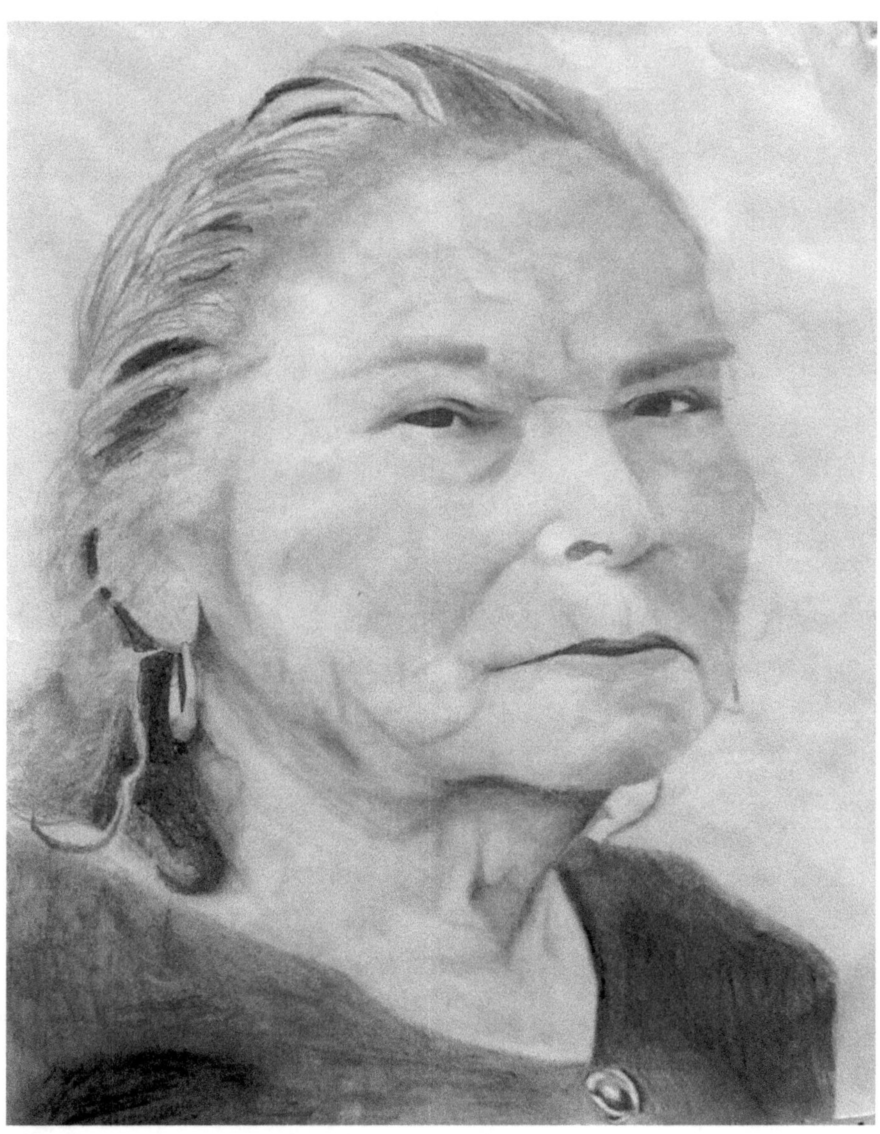

Evangelina Zepeda

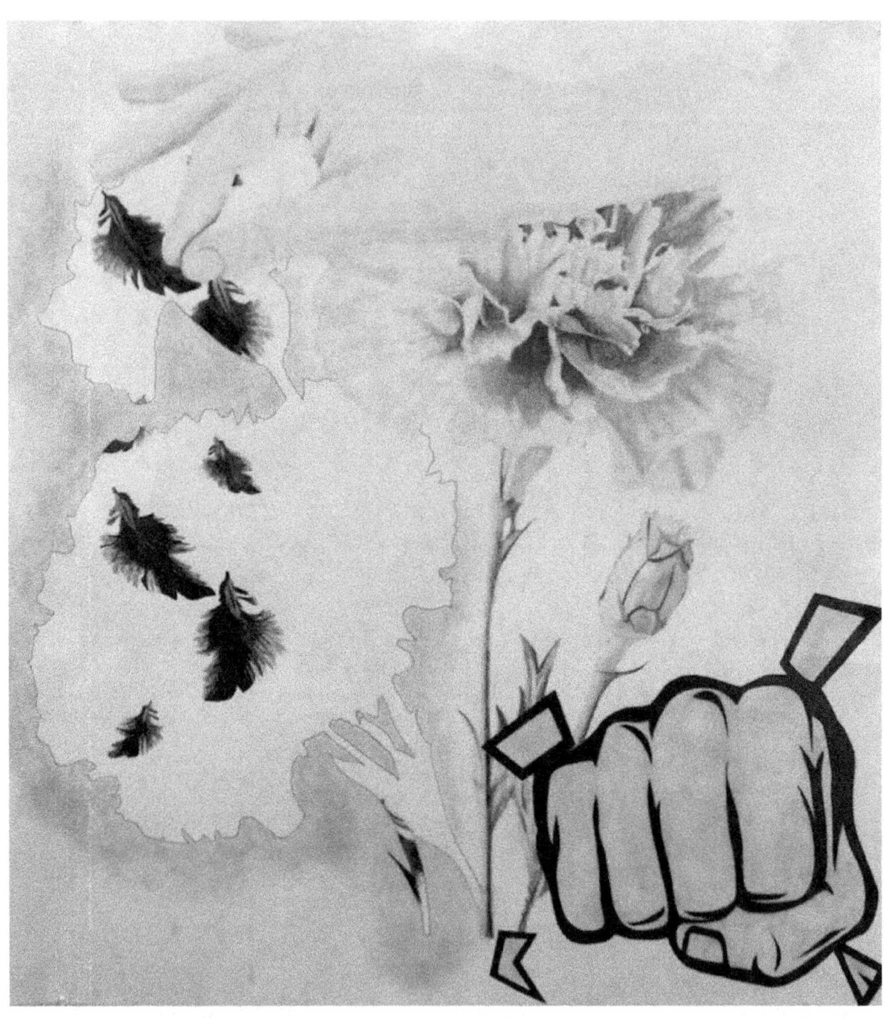

Ariana Ayala

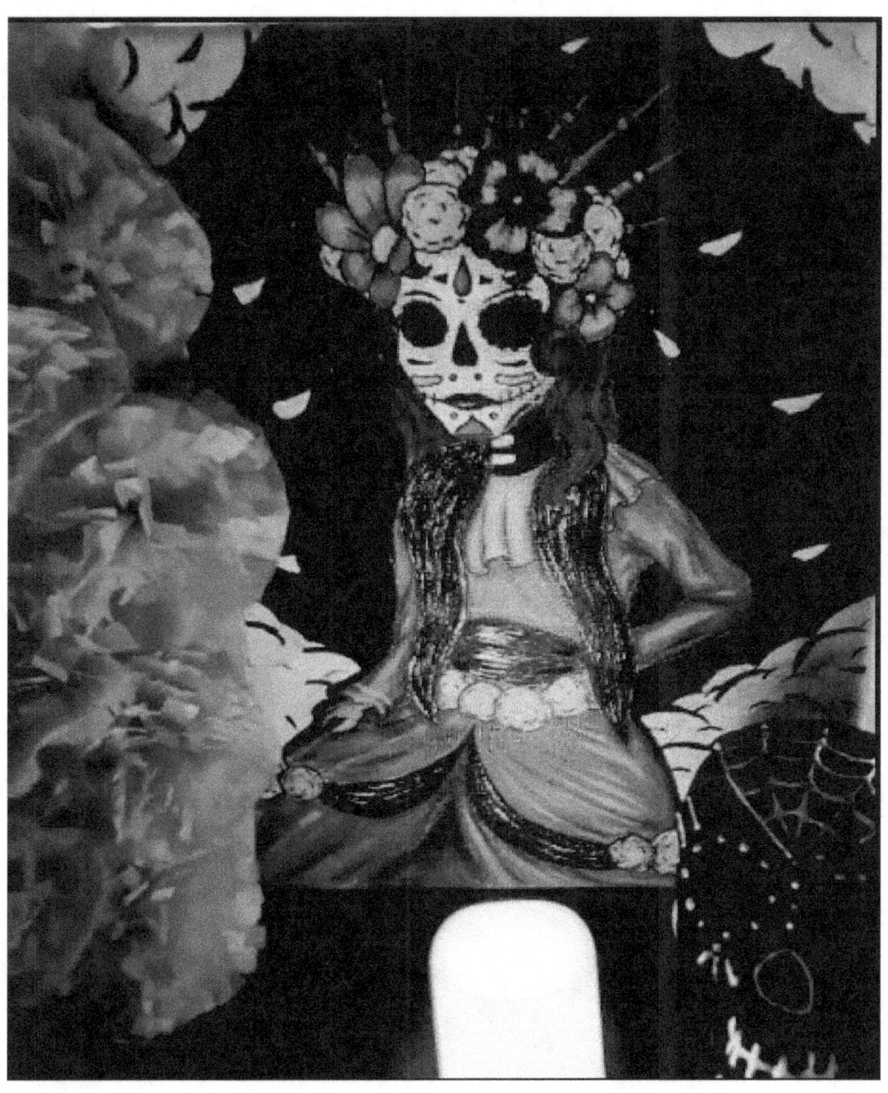

Adrian Rios Cisneros

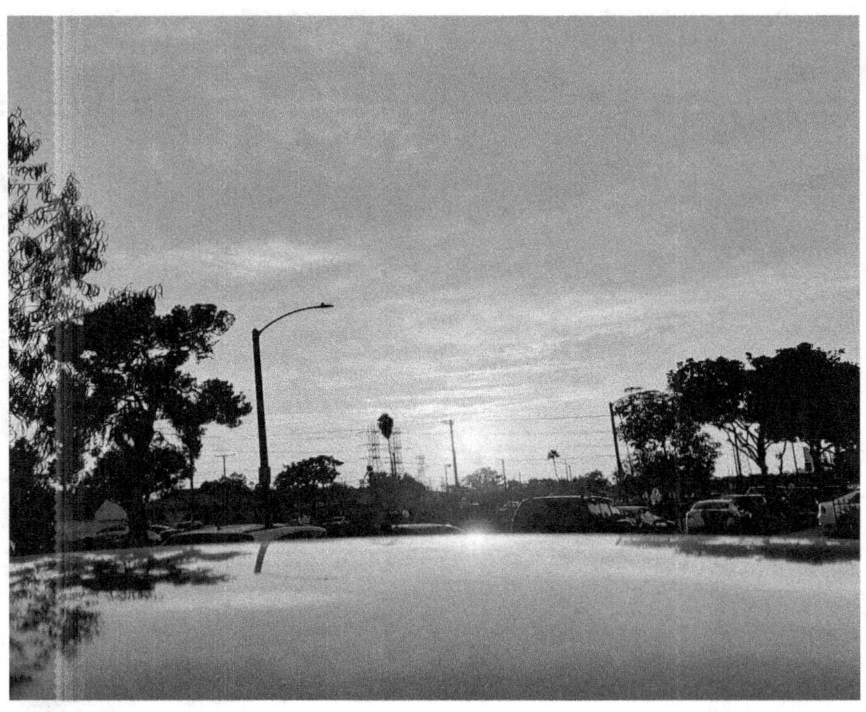

Stephanie Velasquez

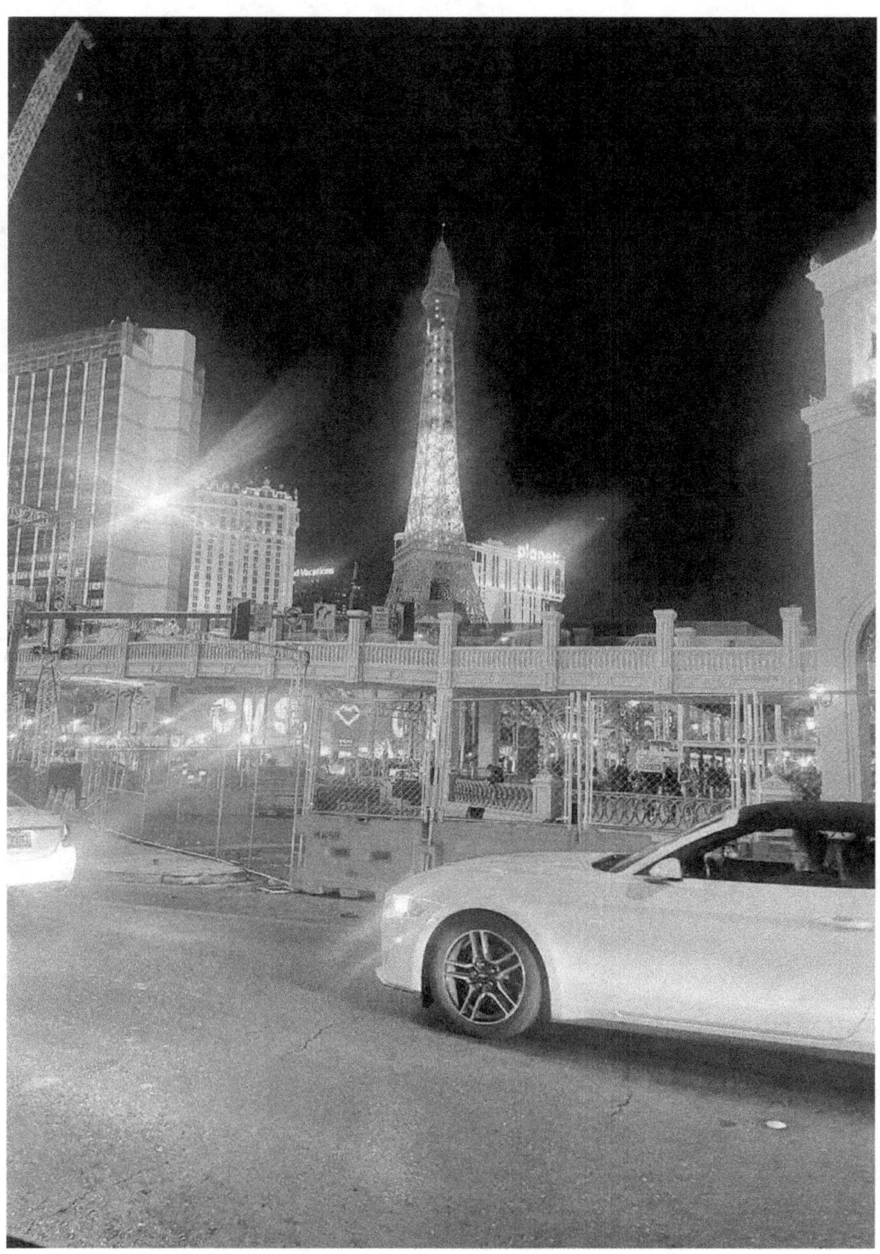

Geraldine Soria Rodriguez

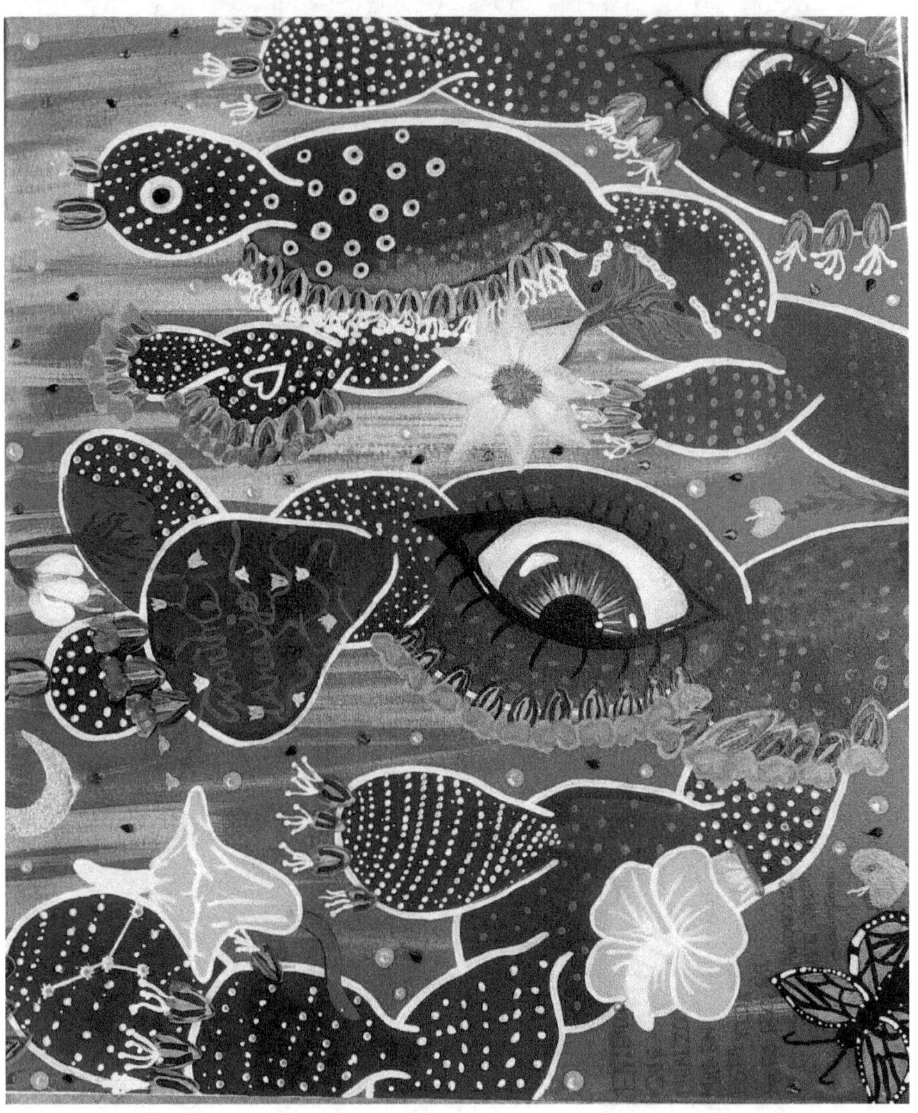

Karime Aruajo

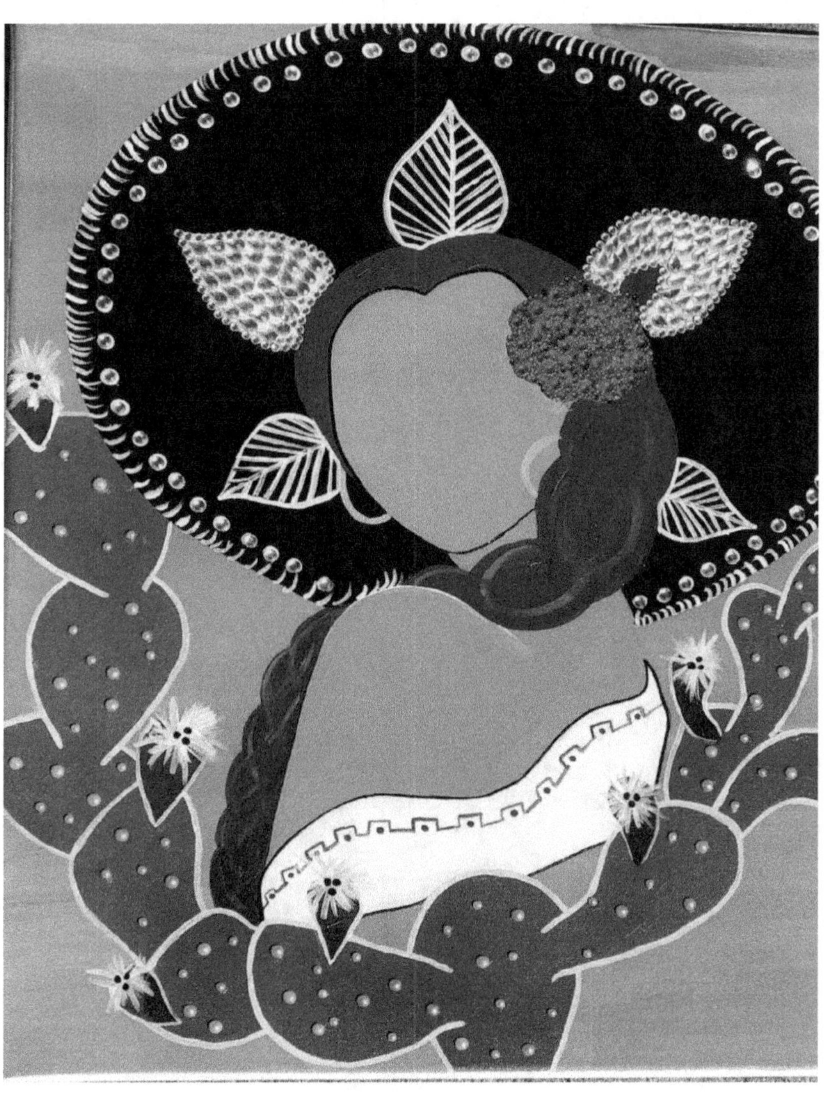

Karime Aruajo

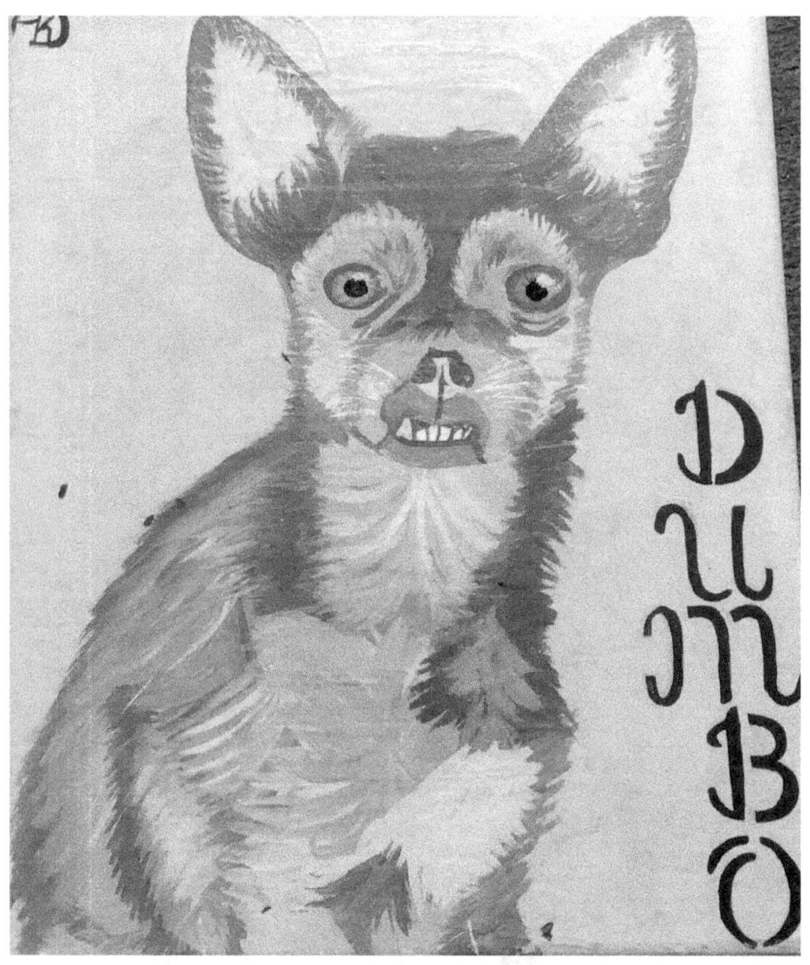

Karime Aruajo

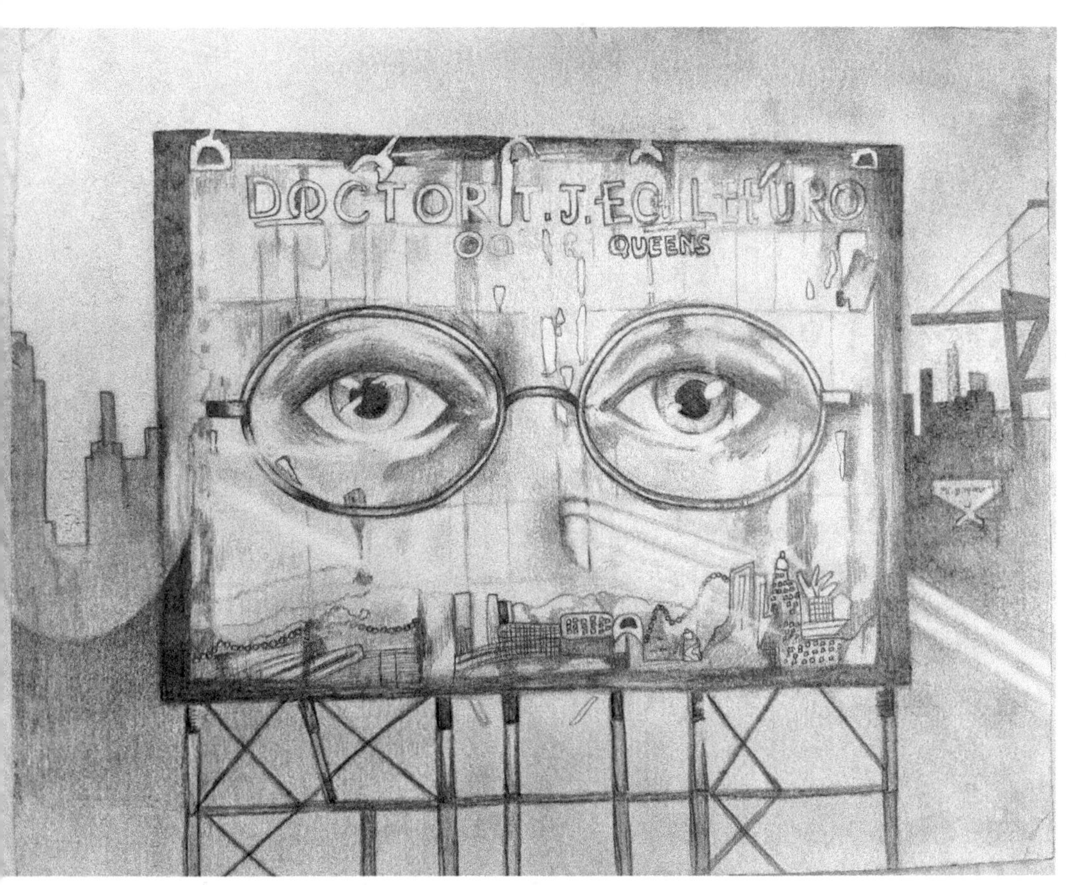

Ashley Lazo-Ruiz

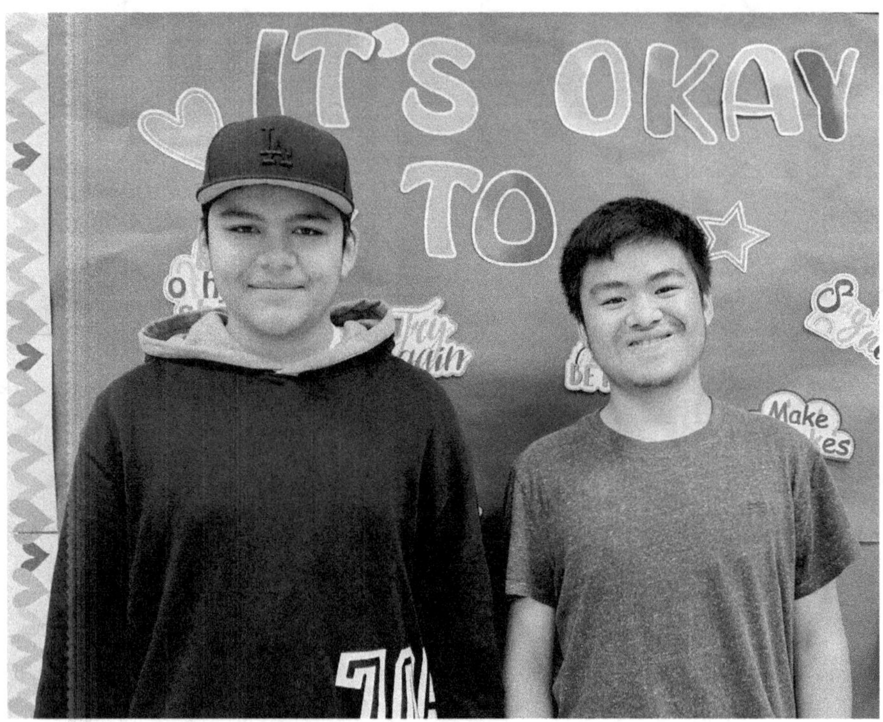

We want to thank all the writers, artists, and photographers who contributed their work. This book would not have been possible without your contributions. Karime Aruajo, thank you for creating the art for our logo. Tyler Alvarez thank you for digitizing the art for the logo. Brayan Sanchez thank you for all your copy editing. Adrian Fuerte-Campos thank you for your support and help with this project. We also want to thank Larry Mckiernan, Lauren Kalmar, Erik Greene, and Nare Movsisyan for all your support. We also want to give a special thanks to Rene Munoz who took time out of his schedule to professionally photograph the art pieces. The quality of this book would not be done well without your contribution to this project thank you. Lastly, thank you Ms. Lopez for spearheading this project. This book production process was a great learning experience for us.

Co-Editors Matthew Genesis Gonzalez Reyes and Ricardo Valencia